IDEALISM AND NATURALISM
IN GOTHIC ART

Frontispiece: The Rose Window of Chartres Cathedral. *Courtesy European Art Color Slide Co., New York.*

IDEALISM AND NATURALISM IN GOTHIC ART

BY MAX DVOŘÁK

Translated

with Notes and Bibliography by

Randolph J. Klawiter

PREFACE BY

KARL MARIA SWOBODA

UNIVERSITY OF NOTRE DAME PRESS

1967

Now that it is translated and complete, anyone can read and criticize it. . . . it is good plowing when the field is cleaned up; but rooting out the woods and stumps . . . that is work that nobody wants!

5064

MARTIN LUTHER
Sendbrief vom Dolmetschen

TRANSLATOR'S NOTE

IT is with a sincere sense of gratitude that I acknowledge my indebtedness to two of my former colleagues without whose aid and encouragement the realization of this translation would have been impossible: first to Professor John Howett, Art Historian and former Curator of the Notre Dame Art Gallery, who brought Dvořák's work to my attention and suggested that I render this seminal essay into English—a suggestion rendered fruitful by his knowledge which was constantly at my disposal; and then to my friend and confrère, Dr. Arthur R. Evans, Jr., Professor of French at Emory University, to whom my debt is far greater than I shall ever be able to repay. I can but hope that he realizes my sincere thankfulness for the countless hours he devoted to reading the manuscript in its various stages and for the invaluable corrections that he proposed.

I am further indebted to Dean Porter, present Curator of the Notre Dame Art Gallery, who provided the information necessary to obtain the plates for this volume; to my wife, Marilyn, and to Mrs. Marcelette Webber, secretary of the Notre Dame Department of Modern Languages, both of whom typed the various versions of the manuscript; and finally to Mrs. Anne Kozak, a most competent and charming editor, with whom it was more of a pleasure than a task to work.

CONTENTS

ILLUSTRATIONS

ABBREVIATIONS

General

a.	article
ad.	answer to the above objection (with reference to the *Summa Theologica* of St. Thomas Aquinas)
Beibl.	Beiblatt, i.e. supplement
bk(s).	book(s)
Br.	Breisgau (Baden, Germany)
c.	chapter (in Latin titles)
ca.	approximately
cf.	compare/see
chap.	chapter (in English titles)
col(s).	column(s)
et al.	among others
e.g.	for example
f(f).	following page(s), year(s), etc.
F.	Folge, i.e. series
Heft	issue
ibid.	same as above
i.e.	that is/namely
Jhrg.	Jahrgang, i.e. annual set
loc. cit.	work and place cited
n.	number (in Latin titles)
Nachf.	successors
n.d.	no date
N.F.	Neue Folge, i.e. new series
no.	number (in English titles)
N.S.	new series
op. cit.	work cited
p(p).	page(s)
q.	question(s)
q.v.	quod vide, i.e. which see (used throughout the text

with reference to proper names, information concerning which is to be found alphabetically arranged in the appendix)

Sent.   Sentences (with reference to the Latin work of Peter Lombard)

St.   saint

vol(s).   volume(s)

Monographs and Periodicals

ADB   *Allgemeine Deutsche Biographie* (München-Leipzig)

AHdlMA   *Archives d'Histoire doctrinale et littéraire du Moyen-Age* (Paris)

AkbGW   *Abhandlungen der königlichen-böhmischen Gesellschaft der Wissenschaften* (Wien)

Altaner   Berthold Altaner. *Patrologie. Leben, Schriften und Lehre der Kirchenväter.* Freiburg im Br.: Herder, 1938 (References are to the 1951 edition).

AÖAW   *Almanach der Österreichischen Akademie der Wissenschaften* (Wien; also referred to as the *Wiener Akademie der Wissenschaften*)

ARB   *Académie Royal de Belgique* (Brussels)

Bardenhewer   Otto Bardenhewer. *Geschichte der altkirchlichen Literatur.* 5 vols. Freiburg im Br.: Herder, 1902–1932.

BCJ   C. Sommervoge, ed. *Bibliothèque de la Compagnie de Jésus.* 9 vols. 2nd edition. Bruxelles-Paris, 1890–1900; Supplements 1912–1930.

Bel   *Belvedere* (Wien)

BFPLUL   *Bibliothèque de la Faculté de Philosophie et Lettres de l'Université de Liége* (Liége)

BGPM   *Beiträge zur Geschichte der Philosophie des Mittelalters* (Münster)

BioJb   *Biographisches Jahrbuch und deutscher Nekrolog* (Berlin)

BioJba   *Biographisches Jahrbuch für Altertumskunde* (Berlin)

BJFkA   *Brusians Jahresbericht über die Fortschritte in der klassischen Altertumswissenschaft* (Berlin)

ABBREVIATIONS

BZ	*Byzantinische Zeitschrift* (Leipzig)
CE	*Catholic Encyclopedia.* 15 vols. New York, 1907– 1914.
CSEL	*Corpus Scriptorum Ecclesiasticorum Latinorum* (Wien)
DBJb	*Deutsches Biographisches Jahrbuch* (Stuttgart)
DnW	*Der neue Weg. Österreichische Monatsschrift für pädogogische Forschung* (Wien)
DTC	*Dictionnaire de Théologie Catholique.* 15 Vols. Paris, 1903–1950.
Dpf	*Die Denkmalpflege* (Berlin-Wien)
DZ	*Deutsche Zukunft* (Berlin)
EC	*Enciclopedia Cattolica.* 12 Vols. Città del Vaticano, 1949–1954.
EPM	*Etudes de Philosophie Mediévales* (Paris)
FcLDg	*Forschung zur christlichen Literatur- und Dogmengeschichte* (Paderborn)
GCS	*Die griechischen christlichen Schriftsteller der ersten drei Jahrhunderte* (Berlin)
GH	*Gelbe Hefte* (München)
Gyd	*Ganymed* (Dresden)
HAR	*Hamburgische Akademische Rundschau* (Hamburg)
HJb	*Historisches Jahrbuch* (Münster, 1880–1882; München, 1883–1930; Köln, 1931–1950; München-Freiburg im Br., 1950 ff.)
Hld	*Hochland* (München)
HS	*Historische Studien* (Berlin)
HZ	*Historische Zeitschrift* (München)
JbBAW	*Jahrbuch der Bayrischen Akademie der Wissenschaften* (München)
JbkpK	*Jahrbuch der königlichen preussischen Kunstsammlungen* (Berlin)
JbSAK	*Jahrbuch der kunsthistorischen Sammlungen des Allerhöchsten Kaiserhauses* (Wien)
JbSW	*Jahrbuch der kunsthistorischen Sammlungen in Wien* (Wien)
JbWK	*Wiener Jahrbuch der Kunstgeschichte* (Wien)
JbZK	*Jahrbuch der Zentralkommission zur Erforschung der Kunstdenkmäler* (Wien)
JL	*Jesuiten Lexikon.* Paderborn, 1934.
JTS	*Journal of Theological Studies* (Oxford-London)

KA	*Kunstgeschichtliche Anzeigen* (Wien, Beibl. to *MIÖG*)
KGW	*Königliche Gesellschaft der Wissenschaften* (Göttingen)
KJb	*Kunstgeschichtliches Jahrbuch* (Wien)
KS	*Kunstgeschichtliche Studien* (Berlin)
KTVÜ	*Kleine Texte für Vorlesungen und Übungen* (Bonn)
KuK	*Kunstchronik und Kunstmarkt* (Leipzig)
Lit	*Die Literatur* (Berlin-Stuttgart: formerly: *Das literarische Echo*)
LTK	*Lexikon für Theologie und Kirche.* 10 Vols. Freiburg im Br., 1930–1938
MGH	*Monumenta Germaniae Historica* (Hannover; Gesellschaft für die ältere deutsche Geschichtskunde)
MIÖG	*Mitteilungen des Instituts für Österreichische Geschichtsforschung* (Innsbruck)
MkkZ	*Mitteilungen der kaiserlich-königlichen Zentralkommission zur Erforschung und Erhaltung der Kunst- und historischen Denkmale* (Wien)
MÖVB	*Mitteilungen des Österreichischen Vereins für Bibliothekswesen* (Wien)
MZKE	*Mitteilungen der Zentralkommission zur Erforschung der Kunst- und historischen Denkmale* (Wien)
NDB	*Neue Deutsche Biographie* (Berlin)
NFP	*Neue Freie Presse* (Wien)
NÖB	*Neue Österreichische Biographie* (Wien)
NPNCF	*Nicene and Post-Nicene Christian Fathers* (New York-Oxford)
OBK	*Offizieller Bericht über die Verhandlungen des internationalen kunsthistorischen Kongresses* (München, Sept., 1909)
PG	*Patrologia Graeca*, edited by Jacques Paul Migne (Paris)
PJb	*Philosophisches Jahrbuch* (Fulda)
PL	*Patrologia Latina*, edited by Jacques Paul Migne (Paris)
PV	*Philosophische Vorträge* (Berlin)
RKwt	*Repertorium für Kunstwissenschaft* (Berlin-Stuttgart)

RMAl	*Revue du Moyen-Age latin* (Lyons)
RpTK	*Realencyklopädie für protestantische Theologie und Kirche.* 21 Vols. Paderborn, 1898–1908; Supplement, 2 Vols., 1913.
SGTK	*Studien zur Geschichte der Theologie und der Kirche* (Leipzig)
SO	*Symbolae Osloenses* (Oslo)
Spec	*Speculum. Journal of Mediaeval Studies* (Cambridge, Mass.)
TUGaL	*Texte und Untersuchungen zur Geschichte der altchristlichen Literatur* (Leipzig)
Überweg	Friedrich Überweg. *Grundriss der Geschichte der Philosophie.* 4 Vols. 12th edition. Basel: Benno Schwabe, 1951
WuW	*Wort und Wahrheit. Monatsschrift für Religion und Kultur* (Wien)
WZGK	*Westdeutsche Zeitschrift für Geschichte und Kunst* (Trier)
ZbK	*Zeitschrift für die bildende Kunst* (Leipzig)
ZGORh	*Zeitschrift für die Geschichte der Oberrheins* (Karlsruhe)
ZKg	*Zeitschrift für Kunstgeschichte* (Berlin-Leipzig)
ZKTh	*Zeitschrift für Katholische Theologie* (Innsbruck-Wien)
ZTK	*Zeitschrift für Theologie und Kirche* (Tübingen-Leipzig)

PREFACE*

AX DVOŘÁK (1874–1921), one of the most important scholars of the Vienna school of art history, was born in Roudnitz, Bohemia. Initially this Austrian of Czech descent had reservations about pursuing a career in art history, for the intellectual upheaval of the last decades of the nineteenth century made Dvořák, a sensitive young man, profoundly skeptical of learning, particularly in its overestimation of the relationship between learning and culture.

Diverse factors deriving from this intellectual revolution apparently influenced him. As early as 1895, he referred both to the overpowering effect of Nietzsche's thought on him and to his exemplary prose style. Northern art and poetry, Strindberg, Ibsen and Eduard Munch, but more particularly the French painters—the Naturalists and the Impressionists—influenced him to such an extent that for a long time he was uncertain whether he should study history or become a writer. His literary attempts, some of which appeared in German papers in Prague and Hamburg, were more important to him at that time than were his professional history studies. "The Relations between Metaphysics and Scholarship," his choice of a topic for a lecture

* I am indebted to Jeanne and Otto Pächt for the English translation.

delivered before the Prague Historical Society, was another indication of his dissatisfaction with the existing intellectual climate. The tension caused by the disparity between his general
cultural experiences and the contemporary position of learning
produced in Dvořák a thoroughly pessimistic outlook.

More the modern intellectual, the philosopher in the true
sense of the word, than the traditional academic scholar or the
learned civil servant, Dvořák became a University Assistant in
Vienna at twenty-four and a Lecturer at twenty-eight. By the
age of thirty-five, he had been nominated Professor (*Ordinarius*)
and had become the successor of Wickhoff who died in 1909.
From what source, one may ask, did this pessimist draw the
buoyancy necessary for such a career and from whence came
his new trust and belief in scholarship? Undoubtedly it derived
from the certainty acquired during his early years in Vienna
that a turning point had been reached not only for the humanities but more particularly for art history.

Dvořák gave expression to this new credo in his essay "Die
letzte Renaissance" ("The Last Renaissance"). He observed that
the prejudices of classicism and a brand of humanism blind to
its own time were responsible for the late nineteenth-century belief that they were an "Epigonenzeit"—a misapprehension of
which he too had been guilty. In addition to Dvořák's essay,
numerous art publications were explicating this thesis and hence
were fostering new thinking.

A great upsurge of art had taken place since the 1850's. In
France it was led by pioneers such as Courbet, Millet and Manet
—all of whom had died in the seventies and eighties but all of
whom had continued and expanded the great line of painting
from Titian to Tintoretto, to Rembrandt and to Velázquez.
That these works evidenced historical progression was not noted
by the advocates of academic aesthetics and history of art.
Rather it was the literary men and artists who championed the
recognition of such a growth: Ruskin who pointed to the his-

torical importance of Tiepolo; Degas who taught a new understanding of Watteau and Fragonard; Meunier who advocated the
techniques of Bernini and Duquesnoy. Thus Dvořák perceived
that a new approach to art was being disseminated and it was this
awareness that spawned his optimism.

Further Dvořák realized that the chief representative of
this new position was Wickhoff whose knowledge of modern
art, as evidenced in his principal work on ancient Roman art,
contained in the introduction to the manuscript of the Vienna
Genesis, led to the discovery of late antique impressionism. The
result was a reciprocal clarification of the course of development
of both antique and modern art. Although Wickhoff made the
initial discovery, Riegl in his book *Die spätrömische Kunstindustrie* further explored it and clarified its implications for the artistic development as a whole. This second great name in Viennese
art history began decisively to form Dvořák's thinking and his
ideas inevitably had a releasing effect on Dvořák and on his artistic disposition. The "Patres" of the new historical approach, represented by Wickhoff and Riegl, were Justi and his work on
Velázquez, Thaussing and his thesis on Dürer and the vast scholarship of Lange and Löwy, for it was these men who effected a
positive appreciation and understanding of the whole field of
both the Greek and Roman development and correspondingly of
the modern development since the Renaissance. Because of its
fundamental importance for modern and contemporary art history, their total achievement seemed to Dvořák to be a "Last
Renaissance."

If art history and art appreciation are to derive from and to
reflect the prevailing *Weltanschauung*, as Dvořák believed they
did, then the role of art history becomes inexorably bound with
life, and it fuses general cultural experiences with the existing
intellectual climate. Thus, it was this belief that fostered Dvořák's
optimism and that remained with him throughout his long and
fruitful career. It remained with him even in the distress of war

and the post-war years; it gave him his confidence, his idealism and the strength to transmit his conviction to his friends and pupils. In this belief and in his fascinating person lies the secret of Dvořák's humane influence.

Whether this confidence was justified in the face of the subsequent development of history is not relevant in assessing Dvořák's importance as an art historian; rather one should evaluate his achievement and eminence in research. Consequently any consideration should involve the goals Dvořák set for himself in the new era of art history, the task Wickhoff and Riegl left him to accomplish and the extent to which he effected them. These aims and the tasks were summarized in Dvořák's essay "Les Aliscans," written for the *Festschrift* in honor of Wickhoff's fiftieth birthday.

The development of ancient art and that of modern times since the Renaissance were now seen in a new light and understood within their historical context; however it was still necessary to integrate the art of the Middle Ages within this framework. Although since the Romantic period, medieval, and more particularly Gothic, art had been appreciated to an extent, though in a purely sentimental way and frequently from a nationalistic point of view, no one would have dared to place the works of the Gothic period on the same level as those of the Renaissance or to regard them as intelligible to the same degree. Rather they were categorized by art historians as something peripheral to the vital forces leading to contemporary art; they were not yet admitted to the status of mature creations. Furthermore the sympathetic interpretation of this art originated with and was sustained by writer-artists and amateurs who discovered in it affinities to their own works. In "Les Aliscans," Dvořák initially posed the problem of the correct historical placing of medieval art, and in all his subsequent works he attempted to resolve it. In "Les Aliscans" he hinted at a possible sociological solution. The new nations had to submit to the stages of development previously experienced by the nations of classical antiquity, but because of the extant heritage of ancient art, it was not a beginning "ab ovo." Since earlier, more primitive forms of classical art had survived, they could, historically speaking, be assimilated by the peoples of the Middle Ages. As evidence of this assimilation process, he cited the primitive forms displayed by the Sarcophagi in the necropolis of Les Aliscans near Arles which still belong to the late classical period and the late classical form of Byzantine painting.

Because of its proximity to Byzantium, this assimilation was reflected more forcefully in the new Italian art—one saturated with classical form and, since Giotto, composed in terms of three-dimensional space. Although Dvořák dealt with this topic in his early years ("Über den byzantinischen Einfluss auf die Miniaturmalerei des Trecento"), he restudied the question of renaissances and of classical survival in the Middle Ages and his conclusions regarding interrelations in wall-painting of the early Middle Ages in Rome comprise the definitive study in this area.

Another aspect of this same question which Dvořák treated in "Die Illuminatoren des Johann von Neumarkt" is the assimilation of the new Italian art in countries north of the Alps. In both the illuminations of the manuscript of Charles IV's Chancellor, Johannes of Neumarkt, and in a group of related panel- and wall-paintings, Giottoesque influences were presented north of the Alps for the first time in a fully developed form. Dvořák pointed out these links, explained how the special features of the paintings depended on such connections and outlined the art-historical, developmental process in a study whose cultural and historical vision goes far beyond that of Burdach. The increasing assimilation of the antique as well as the formal values of the Trecento, which values varied according to the specific artistic traditions of these northern countries, enabled Dvořák to explain the early naturalism in Dutch painting originating with the brothers van Eyck (cf. his study "Das Rätsel der Brüder van Eyck").

In this work he apportioned the respective share of the two

brothers in the Ghent altarpiece. Using external criteria and internal stylistic evidence for an evaluation of the other works of Jan van Eyck, Dvořák demonstrated that his unique naturalism evolved historically because of the assimilation of Italian Trecento pictorial ideas by French book illuminators around 1400. This explication of van Eyck's art, based on a rigorous historical method, still forms the broad basis for all specialized research in art history.

Dvořák's essays, written and published in the period 1900–1903, not only represented a gigantic achievement in art scholarship, but they also enabled Dvořák both to formulate his technical literary style and to set a pattern for his later studies, e.g., an essay on Schongauer reflected the history of German and Flemish painting. In addition, these essays illustrating the historic evolution of painting in the later Middle Ages were unique from an art-historical point of view since no comparable study existed for the period of later Medieval art, i.e., the period around 1500 when Gothic art attained its perfection in France. Although Dvořák did not formally treat this problem in any specific essay, his reflections and ponderings formed a substantial part of a cycle of lectures delivered on post-classical art.

About 1916 the dominant idea of Dvořák's historical vision changed and found its resonance in the weighty paper "Idealismus und Naturalismus in der gotischen Skulptur und Malerei," an essay developed out of his lecturing activities. Previously Dvořák, in line with the artistic creed of his youth, had viewed the whole course of artistic development essentially as an ever increasing drive toward naturalism. But in accordance with the turn of contemporary art, naturalism as a motive power was joined by a second element, idealism, whose function is to express as the first object of artistic creation those spiritual qualities that motivate and propel human beings.

When Dvořák published this essay in 1918, he was quite sick. In Vienna the years after World War I were years of of virtual starvation that told on Dvořák and his family. As head of the Austrian Monuments Commission, he had to use all of his diminished strength to defend the possessions of the Austrian state collections against the claims of the victorious powers.

Nevertheless he found time to enlarge the foundations of his "Kunstgeschichte als Geistesgeschichte," that is his concept of art history as a history of ideas. The expression "Kunstgeschichte als Geistesgeschichte" was not Dvořák's; rather it was chosen by the editors of his collected works as the title for a volume of essays containing among others "Idealismus und Naturalismus." Unfortunately he did not find enough time to pursue this thesis. His only studies in those years were some smaller essays and his lectures on Italian Renaissance art (delivered in 1919 and 1920, but published only posthumously). In these studies, undertaken with the new emphasis on art as an expression of ideas, Dvořák came to vindicate the hitherto ill-appreciated "mannerists" period between High Renaissance and early Baroque art as an artistic growth with a style and laws of its own, and it was thus that he endowed the term "mannerism" with a positive connotation.

SUMMARY OF
Idealism and Naturalism in Gothic Sculpture and Painting

IN THE INTRODUCTORY CHAPTER, Dvořák emphasizes that medieval art is based on the tremendous Christian spirituality of the Middle Ages—a force whose significance for medieval art one can at present only dimly apprehend. He stresses that his intention was not to link occurrences of an economic, social or religious nature with artistic phenomena in a causal connection, nor to derive the spiritual content of works of art from the writings of the great medieval theologians; but rather it was to illustrate that the spiritual content of a medieval work of art and the historic development of its relationship to transcendental ideas and the material facts of life both spring from a common source: the *Weltanschauung* of medieval Christianity. Moreover even the form of the work of art is conditioned by these spiritual forces and since these forces also determined the writings of the great theologians, the latter can be of advantage in establishing standards for the evaluation of the contemporary artistic production.

In the following elaboration of this thesis, some of the ideas of the preceding generation of art history still prevail unchallenged, e.g., the idea of a naturalistic evolution of art. Furthermore Dvořák's terminology is somewhat encumbered by the ambiguities of the terminology of his teacher Riegl, for example, his contrast of the sensualism of Greek art with the "subjectivity" of medieval art. In Dvořák's new approach, the interpretation of the spiritual content of a work of art becomes separable from that of its formal aspect, so that Dvořák in discussing medieval art can speak of a victory of ideal concepts over formal perfection. However the weaknesses of this kind of antithesis may be understood in the context of the radically new turn Dvořák gave to art-historical thinking.

The advance was twofold. Firstly, the *Weltanschauung* of a given historical moment is considered not only as the conditioning factor of a work of art in its specific and singular form, but in addition as an explanation of a specific trend of artistic development—a method of interpretation already adumbrated in some of Riegl's writings. Secondly, this approach is applied in particular to the religious art of the Middle Ages and specifically to Gothic painting and sculpture.

Dvořák's essay proclaims that the artistic creations of the whole Christian era—the smallest details of their formal data as well as the changes of style—derive their premises from the tenets of Christianity and can only be understood from that position. Hence he frees himself from the prejudices of the anti-religious art historians of the eighteenth and nineteenth centuries and claims that the religious element is a moulding force in the creation of artistic form. Thus Dvořák points the way to a genuine understanding of the art of the Christian era; his treatment of the Dark Ages and the Romanesque periods is generalized while his analysis of the Gothic periods is extended and particularized.

For Dvořák medieval art is based on a reassessment of all artistic values of antiquity. This re-evaluation in the Gothic period inaugurates a new orientation of the artist's imagination and is marked by a fresh appraisal of physical reality.

Chapter II treats the basic problem of Gothic art as the relationship between transcendental ideas and the finite world. Anything perceivable by the senses or by reason is for Gothic art a reflection of the absolute, a manifestation of the sensibly and rationally unfathomable thought of God. All substances and relationships are shown to be completely transformed by new concepts of what was deemed spiritually valuable for mankind. Thus postclassical naturalism is based upon an interpretation of man as a spiritual personality, and the world is discovered anew as a reflection of individual consciousness. Hence evolves the special character of Gothic figures as expressions of a transcendental interpretation of ideal images. Artistic invention remains rooted in the experiencing of God rather than nature. Primacy is accorded to the theological structure ordering natural relationships and all objective, descriptive details that have no immediate connection with theological, hagiographic or liturgical meaning are suppressed as far as possible.

Certain views of St. Thomas Aquinas can by analogy throw light on the workings of the Gothic artistic imagination. The source of new significance lies for St. Thomas in man's power to attain to the *vis cognoscitiva* which enables man through divine grace spiritually to penetrate more deeply into the mysteries of external phenomena than he can by means of his frequently deceiving senses. The task of representation—*similitudo*, not *imago*—is to substitute the *imperfectum* of sense perception by the *perfectum* of the divine ideas. Not a uniform degree of nature observation is the aim, but rather a maximum of inner discipline in an abstract structure. Gothic figure art is organized as a hierarchy: 1) the higher the concept that a figure is meant to embody, the more simplified is its form; 2) only minor or secondary persons are characterized in their transitoriness, i.e., naturalistically. But even figures of the higher order should not lack what is intrinsic to their physical nature; in the words of St. Thomas, *claritas* must be joined to *integritas*. Idealism and naturalism appear here not as irreconcilable opposites, but as an illustration of St. Thomas's notion of *consonantia*—a valid criterion for the world of Gothic figures.

In the Gothic Cathedral, the symbol of the relationship between the *Civitas Dei* and the terrestrial world, representational art is not autonomous but acquires its *raison d'être* and significance from its focal position as the nexus of this polarity. It is, therefore, the transcendental interdependence of the figures that conditions their position and shape, their alignment against the pillars of the church as a *sacra conversazione sub specie aeternitatis*, and the upward surge of their endless, drawn-out movement. Their pictorial arrangement in scenes without any real stage and their three-dimensional appearance against spaceless tapestry backgrounds are likewise determined by this selfsame transcendental position.

The conflict of idealism and naturalism in Gothic art has its perfect analogy in the philosophy of the age, symbolized by the dispute between realism and nominalism. Thus even the expanding secularization of form and content in later Gothic art, one of the results of this conflict, would seem to have its roots in the spiritualism of medieval Christianity.

It is only toward the close of the Middle Ages that, under the influence of Aristotle, late scholastic philosophy develops the concept of divine revelation, and thus it loosens the ties that bound the intellect to transcendental thought. The parallel in

"Giovanni Arnolfini and Jeanne Cenami," by Jan van Eyck. *Reproduced by courtesy of the Trustees of the National Gallery, London.*

art, which forms the subject matter of Chapter III, is the new possibility of the coexistence of unfettered idealism and unprejudiced observation of nature. After a transitional period in the fourteenth century, Northern art, mainly as a result of Jan van Eyck's epoch-making innovations, reaches a point where intuitive observation of nature in its self-evidence is regarded as the cornerstone of artistic truth. A concomitant factor is the radically new notion of pictorial space as a cut from nature replacing the abstract concept of the universe dependent on and organized by supranatural factors. Infinity of space is, however, still understood as an integral part of divine creation. Light, which as a source of all visibility is first shown in Jan van Eyck's painting, now becomes the unifying element through which every single figure and object partakes of the world as a whole. By means of their silent detachment from all earthly activity and passion, Jan van Eyck's motionless figures, no less isolated than the statues in the pillars of a Gothic cathedral, display for the first time an inner life which enables them to commune with each other in a common contemplative mood.

Karl Maria Swoboda

IDEALISM AND NATURALISM
IN GOTHIC ART

INTRODUCTION

HE ever expanding knowledge of the political, legal, economic and religious life of the Middle Ages is undoubtedly to be considered among the greatest accomplishments of contemporary historiography. As Georg von Below (q.v.) once noted, the writing of history has never been as objective as it is today. By this he meant not merely source criticism, a discipline only recently raised to the greatest possible degree of certitude, but also the manysidedness of observation as well as the ability to render even the most distant and heterogeneous periods of history intelligible. This progress, which is the natural outgrowth of both the extension and deepening of historical studies and the growing wealth of man's cultural consciousness, can nowhere be more clearly observed than in the treatment of the history of the Middle Ages.

This is true, however, not only for the history of medieval art. To be sure, contemporary literature about the art of the Middle Ages is vast although not nearly as extensive as is the literature devoted to the art of classical antiquity or the Renaissance. An abundance of new facts has been made available, facts which were investigated in all areas of medieval art and by means of which, in certain of these areas, and in exemplary fashion, a permanent basis for every later scientific treatment of the material was established. In this connection one need only refer to Georg Dehio's (q.v.) monumental work on medieval ecclesiastical architecture.[1]

The attentive observer, however, can hardly have failed to notice that the interpretation of these facts has in no way kept pace with the establishment of their validity. This is particularly evident in the critical examination of the works of medieval sculpture and painting. Much excellent work has been accomplished in certain areas, e.g., in the investigation of the external history of their origins; in the notation of time and place factors; in the determination of specific schools as well as delimitation of each; in questions of iconography, or in the critical treatment of existing works of art. On the contrary, however, hardly anything that could be considered satisfactory today has been done in the art-historical explanation of the universal fact of art per se which these works embody, either individually or considered in their totality.

The admirable, indeed grandiose, attempt of Karl Schnaase (q.v.) to deduce medieval art as a whole from the "external and internal motifs" of the Middle Ages is almost fifty years old and rests for the most part on hypotheses that now must be considered superseded and no longer tenable.[2] Since then, however, in spite of more exact knowledge of the past, little has been done to approach historically the artistic meaning of medieval sculpture or painting and little has been learned about understanding them in their individuality as products of artistic endeavors which were characteristic of the Middle Ages and which, objectively speaking, are not less important and noteworthy than the endeavors of classical antiquity or the Italian Renaissance; for in a similar manner these artistic works of the Middle Ages have also influenced the later development of art. Generally speaking a great inner and creative power is attributed only to medieval architecture. The works of representational art partake of this power to only a slight degree and then rather indirectly.[3] With

"Moses," by Claus Sluter; from the Well of Moses. *Courtesy European Art Color Slide Co., New York.*

few exceptions, which I shall treat later, they are consciously or unconsciously treated more or less as "simply historical documents" and "products of primitive stages of artistic development," or as relative values of a period of transition. Only in the rarest cases are they examined for their individual, specifically medieval artistic content. It was against this particular attitude that Schnaase directed his attack.

On the other hand, if one attempts to judge fairly the artistic merits of medieval sculpture or painting, the words of praise usually sound rather hollow, almost like conventional forms of polite discourse. Inherent in such criticism are value judgements that are arbitrarily transferred to the Middle Ages. This naturally influences the total picture of medieval art and renders it uncertain and remarkably lifeless—a kingdom of nebulous, chaotic twilight out of which isolated towering peaks of artistic creation emerge—the immense cathedrals, the statuary of Reims and Naumburg, the rose windows of Chartres—and radiates effects and significances which, although powerful, are more vaguely felt than clearly defined. The majority of the monuments of this period, however, appear to be little more than an indifferent mass which can excite questions of antiquarian interest, vague stylistic suppositions or modernistic emotive associations and which are totally lacking in that historic and artistic vitality that characterizes, for example, even the most insignificant work of Greek art as the necessary flowering of a specific, closed and individualistic development of mind and art.

The causes of this state of affairs will become clear if one considers how the standard, which later critics used to judge the artistic significance of a medieval creation of sculpture or painting, is established. Apart from points of view of content, these works of art are first and foremost examined to determine whether or not they are still "classical" or already "true to nature." Parenthetically it should be noted that the term "true to nature" is to be understood as those demands for external objectivity of description and reproduction of form which developed in the art of the fifteenth and early sixteenth centuries and which since then have remained for the public as a whole the outer limits of that which can be demanded of a representation that is both faithful to its content as well as true to its existential reality. In other words, medieval painting and sculpture are judged by standards of a far distant past or a much later development, standards which forget that between these two extremes lay centuries forming a world unto themselves. Basically this is the standpoint of Italian art theoreticians of the Renaissance and the Baroque ages; moreover this standard remains operative in prolonging the theory of the degeneration and revitalization of art —a theory which in the fifteenth century evolved from the artistic condemnation of everything that could be classified "Gothic" and which, having survived the emotional and historic rediscovery of medieval art some one hundred years ago, has merely assumed new scientific forms.

It was and certainly still is fruitful to trace both the continued existence of classical antiquity during the Middle Ages as well as various incipient influences at different times and in different areas—for example, the impact of various Renaissance movements or the degree of influence of Byzantine art forms. In like manner, research into the medieval origins of an objectively demonstrable fidelity to nature can be both interesting as well as important, for example, studies concerning the extent of positive knowledge of the natural sciences prevalent in the Middle Ages. However investigations of this type can in no way justify the belief that the fields of research have been exhaustively fathomed and clarified with unalterable decisions concerning the notions of "retrogression" and "progress" in medieval art, its general art-historical position or its essence and goals. In paradoxical contrast to the generally prevalent method of research of a few decades ago, the naturalistic advances of medieval art cannot be viewed as irrelevant to the intentions which served as its artistic basis.

On the contrary, these intentions were so variously and inextricably bound to specifically medieval suppositions and problems that were they to be separated from them, they could neither be properly understood nor could they afford a satisfactory picture of the abilities of the medieval artists and the irresistible daemon which drove them to create in a manner so opposed to the commonly accepted artistic credo. What has thus far been said of fidelity to nature must similarly be predicated of individual compositional characteristics, which one (laboring under the influence of classical art and the artistic tendencies stemming directly from the Renaissance) is accustomed to consider inseparable from the concept of every figurative representation that is "no longer primitive." This quality, however, cannot always and with equal validity be attributed to these various compositional characteristics. In many respects the standards by which one judges medieval sculpture and painting are simply incompatible with the art of classical antiquity or of the contemporary era, just as the crusades can in no way be compared to the military exploits of Greece and Rome or to modern colonialism. Were these varied periods of art to be compared, it is not difficult to prove that classical antiquity far outlived its official end and that the Renaissance had started long before its recognized beginning. In doing this, however, what actually constitutes the peculiar individuality of medieval representational art is lost and that very element essential to its own values and basically new tendencies is completely ignored.

Nevertheless one must not conclude that the specifically medieval artistic qualities of Romanesque or Gothic sculpture and painting were never the objects of historical research. Rather they were repeatedly stressed and examined with reference to individual monuments, schools or periods. And yet the obviously prevailing uncertainty of these studies, vacillating between a wholly subjective emphasis on the one hand and totally incoherent observations on the other, clearly demonstrates that both

sound bases and historically clarified perspectives were completely lacking. Contemporary art historians have come to recognize this deficiency and have repeatedly endeavored to overcome it by means of a broadened understanding of the values
serving as the basis and the particular individuality of medieval
art as well as by a unified and vitalized interpretation of its total
character—an interpretation that to a certain degree had already
been accorded the Romantic period. This Romantic interpretation, however, was so incredibly and one-sidedly based on current
intellectual movements that it could only gradually disappear,
without being replaced by some similar theory, when artistic
naturalism and historical criticism came to dominate even the
concept of classical art.

The favorable reception of Wilhelm Worringer's (q.v.) attempt to rend with one blow the veil behind which, until now,
the essence of medieval art had remained concealed from the
contemporary public proves how quickly and vigorously the recognition of this critical deficiency has spread.[4] Irrespective of
the actual historical facts and by arbitrarily limiting himself to
one very characteristic trait of medieval art, Worringer based
his brilliantly written observations upon an ethnopsychological
concept of the Gothic "will-to-form." It is this ethnic will-to-
form that distinguishes everything artistically created by the
younger Nordic peoples of their own initiative from the artistic
artifacts of the older oriental and classical civilizations. That
which is essentially Gothic in medieval art can, therefore, be interpreted as a latent or typical characteristic of its entire artistic
development until it was interrupted by the secularism of the
Italian Renaissance. The elaboration of this Gothic quality was
resumed at a later date but only to the extent that art was lib-
erated from the mannerisms and goals of the Renaissance. As
brilliant as Worringer's proof may appear at first glance, a closer
examination of his initial premises reveals them to be little more
than an arbitrary construct. His whole theory is based on the

idea of an a priori Gothic concentration by the younger Nordic peoples on the intensification of the expressions of the transcendental; this concentration is not only at variance with reality but actually inimically opposed to any form of naturalism. Although clarifying many important phenomena of medieval art, this theory when judged by the complexities of the period proves to be even more fantastic than the abstract stylistic concepts of the Romanticists. A few studies in the field of ancient Christian and medieval architecture and sculpture, to which I shall return later, have proven to be much more fruitful, but in essence they contain hardly more than the isolated beginnings of an interpretation of the artistic significance of medieval sculpture and painting; this interpretation is independent of commonly accepted but no longer tenable notions.

The difficulty in establishing a more compatible relationship with the sculpture and painting of the Middle Ages rests primarily upon the fact that the common spiritual foundations of medieval art have been neither sufficiently known nor adequately taken into account. To be sure, it has been repeatedly emphasized that medieval art was based entirely on a religious *Weltanschauung*, but for the most part one still fails to realize that this *Weltanschauung* influenced the development of art positively as well as negatively and in so doing created points of view and values that are incommensurable with everything that preceded them. It must also be borne in mind that modern art historians are in no way justified in assessing these values and viewpoints and their determining *Weltanschauung* as of lesser historical worth than the guiding values of any other age since they too influenced later art forms. Certainly no one today can still maintain, as many did so vociferously in the past, that medieval theology was nothing more than a sterile hiatus in the mental development of mankind, a muzzling of the human spirit by means of an obscurantist dogmatism. On the contrary, man has come to realize that this religious philosophy of the Middle Ages is an important stage in the spiritual development of the European peoples, as necessary to contemporary intellectual life as are the spirit and achievements of the Renaissance. The same is true for medieval art. The far-reaching distinctions differentiating contemporary art from that of classical antiquity have their roots, for the most part, in the Middle Ages and more precisely in those developmental stages of medieval art which are as far removed from classical antiquity as they are from contemporary thought and feeling, that is in the particular relationship of medieval man to the life of the senses.

How is one to learn to understand and to interpret all of these factors which at first glance seem to prevent any appreciation on man's part since they have their origin in a particular artistic sensibility with which modern man lacks almost every immediate contact? Thanks to an extensive, systematic intellectual formation, classical antiquity has become an integral part of the spiritual heritage; most of the general intellectual principles that have gained ascendency since the victory of the Renaissance over the semi-closed ecclesiastical system of the Middle Ages continue to exercise an influence on man's intellectual and artistic consciousness. On the other hand, despite the exuberant enthusiasm of the Romanticists, the spiritual culture of the Middle Ages remains for man today, in the fullest sense of the word, a foreign world, a clear picture of which can be gained only gradually and after much persistent, concerted effort. In this task the outstanding survivals of those spiritual and material values that the Middle Ages deemed worthy to be artistically exemplified and immortalized can doubtlessly serve as guides.

Further I would not hesitate to emphasize that the most important results which one can expect from a history of art thus oriented must stem precisely from those very goals which differentiate art history from the other humanistic studies, namely the observation of artistic endeavors and forms of expression in their immanent and autonomous development. However this does not mean to imply that the justifiable pride of having solved certain artistic problems within one's own particular field must axiomatically ignore other more or less extraneous sources of data which can be utilized in the critical examination of the general intellectual situation of the Middle Ages—whether they be the progress made by research in other fields of medieval spiritual life as a whole or the analysis of original literary monuments through which this spiritual life expressed itself. I do not suggest that one should attempt to relate artistic phenomena in any causative sense with the development of new economic, social or religious conditions or to deduce the specific spiritual content of medieval works of art from the writings of the great contemporary theologians whose influence on art, if it had ever existed at all, could hardly be historically comprehended. Schnaase and his school of historical interpretation attempted to do just this and it was not long before the sterility of such an approach was recognized. However those factors which can afford man the most valuable means by which to adjudge medieval art, namely its spiritual content, deviating as it does sharply from those values with which man is familiar today as well as the immensely important development of the relationship of art to transcendental ideas on the one hand and to the actual facts and goods of nature and life on the other—the most important source of inner mutations in medieval art—all of these were naturally not limited to the field of art alone but were common to all movements of the time and to the historical verities upon which the medieval Christian *Weltanschauung*, the fundamental basis for everything here under consideration, exerted an untold influence.

Therefore, in pursuing the study of the history of art, one will encounter stages of development which derived those elements normally expected of art not from any theoretical speculation but rather from a direct contact with various fields of human activity. Thus in medieval literature or in the great theological confrontations and systems as well as in the scientific endeavors and the general educational tendencies of the Middle Ages, this interplay of thought and a unified world outlook is, for the most part, either unambiguously expressed in the documents pertaining to each field or is made so clearly evident through comparative research that the significance of corresponding analogies in art can hardly be doubted. It is indeed not the scanty registers of the alchemists' workshops, the recipe books, which recently have assumed such an unwarranted importance,[5] that are the true theoretical commentaries on the rebirth of an idealistic-monumental art in the Middle Ages and the new forms of creation which this art derived directly from nature; rather it is the works of the great medieval thinkers whose main preoccupation was for centuries the problem of man's relationship to compelling intellectual abstractions and his interpretation of the world of the senses as determined by these concepts.

The decisive, artistic goals and interdependencies in the history of postmedieval art can be understood only to the extent that during the period of their ascendency (in spite of occasionally evidenced arbitrariness) they were accompanied by theoretical discussions on the nature and techniques of art, the principal result of which was that later art-historical investigations were able to establish contact from the very beginning with a continuous body of knowledge of the most important changes in the interpretation of artistic problems. This was, however, almost completely lacking in the Middle Ages where formal objectives had to be subordinated to a greater or lesser degree to a common spiritual content. However this deficiency can be compensated for, in part, by the works of the great theologians dedicated to this problem.

Although the ultimate goals of art-historical investigation are uniform, obviously the great periods of art demand a special scientific treatment, and it would indeed be unwise were the above named aids to be disregarded only because they seem to pertain to fields extraneous to the principal object of art history or because in the past they have not always been felicitously applied. The point is entirely missed if these secondary sources are indiscriminately used to construct a presumably definitive description of the artistic conditions of any given period. They can, however, render an indisputably heuristic service (as I shall attempt to demonstrate in the following study of one particular concrete problem) in establishing a new set of criteria by which to judge works of art—which is perhaps one of the most important desiderata in the contemporary study of the history of medieval art.

I. IDEALISTIC FUNDAMENTALS

HAT does one really mean when he speaks of the idealism of Gothic art? As opposed to the idealism of classical art, Gothic idealism had its origin in the spiritualism of the Christian *Weltanschauung* and was based on the victory of an abstract, ideal significance over formal perfection, the mastery of spirit over matter. This dominance was not limited to Gothic architecture and sculpture alone; it is equally applicable to all aspects of medieval art and life. Indeed its influence even predates the Middle Ages since it is also a characteristic of the late classical spiritual development and as such belongs to the many bonds uniting Christianity and the culture of classical antiquity. A purely semitic Christianity, that is a Christianity bitterly opposed to any union of the concept "God" with figurative representations thereof, is just as unthinkable among the peoples who inhabited the Mediterranean seacoasts as was the acceptance by these same peoples (and by this same Christianity) of the strictly materialistic anthropocentrism of Greek-Hellenistic art. A desired compromise was effected by combining the forces of neo-Platonic philosophy and the new illusionistic art; moreover this compromise enabled the new religious beliefs to be fused with the classical world of culture in the field of art.

A form of art that apprehends physical reality as nothing more than an endlessly flowing and variable optical impression and that constantly refashions material being as merely the reflected image of subjective sensation could very easily shift the main emphasis in artistic creation in the direction of a spiritual subjectivism and thereby replace the preponderant sensualism of the older classical art with that stress on spiritualism which was to be the basis of the entire art of the Middle Ages.[6] This new basic orientation of the imagination, enabling the Germanic peoples to enter into the formerly closed province of Mediterranean art, gave rise to a wholly new art that, alternating between a slow ordered development and sudden drastic change, would seem to be a decided retrogression because it was moving in a direction different from that which man formerly was accustomed to consider progress. It removed from artistic forms anything that could be considered an expression of the artistic apotheosis of either the strikingly physical in man or those rational powers which control matter, thereby converting dead architectonic masses into aspects of mathematics, and then, as a matter of principle, idealizing their heavy amorphous, "barbaric" formlessness by means of rhythm and a "secret" construction. As an expression of abstract ideas, art was therefore to be transformed from that of a cult image to the level of a religious confession; consequently it demanded of all figurative representation a deeper meaning, a fundamental spiritualization. This shift in interpretation and emphasis, so decisive at its inception, was to remain equally so in all future forms of art.

If this study is based on objectively historical points of view, it becomes obvious that these and similar considerations will enable early medieval and Romanesque art to appear in an entirely new light—as an art which not only throve on inherited classical traditions, while striving simultaneously for newer naturalistic and technically practical solutions, but one which also in its own right, as an independent phase of a great spiritual-idealistic

Queen Mary's Psalter, Christ Preaching. *Reproduced by courtesy of the Trustees of the British Museum, London.*

period of art, created new values and principles for the development of mankind, not solely in art but in every area of cultural endeavor.

However Gothic idealism was essentially different from the antimaterialism of late classical antiquity and the early medieval period. While for the latter, matter was per se null and void, or at least immaterial from the standpoint of a spiritual elevation via art, and all but eliminated wherever possible. The relation between the physically perceivable and the transcendental became extraordinarily complicated during the later Middle Ages.

Since this is true not only in the domain of art, the clarification of the entire problem will be greatly facilitated if one bears in mind how this particular relationship developed within the framework of the total *Weltanschauung* of the later Middle Ages. One of the cardinal errors traceable to the literature of the early Humanists is the belief that the *humaniora* were the only legacy inherited by later ages from classical antiquity. As an integral part of the militaristic and polytheistic national states, founded on natural law, they too were doomed to dissolution once the might of these states was crushed and consequently nothing but *membra disjecta* remained. Because their meaning, based on a naive materialism, was lost, they were rendered as valueless as a manuscript which cannot be deciphered. The *humaniora* were replaced by the idea of the absolute worth of the human soul and by an ethos that was based not on might or law but rather on conviction and a feeling of communal sentiment. This new theory was a combined product of classical philosophy and Christianity; that it was able to assume its dominant position almost without a struggle illustrates far more cogently than do external revolutions the deep abyss which separates a new age, indeed a new mankind, from classical antiquity. The new spiritual goals that alone guaranteed truth and moral rectitude appeared so valuable to this "new" humanity that every other consideration was temporarily shunted aside as something superfluous and indifferent.

EIGHTEEN

Classical culture declined not because it was inundated by barbarians, nor because it lost its best representatives (e.g., Otto Seeck [q.v.]), but rather because these same great minds were now engaged in pursuits other than those which underlay the whole structure of classical institutions and attitudes toward life. The positive sciences, national literatures, naturalistic art—all of these fell into decay because the great thinkers were now faced with a totally new question as to the ultimate meaning of existence, a question which far surpassed their former humanistic endeavors; moreover what these minds were then to create was much more than the mere internal and external formulation of a new religion. The great dichotomy that separates classical antiquity from the world of the Middle Ages is perhaps nowhere better summarized than in the words of Wilhelm Dilthey where in essence he states that although the civilizations of Greece and Rome had produced an aesthetically sensuous culture, it was only the intense, century-long concentration of man's imagination and speculative faculties on purely spiritual ideals (ideals which characterize the intellectual life of Christian antiquity and of the earlier Middle Ages) which made possible that penetration of all phases and problems of life by purely spiritual values and that predominance of objective truths and ethical feelings recognized by man as both self-existent realities and as the most important presuppositions of all later cultural progress.[7]

This transference of emphasis from the sensually perceivable and from an organization of life based on will and power to a system rooted in spiritual trends and emotions could hardly have had such far reaching effects had it not begun its ultimate victorious conquest as an unconditionally religious challenge that recognized only supernatural goals. Sooner or later this unrestrained spiritualism, having undermined and deprived the older cultures of their values, had to come to terms with existing conditions to the extent that, in ecclesiastical guise, it began actively to intervene in all the activities of daily life. A similar crisis had engulfed the religious, political, social and cultural conditions of the early Middle Ages when, in the throes of a great spiritual catastrophe, they had emancipated themselves from every cultural dependance on classical antiquity in order to reorient their psychic energies under the influence of the younger European peoples. Out of this struggle arose, however, that problem in which all of the spiritual interests of the Middle Ages were to intersect and which, occupying all of the great medieval minds, was to prove to be the key to the entire medieval *Weltanschauung* and world order. This problem involved the proper relationship between transcendental ideas and the "world as such," between natural and supernatural law or, in other words, between the absolute spiritual principle of a transcendental determination of life and everything else which nature, life itself and the historical development of earthly goods and preconceptions offered as opposing determinants.[8]

From this problem, or rather from this complex of problems, emerged the remarkable system of the spiritual life of the later Middle Ages whose point of departure as well as its purest embodiment was the medieval church. In her role as guardian and mediatrix of God's grace and revelation, of those most profound and ideal of all spiritual possessions which, according to Christian interpretation, are to be considered higher than everything else, the church was also automatically the mediatrix of a complete revaluation of all worldly values. As an institution, the church was founded on the theosophic principle of a divine state and on concepts concerned with the hereafter that, according to the position of the Stoics, expressed not only a negative but also a positive relationship to life here on earth with its worldly goods and rights, goals and duties. This relationship to the here and now was based on the force of actual situations, and above all on the consequent autonomous development and application of basic Christian ideas. In her role as arbiter of the rights of this world, the church would no longer negate her claims on man's attention to the extent that she had done so earlier but rather endeavored to give them a new content and meaning. The world was discovered anew and interpreted not in accord with new theories or residues of older ones but principally from the standpoint of that all-pervading medieval spiritualism that gave birth to a new worldly ethos, a new science, a new poetry and a new *Weltanschauung* whose basic character was a religious, philosophic and historic relativism. As the stage for meritorious works, life assumed fresh meaning and nature, a new significance as the evidence of God's omnipotent power and wisdom. The natural, social and political institutions with their varying gradations of duties and rights, were annexed to the intricately organized hierarchy of the church which—considered as both a work of Providence and as the necessary stage in the supernaturally determined development of mankind—although frequently forced into violent or sophistic compromises, must be recognized as the first great successful attempt, unexcelled in the boldness and energy of its execution, to erect upon a spiritual basis a total culture in all its natural and historic ramifications.

The church was founded on the most important philosophic and ethical accomplishments of classical antiquity—on Plato and Aristotle and Cicero, on the Stoics and Roman law, on the development of Christian ideas as well as constitutive elements of the emerging nationalities.[9] However the end result of this union that ensued (somewhat analogous to the fusion of heterogeneous chemical elements under high temperature) from an intense absorption with the basic problems of being, an involvement pushed to the ultimate of energy and concentration, was entirely new and independent. It was not only a *politeia* or *civitas Dei* (worthy of the boldest dreams of a Plato or Augustine) but something far more essential. It was a complete reconstruction of all avenues to knowledge and moral consciousness, a new unified and forceful system of thought and emotion into which the entire criteria of earlier spiritual values were assumed—a system which encompassing both philosophic scholasticism and religious mysticism contained the first beginnings of the rationalistic as well as the idealistic tendencies of the modern world. Thus in this system, classical antiquity not only actually faded into the past but was virtually overcome as a vital coeval force for all times to come.

This remarkable, complicated and profoundly artistic system was reflected in the art of the later Middle Ages. With reference to the subtlety of its constructions, this art has often been referred to as petrified scholasticism—a metaphor which is justified only insofar as it concerns parallel aspects of a more deeply rooted, all-pervading cultural transformation. In Gothic art one will also find a fundamental compromise between a supernatural interpretation of life and a qualified recognition of the rights of this life on earth, a fact which is of the very essence of this transformation. This art found its highest and richest expression in the immense cathedrals of medieval Europe, not because it was purely hieratic as old Egyptian art had been and certainly not because solutions to problems of this religious art offered absolutely the only source of artistic imagery. Rather the answer lies in the fact that the huge cathedrals were the purest embodiment of the ecclesiastical world dominion, as it were a symbol of their age, just as the teeming metropolis is a symbol of the twentieth century. One must beware, however, of interjecting contemporary concepts into these questions. All comparisons aside, the Gothic cathedrals were a completely unique, specifically medieval creation. The same men who inhabited dank little towns with narrow alleys and gloomy dwellings, both mentally and physically penned in, executed religious edifices which seem to burst every narrowness of earthly constraint and towered heavenward through endless space at vertiginous heights. There is nothing, or very little, that can be considered massive or solid in these cathedrals—the common endeavor of artists from near and far. These communal projects of generations and nations, indeed of all Christendom, arose as the mighty symbol of God's divine kingdom on earth, the expression of ideas which held before the eyes of man a higher form of being, the purified essence of mankind's earthly existence.

In these cathedrals one encounters the relationship between the world and the *civitas Dei* in a new form, that of matter and spirit. Gothic architecture did not seek to eliminate matter, for the cathedrals are enormous stone structures and as such were meant to create an overwhelming physical effect. But by artistic design they are radically different from the early Christian basilicas in which the material nucleus of the structure had no artistic function for the viewer and which, therefore, was made to disappear in a dissolving play of movement, vanishing perspectives, light and shadow effect, and the interplay of color.

In no sense can this be asserted of Gothic structures that never attempted to deny their basic stone character. In this they are more nearly akin to earlier Romanesque architecture—and yet even here a profound difference separates the two. In Romanesque buildings the dualistic *Weltanschauung* appears as a harsh juxtaposition of matter (wall and pillar) and abstract compositional regularity. In Gothic architecture, on the other hand, this basic materiality, this architectonic mass of stone as a requisite element of construction, surrendered its independence and self-determination without losing its forcefulness, and became rather (as it had previously been in Grecian architecture) the expression of a unified, subsuming artistic idea. Even here a distinction must be made. Whereas in Greek architecture the principal concern in artistic creativity and figurative representation was the embodiment and transfiguration of 1) the objective, material forces inherent in a building as mass, 2) the center of equilibrium and 3) the physical resistance and the means of overcoming it in order to breathe life into concrete matter; in Gothic architecture it was these very forces of artistic effect that were, wherever possible, excluded or at least concealed so that the material mass involved was compelled to submit to other forces not present in its natural state or particular condition. By means of a highly ingenious method of construction, itself a technical advancement signifying a new era in the history of mankind and becoming indeed a significant symbol for all positivistic systems and interpretations of history devised not primarily as a technical accomplishment but rather as a furtherance of purely spiritual goals,[10] two basic characteristics of material mass could be overcome, namely its earth-bound stability and its compact coherency. Thus without wholly freeing it of its matter, this mass could be rendered subservient to a transcendental, artistic will, based not on the will of various individuals (as it was to be during the age of Baroque art) but on the universal ideas which dominate mankind. Seeming hardly to rest upon the earth, monstrously huge and yet never ponderous, the Gothic cathedrals tower within a limitless verticalism far above the cities below them; though dissolved in space and as seemingly independent in growth as vegetative nature, these cathedrals were unified down to the last turret by an immanent ordering which regulates their every detail. Moreover this regulation of detail makes them analogous to the divine law and to that ecclesiastical and secular authority which represents it within the life of Church and State, and in addition it draws together each architectural feature into a universal, ideal unity.

Imitative art was unable to obtain an independent importance in this artistic organism which flourished for decades and centuries without losing its unity, primarily because it rested on an immaterial principle and not on an isolated, self-contained form.[11] This sounds almost paradoxical if one considers the incalculable number of statues that embellish these Gothic cathedrals and that definitely signify a renascence of monumental sculpture; or if one recalls the quantity of stained-glass windows and murals that have either survived the ravages of time or have been destroyed since the Middle Ages, the sum total of which in their abundance of motifs and portrayals would alone be of value as the most exhaustive illustrated chronicle of all times.

In spite of these considerations, this wealth of material was

Amiens Cathedral, west facade; rows of statues with quatrefoils showing prophets and Old Testament kings. *Courtesy Jean Roubier, Paris.*

fettered, exteriorly and interiorly enchained, with respect to the cathedrals to which they were allied as well as in their relationship to nature and life. Renaissance paintings of Raphael or Titian are a microcosmos, a world unto themselves not only in the sense that their value and effect are not essentially dependent on the effect of the building for which they were commissioned but rather because the greatest part of their artistic content was autonomous and could be understood and enjoyed without a direct relation to any overall artistic system. This is not at all the case with Gothic sculpture and painting. The series of statues which adorn a Gothic facade form an integral part of it, and not merely as a form of decoration as has been occasionally asserted whenever the decorative significance of Gothic sculpture and painting has been discussed. If the literal meaning of the word is not entirely to be distorted, one can speak of art forms that are "decorative" only if they form an aggregate which is designed to heighten the effect of an art work—forms which can be omitted, however, without destroying the inherent value of the basic form. Gothic ornamental statuary is a part of this form and in conjunction with other architectonic factors expresses the movement of the building and its tectonic sense, the unhampered growth, the free dissolution of a compact mass. In like manner, Gothic monumental paintings are the unmistakable expression of a form of architecture which has withdrawn the predominance of effect from firm walls, circular forms and self-enclosed space.

It would be totally wrong, however, if Gothic sculpture and painting were seen only as an embodiment of the architectural principles of their age. Within the framework of architectonic constraint, Gothic imitative art was, as it were, a new and independent attempt to solve the perennial problems of plastic and figurative art; this attempt was based on the idealistic character of early Gothic art. Moreover it is this basic character of early Gothic art that must also serve as the point of departure in this present study, even though from the very beginning one encounters innumerable difficulties. The terminology of artistic characteristics itself is one such source of confusion since the vocabulary of art in current usage stems from a period in history which neither could nor wanted to acknowledge the artistic significance of the older Gothic art. In addition there exist rather objective reasons for this lack of sympathetic appreciation, reasons which deserve a more penetrating analysis.

Between the Middle Ages and the present day the concept of what constitutes art has changed radically (even there where irrational material is the principal subject of treatment), since the modern interpretation of art is based on varying relationships to real being, to nature and to the sensuous life of man on this earth. For this very reason it is not at all easy for one to penetrate abstractly a world which conceived all values of reality, or everything graspable by the senses or by reason as well as everything finite and limited, as simply reflections of the absolute, the eternal, the infinite. Moreover Gothic ideology envisioned reality as manifestations of the sensibly and rationally unfathomable thought of God, which in the words of Hildebert of Lavardine (q.v.) is "above all, under all, exterior to all, in all" and to which alone every causality, every creative agent and every created reality must be reduced. The originality of medieval art does not lie solely in its religious character to which repeated reference has been made—the art of the Counter Reformation for example was not less religious, and yet despite many points of similarity it is far removed from Gothic art. Rather it is to be found in the all-pervading force of a spiritual construction situated beyond material experience, a force whose influence was so extensive that any direct reference to sense experience in spiritual matters was considered to be a foolish and self-condemnatory abuse of truth and human reason. Today the situation is reversed, for any arbitrary disregard of sense experience is considered now to be equally absurd and bordering on the fallacious and detrimental. The whole attitude of the Middle Ages is perhaps most aptly summed up in the words which Anselm of Canterbury (q.v.) directed against Roscellin (q.v.) and his disciples, when he said: "In their souls thought is so ensnared in corporeal matters that it never will be able to extricate itself from their clutches."

It is precisely this subordination of all that is corporeal, of all sensible values and material relationships, to a purely spiritual and transcendental point of view that was the primary source for the progress made in the development of medieval art; consequently it must be regarded as an independent and self-contained phase in the general evolution of European art; this phase is equally as important as that of oriental, classical or modern art. In addition medieval art illustrates the general cultural growth that in classical Christianity and in early Christian art led from the dream-like spiritualization of matter and of the entire universe to the barbaric, volcanic, almost cruelly revolutionary disregard of sensuous beauty by the younger peoples and the newer culture; this development drew a sharper line of demarcation between the new spiritual truths and convictions (and the activity of the imagination based on these new verities) and the "illusory existence" of former worldly goods and sensible impressions—a division which led to the eventual destruction of all the older cultural concepts.[12] After having been forced by the influence of new political and social circumstances to seek a compromise with earthly existence and its values (and it is precisely here in this compromise that the most direct cause of the Carolingian Renaissance is to be discovered) and after the unconditional, transcendental religious determination of human conduct had ceased to exercise exclusive dominance in the life of man the Carolingian Age began to return anew to these once discarded concepts. Again it was the predominance of spiritualism which, in the final analysis, exercised a decisive influence on art, irrespective of all new demands and goals. In like measure, it was this renewed spiritualism that directed art along the path of a gradual revaluation of all sensuous elements, and this reinterpretation based on spiritual principles could only lead art further and further away from the guiding aspirations of classical Greece and Rome.

It would be important and very tempting to discuss in detail how, out of this process in all of the arts, the first stages of development resulted in Romanesque art with its remarkable parallelism of effect embracing both the finitely material and the abstractly transcendental; and how the second developmental stage was to terminate in Gothic art with the total transmutation of inherited art forms by means of a complete penetration and transformation of all real substances and relationships by new concepts of what was deemed spiritually valuable for mankind and of itself worthy of being immortalized. It would be equally tempting to determine how this transmutation of artistic values affected every other relationship to the social, political and cultural milieu and gave rise to new artistic concepts, formal goals and points of view. In addition this transmutation encouraged a new, progressive elevation of the world of the body that, although entirely different from classical perspectives, was to realize its artistic ends by a reversed utilization of classical means. Whereas classical art sought to raise the sensuous to the level of spirit, Gothic art endeavored to clothe the spiritual—and indeed at first the supernatural—in sensuous forms and thereby to elevate a transitory, finite materiality into the realm of ideal human values by means of formal beauty and artistic abstraction. Finally one could consider the problem of how all forms of tradition were revaluated in terms of this universal, radically new art, the essence of which was an entirely new *Weltanschauung* and because of which new problems, new laws of monumental harmony, artistic perfection, size and general validity were to evolve.

Were the above considerations, substantiated and illumined by the vast store of factual knowledge at man's command, to serve as the incentive for an historical study of medieval art, a drama of artistic development would be unveiled before one's eyes which, with respect to the consistency of its inner structure, the compactness and severity of its form, and its value for all future times, would find its only parallel in the artistic genius of classical Greece.

This, however, is a task for the future. Today I will only consider, at least insofar as they are necessary for my purpose, a few of the characteristics of Gothic sculpture and painting which resulted from their transcendentally idealistic origins. Inasmuch as figural representation completely dominated the scene at first, it would behoove one to proceed from it and attempt to investigate the points of view which were decisive in the creation of each individual figure.

The objective content of Gothic statuary stems from two sources: tradition and, as is occasionally emphasized, "a personal relationship to nature." In the perceptive words of Wilhelm Vöge (q.v.), this content is "retraced by the artist as though it were reflected in a concave mirror,"[13] or, in other words, as though it were adapted to some formal pattern. However this pattern was certainly not based on primitive images residual in the collective memory as has been assumed by Julius Lange (q.v.) and Emanuel Löwy (q.v.) who considered such subconscious collective memories to be the natural fount of primitive Greek art as well as of every other primitive art.[14] Furthermore this scheme cannot be deduced directly from the structural and aesthetic presuppositions of the new architecture as was most ingeniously attempted by Vöge.[15] It was rather an extraordinarily complicated product of the entire development of medieval art which could be explained far more readily in terms of the idealistic norms of the golden age of Grecian art. However the main difference is that in Gothic art it was not natural function and its corresponding beauty and forms of expression which were of primary concern, although the medieval artist did strive for a perfected execution of these factors in his art. Of far greater importance was the refashioning of concepts and relationships,

Chartres Cathedral, south portal; trumeau of the central bay, "Le Beau Dieu." *Courtesy Giraudon, Paris.*

based on tradition or direct observation of nature, into expressions of a transcendental interpretation of ideal images. They were not only to embody artistically intensified impressions of reality and those natural powers which dominate all living organisms, but they were also to combine with the concrete form those qualities which would best reveal to the viewer, under the aspects of a transcendental conformity to norms, the substance of the divine and its all-pervading governance.[16]

It is doubtlessly correct to refer to the didactic meaning of medieval sculpture and painting, this "Bible of the poor in spirit," as one of their most important characteristics. It should not be forgotten, however, that over and above the instructive, historical and dogmatic content of these works of art, their *raison d'être* centered in their power as morally edifying agents, whose object was to demonstrate the sovereignty of spiritual insight and revelation—a demonstration based on a "metaphysical transubstantiation" of all formal elements and relations (if I may be permitted the expression)—as opposed to "impure" and "deluding" sense perception, i.e., the *lex Dei* versus the *lex naturae*.

The concept of the *forma substantialis* as the reflected splendor of primal beauty (a beauty hidden to the naked eye and, in its total independence of all mutability, comprehensible only to enlightened intelligence) and the synthesis of secret causes and effects, which would reveal themselves only to the "spiritual eye," was taken directly from neo-Platonic philosophy and applied equally directly to the developing Christian *Weltanschauung*.[17] In the literature of the Middle Ages from St. Augustine to St. Thomas and beyond, this concept was subjected to ever deepening and broadening reinterpretations and was to play a role, though a far more important one, in the Christian conception of truth and beauty analogous to the classical-material ideal of beauty so prevalent in contemporary theories of art. That this was more than a mere apologetic attempt to rescue representational art becomes evident if one considers the entire progress of artistic development during the Middle Ages.[18]

At first glance, this progress will appear faltering and disunified when contrasted with the improvements made in the objective reproduction of nature, but if the striving for concrete values of expression, with which the Gothic system of figural creation sought to illustrate the new metaphysical relationship of man to his milieu, is taken into consideration, the logical consistency of the advances in artistic portrayal becomes obvious. For this striving, sense perception was hardly more than a beclouded source of artistic truth and beauty which can only be purified through the higher insights of the human spirit. The essence of this purification is, however, not an experiencing of nature but rather an experiencing of God, a gradually evolving process of the consciousness of self and an artistic endeavor to realize the deeper meaning of all artistic creation as a reflection of the Divine Intelligence shining forth in the wondrous cosmic order of all created matter.[19] In other words, natural causality, or subjection to natural laws, was replaced by an entirely different causal force which had its origin in the relationships of psychic life to the primal source of all being, limited neither temporally nor materially and thus devoid of all subjective determination, and which approached rather the state of a divine *fiat*. The question naturally arises then as to how this new causality was to be expressed in art. The most obvious answer lies perhaps in the conscious attempt of medieval art to avoid direct imitation of nature and thereby to divorce artistic creation from any external fidelity to concrete reality. Since medieval literature emphasizes again and again that a work of art must be truer than nature, one can assume with certainty that what in medieval art appears from a naturalistic point of view to be a decided lack of ability was, for the most part, the product of a well-considered artistic intention.

It is self-evident that, in consequence of such a reorientation of art, the experiencing of nature or the technical ability to reproduce it must inevitably decline. A somewhat similar phenomenon, albeit far more confined in time and space, occurred in the last century in the historical idealism of the classicists and the Nazarenes (q.v.), with a commensurate loss of certain older accomplishments and techniques in the art of painting. But in this instance, as in the Middle Ages, the loss of either technique or content was a willed renunciation of details which had become valueless for an advancing art under the influence of new tasks and views. This rejection was then not the cause but the consequence of a development whose point of departure was the disdain of any form of the cult of nature as the sign of a reprehensible heathenish sentiment. Thus any approximation of nature, be it via tradition or the result of new imaginative activity, was only a means to an end, ordained from the outset to serve higher artistic intentions and to be excluded from all consideration wherever it might countervail these purposes.

If, however, one inquires about the positive content of these artistic goals, primacy must be accorded first and foremost to a theological order of precedence and significance concerning natural relationships. If divine or holy persons are presented as venerable symbols, or miraculous occurrences as evidence of the redemptive process, it is done in a way demanded by the purposes of such artistic creations. Irrespective of experience or the possible reality of a given situation, the figurative task as such is placed in the foreground by either completely suppressing, or limiting as far as possible, all details of objective description which have no immediate connection with verbal statements or the theological, hagiographic and liturgical meaning of the persons being portrayed. On the other hand, everything that has any relationship whatsoever to the persons or situations being depicted is executed with the greatest possible emphasis, clarity and perspicuity. To the degree that the representation of natural space relationships and the establishment of each figural creation

"Adam and Eve," by Jan van Eyck; from the altarpiece of St. Bavo's at Ghent. *Courtesy l'Institut Royal du Patrimoine Artistique, Brussels.*

THIRTY-FIVE

in a real action, position or movement were not forgotten (and how could they be forgotten) but rather became meaningless, to that degree figurative representation was converted, as it were, into a type of hieroglyphics whose character and composition were determined primarily by preordained ideas of the "what" to be demonstrated and only secondarily by the "how" of real situations. Trees are only intimated by means of a few leaves, buildings by a few conspicuous structural elements; each such detail functions more as an abbreviation of reality which, in its unnaturally diminutive form, had only a relative independent importance. In contrast to this apparent indifference toward accuracy of detail, all of the means of artistic composition were concentrated on rendering intelligible to the mind alone the spiritual nucleus of composition, the venerable personality or the miraculous event in their compelling transcendental determination, being and effect. In essence, then, medieval art sought to give form to that which is immortal and invisible and to embody in concrete image the spiritual revelation of God; thereby medieval art transformed, under the aegis of art, the deepest secrets of the redemptive act and the omnipotence of supernatural powers into an edifying and soul-stirring present.

Because of this exemplification and unsubstantial illusion, not only did the traditional late classical figurative devices based on natural laws and sense perception have to be dissolved and re-formed, converted, as it were, into a semblance of forms [German original: *Spoglien* = spoils] with which entirely new creations of the imagination could be fashioned, but even the formal elements of representation, its picturesque and plastic language, had to be changed also. The forms of expression of early Christian art in which the old models had been executed were based on presuppositions directly opposed to the fundamental principles of medieval art. The distinction is not one of degree of ability to represent nature, for in this respect it is a matter of completely heterogeneous constituent elements. The late classical dissolution of form into color values and factors of light and shade was the extreme limit which classical art attained in its endeavor to objectify natural phenomena. For in the acknowledgment that these phenomena were conditioned by transitory space factors as well as by the attitude of the observer toward them, this art destroyed both its own past and the secret of its meaning as well.

It was not difficult to associate this dissolution of form into varying degrees of light gradation with the early Christian ecstasy which had its source in a realm transcending all material goods; and to a certain extent it could even ally itself with the early medieval renunciation of every objective form content, since it was the total dissolution of the older spiritual and social superstructure into unrestrained subjectivism and spiritualism that was to serve as the bridge spanning the chasm between the old world and the new. However when the attempt was made namely to inject this form dissolution into the new system of a spiritual *Weltordnung* no longer based on natural causality—an attempt one might add as observable in all aspects of life as it is in art, characterized by a marked de-emphasis of the original emotional radicalism that had sought an unqualified emancipation from the world of material values—the older illusionist style of art founded solely on a sensuous power of persuasion had to lose every significance and value, becoming totally inapplicable from the point of view of the new concepts of artistic truth and effect.[20] The reverse is equally true, for an artistic representation based on medieval concepts of the supernatural union of all phenomena would hardly serve the purposes of a modern scientific illustration.

Thus there gradually arose in the Middle Ages a new type of form reproduction which has often been described as the first attempt at representing a newly awakened appreciation of nature in sketching, sculpture and painting.[21]

This is the very kind of designation which is thoroughly

false and misleading. It is completely impossible to speak of a "beginning," of a medieval art which commenced at some time and in some place to imitate nature in a childlike fashion. There was neither the possibility nor the cause for such an eventuality. Two of the most striking historical characteristics of medieval art are its originality, initially rather negligible to be sure, and its remarkable independence of the formal and inconographic tradition inherited from classical antiquity—an independence moreover which persisted for several hundred years. The point of departure for this tradition, early Christian art itself, developed wholly within the framework of late classical conditions, both cultural and artistic, became as it were their very fruition and modified them only insofar as was demanded by the new Christian principles of a spirituality oriented solely toward otherworldly concerns. Even in the course of the following centuries, during all of the stages of the progressive development of the new Christian culture, involving as it did so many ethnic, political and social revolutions, no attempt was ever made to find a totally new substitute for the inherited legacy of figurative concepts and formal solutions, an ersatz wholly independent of tradition or one derived either directly from nature or from a new and radically different consciousness of secular culture.

How could such an attempt have been made? It should not be forgotten that the great revolutionary, progressive and reconstructive force behind the growth of the medieval world was basically religiously orientated; it was a struggle as it were for a new inner man with new moral obligations, or in short, a spiritual reform of the world which did not attempt on principle to annihilate or even subdue the objective and formal accomplishments of the preceding secular culture in order to replace them with one resulting from a new objective relationship to mundane realities. In the course of its development, however, the former cultural values had become merely external forms of various fields of spiritual and material activity that, having lost the unifying bond of that *Weltanschauung* out of which they had arisen and thereby having destroyed the fundamental principles requisite for their further growth, were transformed into internally disjointed fragments.

In the barbaric, pre-Carolingian art, i.e., the art of those tribes who, in no way encumbered with the older material cultural needs, had assumed the lead in the transvaluation of all values through the new spiritualism, these fragments were reduced to a form of shadowy existence, without ever really completely disappearing, solely because they were no longer considered important. In the spiritually and politically stormy period following the reign of Charlemagne, the actual development of these relationships demanded a compromise with the physical world, a reorganization of secular and ecclesiastical institutions based on a direct relationship to natural events and circumstances as well as a reorientation in the domain of spiritual creation. Thus these traditionally accepted values and usages were once again pressed into service, although not with their former vibrant power, significance and coherence; rather they functioned as a given means of expression or as accepted formulas for specific patterns of thought which were employed, somewhat analogous to an established vocabulary, only because they were available and because even in the art of this period with its relative return to the world of objective nature they would be solely auxiliary aids while the real problems of spiritual importance were as usual sought elsewhere. Ignoring the individual value of the language as such and concentrating rather upon its aptness to convey a spiritual content pertinent for mankind, men employed them as one would use a dead language. Once adopted, these were the forms used to express all new perspectives, rather than relying in this regard upon an entirely new and primitive representation of nature independent of the past.

The foregoing considerations naturally do not mean to imply that the old formal elements represent only a retrogression and degeneration of art, completely devoid of any subsequent expansion of the inherited means of artistic expression. On the contrary, these formal elements issuing from the most divergent sources were borne along by the mighty stream of unconscious or conscious tradition—the inherited working capital of art inasmuch as it had to represent natural objects—and were repeatedly augmented by ever increasing acquisitions from the older masters. Just as early Christian buildings, with reference to mass and spatial elements [German original: *Block-und Raumbauten*], were not gradually displaced in the Middle Ages by new forms of architecture, but rather were artistically revaluated and replaced by an organic unity of new architectonic effects whose significance even the traditional form of classical tectonics had to take into consideration, so also in the areas of painting and sculpture a new interpretation of formal values vis-à-vis the accumulated riches of traditional paintings and statuary slowly emerged. By degrees everything that had lost its original meaning was radically transformed into a new vivifying factor so that out of the new as well as the old elements an entirely original figurative composition and formal idiom were created, both of which herald the medieval advance over classical art. Its growth extended throughout the entire Middle Ages, analogous to the development of Gothic architecture, and consisted in the triumph of new demands for the reproduction and creation of forms—demands which, in various periods and various regions apparently independent of one another, nevertheless serve in a logical fashion to augment their development even when dependent on classical prototypes. The transformation of all formal means in Gothic art and architecture by these demands for a fresh interpretation of artistic meaning signifies in this respect not the beginning but rather the perfection of a new art, or rather a new principle of figurate representation based on complete purity and universal application.

At first glance this principle is distinguished from the directive goals of the late classical period by a conspicuous reduction in the means of representation. An abstract selection of specific lines, plastic forms and colors, replaced by the detailed and most exhaustive description possible of the plastic and color phenomena of objects, that were characteristics adopted from classical painting and sculpture and that continued to exist in the developing art of the Gothic age in the form of scattered and disjunctive residues, completely disappeared. By means of this simplicity of description, the newer representations seem to approach the art of periods long since past,[22] and in a sense constitute a continuation of them, inasmuch as between periods in which art sought its ideals beyond the limitations of conformity to natural law, there doubtlessly exists an historical continuity as close as between those periods in which art found its highest goals precisely in subservience to a rigid conformity to law. However in no sense is this indicative of a retrograde movement. Basic norms of classical artistic reconstruction of natural or formal constructs and relationships, as for example consideration of the organic structure of bodies, the unity of group phenomena, their natural proportions, organization and coloration or the foreshortening of objects conditioned by their spatial positions, were never entirely lost but remained technical skills which were pressed into service wherever the higher precept of art's new significance allowed.

The source of this latter significance was undoubtedly the ever-recurring accentuated relationship to the powers of human reason, to the *vis cognoscitiva*,[23] which enabled man through divine grace to penetrate in spirit (*spiritualiter*) deeper into the mysteries of external phenomena than he can solely by means of his frequently deceiving senses whose illusions art must combat by presenting to man a form of reality purified by a higher, spiritual insight. For medieval man the nucleus of this insight was not nature but the teachings of God—the consciousness granted to mankind by God's grace that above the merely relative values of nature dwells a world of supernatural order, determination and finality which lies only within the ken of the reflective soul and inner experience, a structure of conceptual being in which the truly real substances are contained (opposed to which the phenomena grasped solely by sense experience are but its last and most insignificant emanation) and out of which the world must be understood and evaluated.

According to this principle of the spiritualistic *Weltanschauung* of the Middle Ages, even art could not attain to its highest goals were it to proceed from an imitation of nature. It proceeded rather in a reversed direction and sought to exemplify through natural forms an ideal conception based on a priori assumptions. It is not as an *imago* that the artistic form is to oppose its counterpart in nature, but instead it is to be united to it in the manner of a *similitudo;* its task consists in compensating the *imperfectum* of sense perception by means of the *perfectum* of the divine ideas which, revealed to the intellect of man, underlie all perceivable phenomena. Therefore it is not a question of uniformity of degree of one's perception of nature, but rather the inner discipline of the abstract structure. It is important for further observations to bear in mind that while the approximation of reality remains variable, the new ideal schemata are continuously developed in a logical manner. Their norm is so binding that they are applied even where the aim of the representation is the very intention of the reproduction of nature—one might even assert that in this instance the norm is one of a more subtle technical knowledge, analogous to a certain extent to a contemporary scientific representation of a linear abstraction which seeks to emphasize the "essence of the matter" by employing all the aspects of the perceptible phenomenon.[24]

Were this comparison to be further extended, the next question should be: "What exactly was the essence of the matter for the medieval artist? or, in other words, how did the norms of nature-representation, honored more highly than nature itself,

Naumburg Cathedral, choir screen; John from the Crucifixion.
Courtesy Marburg–Art Reference Bureau.

arise?" In order to understand the genesis of these norms, one must again realize that they did not originate in new impressions of nature or in pictorial conceptions but developed through a gradual transformation of traditional artistic techniques whose primary figures were at the same time ideally the supreme synthesis of the Christian *Weltanschauung*. However if one traces the development of these basic iconographic types of medieval Christian art, for example, the representation of the persons of the Trinity or the saints, it becomes evident that in the first period of their medieval development they lost their original character as an expression of naturalistic or historical determinism and were transformed into abstract and almost amorphous concept-symbols when compared with their original form.

The concepts themselves, the spiritual substratum, which the sculptural or pictorial images were to call to mind, were not hieratically established (wherein a basic difference exists respective to all older periods in which art was to express abstract ideas as well as external forms) but on the contrary were conceived as stages in an uninterrupted development that had to be operative even in the symbols representing them. This ceaseless evolution consisted on the one hand in the fact that these artistic creations embodied a world of supernatural, religious, moral and historical forces applicable to all men, times and circumstances, since they were independent of all temporally and spatially limited events; on the other hand this belief in such forces was linked with the attempt to fuse them with the classical heritage of thought and attitude systematically schooled in the observation of conformity to the laws of nature as well as with the demands and points of view resulting from the social and political organizations and cultures which emerged from the enormous energies of the younger nations; moreover these forces were released and accelerated by the expansion of the physical might and the psychic life of these newer peoples. The aim of this endeavor was to harmonize traditionally established values and techniques with the ever increasing innovations of a rapidly emerging society. Thus it is that tensions arose in which is to be sought the explanation for the impetuous inner movement of medieval formal representation, its searching, now inflexibly conservative and now wildly revolutionary character, its abrupt reversals as well as the extensive ramification of its energies in schools of thought and fields of art apparently so diverse as to be mutually exclusive.

And yet throughout it is but a matter of various stages and results of a unified process within the motivating forces of the culture as a whole, as is evidenced by the ease with which even the more formal solutions of the artistic problems can be classified within certain specific categories. Again and again formal elements of pictorial reproduction and their individual parts are dissociated from the framework of the natural relationships upon which they are based and are inserted into other systems of reference which did not result from a strict imitation of an actual situation but functioned rather as the reflection of psychic processes in the "meaningful" arrangement of lines and surfaces and in the actualization of rhythmic combinations or the dynamic consequences of motion itself.

In addition to these general metamorphoses, which are in a sense comparable to the remarkable extension of classical philosophy to medieval theological speculation—in part in conjunction with these same transformations, in part independent thereof —the objective character of the forms themselves underwent a process of change. In place of detailed descriptions of optical and tangible, material and functional characteristics, abbreviated forms were employed, which are not arbitrary symbols but result rather from a systematic reduction of their objective thought and matter. With justification they can be designated a legitimately progressive simplification.[25]

Their point of departure was the condensation of all mundane and supernatural realities into a graduated system based upon the importance of each entity. In the medieval view nothing in the universe is without significance, even the most seemingly inconsequential object stands in some relationship to the wisdom of the eternal *Weltordnung* which governs all. The degree of significance, however, varies and unfolds in a hierarchical order of precedence from the lower limited and objectively differentiated material objects to ever higher beings, the higher rank characterized by the measure of universality and permanence possessed by each being as opposed to individuality and transitoriness. It is in this universality of the higher beings, that the ascending simplification of reality resides—temporally and materially conditioned *discrepancy* is replaced by the unity of the all-encompassing idea in an unknown ascent to the very highest idea of the eternal divine Being who is above every form of differentiation.[26] The system of artistic abstractions in the Middle Ages can be compared with this philosophic construction that, regardless of how ambivalent it may have been in the cogency of its explanations as well as in its application, must, nevertheless, be recognized in general as the basis of the medieval interpretation of the world. Although the figures and scenes which depict man and events in their earthly limitation contained more frequent changing and indiscriminate allusions to an individuated reality than did the older periods of classical art,[27] the attempt was repeatedly made throughout to portray the figures signifying the permanent ideals of Christianity even with respect to corporeal phenomena as paradigms of concentrated reality which, lacking all temporal or spatial limitations, contain only that which is commensurate with the ideal construct of a higher, generalized degree of being to which the lines, plastic forms and colors are to be reduced.

It is in this sense that one is to understand St. Thomas whose theories in general (and in this instance respective to aesthetic demands in particular) are not to be conceived solely as a speculative system but contain rather a synopsis of the spiritual progress

"Madonna of Canon George van der Paele," by Jan van Eyck in the
Musée Communal, Bruges. *Courtesy European Art Color Slide Co.,
New York.*

of mankind during the course of the Middle Ages—a philosophic compendium which demands from any artistic reproduction clarity as the first of the three criteria of beauty,[28] namely
that clarity, which is not conceived in any material sense but signifies on the contrary something illumined and illuminating. The
essence of this clarity consists on the one hand in the ability of
the artistic creation so to fashion the sensible characteristics of
things that they become an adequate expression of the ideas
which serve as a basis for the physical objects, and on the other
hand in the artist's skill to convert these basic ideas into vehicles
of "spiritual insight," intelligible symbols of the higher organization fundamental to all being. This organization is rendered
accessible only through the spiritual knowledge of mankind.

This method, replacing forms of nature by conventional
symbols to an ever greater extent, could not have but led art
further and further away from nature, had not a counteractive
agent effectively and repeatedly intervened, namely the second
of the above-enumerated components of medieval development,
classical objectivity—an objectivity viewed not as an end in itself
but as a way of viewing reality which, like all other aspects of
art, demanded that the nature of the concrete world be taken
into consideration. According to the aesthetics of the Angelic
Doctor, *claritas* should be complemented by *integritas*, that is a
perfection relevant to both the spiritual and the physical aspects of
reality and which, with reference to the latter, is present when
no quality essential to their nature is lacking.[29] When applied to
representational art this means that the invention of even the
most highly formal constructs was subject to a certain degree of
subordination to the laws of nature, a postulate that more than
clearly illustrates, by the very fact that it had to be expressly emphasized, how far the bases of art had moved from the guiding
principles of classical antiquity and how the relationship between
art and life had become something radically different.

From what has been said above, one is not to conclude that

idealism and naturalism, in the modern conception of the terms, had existed side by side in perpetual discord in the pre-Gothic era of the Middle Ages. On the contrary, the primacy of a spiritually idealistic world construction was fundamental to both philosophic directions; and thus this dualism in medieval art, as well as the resultant progress it achieved after protracted endeavor, consisted in the variously sought after or attained union of the old or new elements of natural experience with the symbols of a transcendental spiritual community. Since the point of departure for both schools of thought was a unified one, the contrast between the two was not unbridgeable and the endeavor to replace it with a harmonic unity gradually formed not only a third factor in the stylistic development of medieval painting and sculpture, but in the final analysis became its most significant problem whose solution, inasmuch as it was attainable at all, is to be reckoned among the constituent accomplishments of Gothic art. It corresponds to the third quality that St. Thomas includes in the concept beauty, namely *consonantia*, by which he meant that just as a man is considered beautiful if his members stand in correct relationship and proper position with the body as a whole, in like measure a reflection of the harmonic reciprocity between the ultimate "ideas" of creation and its radiation in earthly things must be demanded, for the truth, beauty and goodness of material objects are to be sought ultimately in their agreement with the infinite divine ideas which brought forth their temporal finite existence.[30] The bond that united Gothic architecture with Gothic sculpture and painting within the framework of a necessary homogeneity consisted in this harmony between the presence of worldly limitation and the unhampered flight of the soul bursting its earthly fetters, a harmony so eagerly yearned for by the entire High Middle Ages, and one which reached its fulfillment in Gothic art through a compensatory spiritualization of material factors equalized by the materialization of all spiritual elements.

It is in this sense alone that one can fully comprehend the concave mirror in which the great masters, who executed the Royal Portal of Chartres, saw and then reproduced nature. In the plastic arts this remarkable process resulted in the fact that those holy figures, who were the most important pillars of the described development, not only remained personifications of a metaphysical abstraction, an ideal state to which they had developed from their original historical or concretely symbolic significance, but at the same time they became dominant types of a new conception of nature, a situation somewhat analogous to the position of the gods of Greece, but realized in the Middle Ages under other circumstances and in a different context. Since, according to the medieval conception, they embodied the *summmum* of instruction, edification and knowledge transmitted through art, their type-characterization became the model of perfection and at the same time the standard of fidelity to nature as expressed in art; consequently they became prefigurative for every representation that strives to bestow on natural forms the stamp of a universal validity and an artistic insight elevated above merely accidental or immaterial considerations.[31]

The rapidity of their dissemination throughout the entire art of Europe finds its explanation in the conviction of the absolute ideality and imitative qualities of the "finally" discovered norm. At all times idealistic schemata have quickly become a part of the common spiritual heritage and have tended to exercise an equalizing effect on the schools and areas of art separated by opposing naturalistic goals. However inasmuch as a relative approximation of nature was an inherent quality of the content of Gothic art, the possibility of a new naturalistic development was axiomatically contained within both form and content, a development which can hardly be compared with the imitation of nature perfected by classical art. The distinction consisted above all in the fact that objectivity was transferred from the object to the subject. It is in this respect that the *mens* and the *scientia artificis* are to be understood as the *causa efficiens* of a work of art by means of which the elements of sense perception are ordered,[32] however, not spontaneously and isolated in single individuals, but rather as necessitated by a higher truth revealed to mankind. In other words the new discovery and artistic mastery of nature resulted conjointly, and therein existed a further difference vis-à-vis classical art. This distinction was based on general spiritual truths of which art had become the harbinger and to which from thence forward all progress in the representation of nature would be referred, even then when art was no longer exclusively dependent upon divine revelation but had begun to finds its source in a natural, rational knowledge of the relationships which, discernible only by the spirit, govern the course of the world.

Nothing would be more erroneous than to believe that the question of the origins of the symbolic language of Gothic art were exhausted when considered only from the points of view already treated. Other factors played a hardly less conspicuous role in its development; these were considerations concerned less with problems of epistemology than with the endeavor to effect, by means of pictorial inventions, feelings and conceptions of a complete divorce from concrete being in favor of a transcendent, spiritual event.

The writings of Felix Witting[33] (q.v.), so fertile in their ideas as well as the excellent investigations of Wilhelm Pinder[34] (q.v.) concerning the system of rhythmical forms employed in the interior spaces of the Romanesque architecture of Normandy have taught one (in a manner which the positivistic philosophies of the last century could scarcely have comprehended) how basic stylistic facts and stages of development can be explained by means of the particular spiritual importance accorded the sacred space of churches during both the early periods of Christianity and the Middle Ages. The individuality of these ecclesiastical structures constituted in their very *raison d'être*, namely the faculty to induce in man certain psychic impressions which sustain the feeling of a spiritual participation in supersensual and suprarational mysteries.

Doubtlessly even in the sculpture and painting of the age, similar factors were operative in determining their artistic creation; these factors not only awakened pictorial images in the sense of concept symbols or a visual illustration of divine truth (through whose mediation already known secular truth would then be concretized in symbolic form), but they also mediated to the human soul by means of the dynamism of an abstract artistic organization a solemn and devotional mood, the consciousness of being present at the scene of holy and edifying ceremonies and profound mysteries which have the power to redeem man from the afflictions and monotony of everyday life. The correlation between God and man which constitutes the essence of Christian religiosity was perfected in the paintings and statuary of the churches as it was in the domains of prayer and hymnology, and thus it was that a specific, spiritual content, completely detached from all objective being, actions and events—a phenomenon not limited to representational art alone but observable in all fields of spiritual endeavor—and its necessary concomitant artistic abstraction were inextricably bound to the enormous complexities of emotional response, organized as it were by Christianity and thrust to the fore of a rich spiritual development. If through this process, art became the immediate organ of a religiously subjective emotional life, the first step in its gradual transformation into the organ of subjective psychic life in general, the artistic means of expression of this immediacy—namely abstract forms established by accepted norms, whose task it was to awaken psychic emotions and guide them in predetermined directions—attained a degree of independence hardly inferior to that enjoyed in classical art where they were limited to a far greater extent by their subjection to the objective content of what they sought to represent.

Out of this peculiarity of medieval art, in which alone one

should seek the origins of that subsequent contrast between a primarily abstract, artistic disposition on the one hand and a natural subservience to established law on the other—a contrast as fruitful as it was frequently recurrent—out of this arose a multiplicity of style-determining processes which must be thoroughly investigated before one can hope to attain an insight into the inner wealth of medieval art; it is these style-determining processes that span the distance between this era and the Middle Ages, an era filled with the storms of violent moments interspersed with the calm of decades of a more slowly maturing growth.

The successive arrangement of figures, their movement and their relationship to the representation of space constitute the threefold manner employed by Gothic representational art to express most clearly the compositional elements flowing from the striving after transcendental relationships in spiritual consciousness. And it is precisely in this threefold manner of expression that Gothic art can be seen to be the result of the total artistic development preceding it.

To the extent that the groups of saints which adorn a Gothic cathedral form, from the point of view of a *sacra conversazione* viewed *sub specie aeternitatis*, both a union in time and eternity, in both terrestrial mutability and celestial permanence, and a sacred dialogue to whose level the viewer is raised, to that degree are they united, although not formally, not by means of a group formation participating in some specific event conditioned by time and place but rather solely through their rhythmical arrangement. The figures in these group compositions stand alongside one another almost as though magically transfixed and resemble essentially equivalent vertical schemata; again at times they appear in several rows one above the other as coordinated members, completely devoid of any union corresponding to a real situation and hovering in space as it were; at times they are harmonized in the sense of musical accords or accord progressions, yet without any terminating, formal limitation, and thus enable the imagination to continue the series ad infinitum.

It is customary to refer to some form of tectonic constraint as the cause of this arrangement, and yet (as has been assumed) it is not a matter of any constructive force which doubtlessly would permit numerous other distributions and organizations of the decorative statuary. It is far more a spiritual force that dominates the structure and its decorative accessories; this force is so powerful that it has not remained without influence even within those very reliefs and paintings whose story-content it contradicts; furthermore it unites the structural organism and the statuary governs independently in the former and the latter alike and expresses itself poignantly in both. It is precisely this relative self-liberation of the plastic formations that can be viewed as an essential advance of Gothic over Romanesque art. In the latter art these formations, their verbal significance notwithstanding, were more or less a harmonic tone in the chorus of the architectonically rhythmized structural mass; in Gothic art, however, they were able to assume the artistic function of the Romanesque forms but vicariously and within the sphere of their own individual power. This was the origin and the inner meaningfulness of a new monumental sculpture and statuary art whose freedom and future consisted not in continued reference to its classical determining principles but rather in the fact that a new task could be found for it within the framework of the new, internally rabbeted world of artistic significance; moreover it was a task which could likewise serve as a bridge to equally new monumental effects and statuary problems. The statues assumed the form of columns in order to fulfill their higher artistic purpose, a purpose which now demanded figurative representations larger than life size and about which one is so clearly informed through the rhythmic arrangements discussed above.

The statues were arranged either individually, in groups or in their totality in an ideal ordering of artistic relationships, somewhat analogous to a geometric figure in a symmetrical triangular group of Leonardo Da Vinci. However this arrangement did not rest on an exterior formal unity (as it did with the masters of the High Renaissance) in which natural relationships and sensible impressions were to be elevated to a heightened artistic effect by means of the force of the artistic insight embodied therein, but rather was constructed upon the assumption of a transcendental unity to which all bodies were related over and above their natural, mechanistic and organic function and union, since according to their general form and arrangement they had become excitants and exponents of concepts and emotions projected without temporal limitation into infinite space. Via the connection with an artistically articulated sequence of tectonic and plastic basic forms, adapted to embody the direction of spiritual movement, mankind was borne aloft into a world of purely spiritual events and substances whose artistic reflection was so constituted— and herein lies the advance of Gothic art—that even statuary solutions could be included in its ideal conception and structure and thereby be monumentalized anew. Thus the figures from the vantage point of the viewer were composed as pillars; the pillars were then arranged row on row in a manner best described in terms of the rhythmic fuges of a symphony which in its ascent heavenward slowly dies out in all directions.

To its effect, however, also belonged movement, which independent of all natural spatial and locomotive factors, in part even in contradiction thereto, concentrated lines, forms and bodies into a unified supernatural directional path and caused them to appear as entities caught in the current of an overpowering force before which bodily weight as well as the effectiveness of mechanical and organic forces must forfeit all decisive significance.

This impetus toward movement was realized at first (as it had been in architecture) in the verticalism and proportions of the figures and forms, which in opposition to real mass proportions were elongated; this caused their subtle slenderness to function as an expression of victory by spiritual forces over material constraint and avoided in the very lithesome carriage of the figures everything weighty or anything reminiscent of earthly existence.

When, within this general *sursum*, specifically statuary objectives, and with them endeavors to achieve statuary formation and vivification of the bodies represented, asserted their claims with ever increasing insistancy, a more restricted statuary and then gradually a more generally concentrated figural-representational norm of movement for the vaulted bodily lines, spiralling upwards flexibly and melodiously, was established. The ascending course of these bodily lines in all the contours of their members and vesture was expressed for the most part in gentle curves, giving way at times, however, to a far more passionate agitation —both tendencies being transferred later to every aspect of the decorative forms.

This axiom of movement as developed in Gothic art did not arise, as is customarily assumed, from the necessity of accommodating moving figures in the traditionally established block-form architecture;[35] it embodied rather, in a mode analogous to the *figura serpentinata* of the sixteenth-century mannerists, an ideal solution of the problem of statuary motion, one conceived in terms of the perspectives of the dominant artistic points of view. Its advantage consisted in the fact that it enabled all aspects of the figures to be released from a state of rest and thereby to contribute to the expression of an ascending movement and this—in contrast to Baroque art—without the assistance of a dynamics of corporeal movement which in Gothic art would have contradicted the antimaterialistic ideality of the representations. In this sense the vaulted Gothic lines of the bodies and forms, into which converged not only newly acquired presuppositions but aesthetic energies and accomplishments extending far back into the distant past,[36] belonged without a doubt to the characteristics of a new

Chartreuse of Champmol; Madonna, by Claus Sluter. *Courtesy Giraudon, Paris.*

bodily beauty with transcendental overtones which, assured of divine immanence, elevated mortal forms into the spheres of an immortal reality and bore them into this reality on the gossamer wings of a lyrically delicate, mystically unstable, spiritualized victory over the gravitational pull of terrestrial mass weight. Because of these mystic qualities, this lyrical beauty was made to radiate through figures which were to the medieval imagination in the highest degree the very essence of a divinely animated beauty, the goal of which was the blessedness of man. Therefore it is not by mere chance that this determining canon of movement can be attested in its most pregnant and perfected form in the representations of the Virgin Mother of God, its highest and purest embodiment.[37]

This principle of movement, however, was not the only factor to be considered. Representations of the Savior and his Disciples, or the Prophets and Fathers of the Church, men who were to embody the majesty of divine wisdom or the Christian ethos, the source of which arose in the belief of an afterlife, lacked for the most part these soaringly graceful curves, but found a surrogate expression in a more weighty vertical bodily stance, the effect of which, however, was not ponderous, as it was in the firm and heavy postures of related classical motifs; it appeared on the contrary as an irresistible upward growth, at times even as an unswerving heavenward flight. This impression is bolstered by means of an unnatural counterstance of the upper and lower halves of the figures which are placed in a diagonal position to the viewer by thrusting their feet forward. This counterstance is so unnoticeable that at a fleeting glance it is hardly perceptible and seems rather incompatible to an organic bodily movement. It nevertheless suffices gently to shift all the forms from their position of rest, conditioned as it is by the natural interplay of various forces and thereby to transform the vertical lines, which dominate the appearance of the figure, into an expression of completely independent, freely soaring movement. In this way, having united the arrangement of the figures on a narrow basis (or often even *in punto de'piedi*) with a limited accentuation of the bodily qualities, the artist converted the classical motif of statuary position (either firm or elastic), with respect to the ground on which it stood, into the illusion of a posturing hovering freely in space.

Another legacy of early Christian art was the representation of divine and holy figures in soaring flight wherever in monumental grandeur they were to draw the viewer to themselves as representatives of the governance of supernatural powers. This legacy was faithfully preserved even when statuary corporeality was once again introduced into the circle of artistic interests. From this basic conception and in accordance with its demands, the two guiding schema of movement in Gothic sculpture evolved—the one a completely new creation, the other a reinterpretation of the important classical motif of bodily position. Both of these schematic patterns of motion—derivatives of older classical and newer Christian medieval elements which were operative in the spiritual life of the Middle Ages, forged as it were into an inner unity by the higher instance of the great idealistic system of the Gothic age—became the point of departure for the solutions of the most important problems of statuary art as well as the further extention of that art itself whose origins may accordingly be considered in a completely new light.

The reintroduction of corporeal mass into the flight into the transcendental that, uniting both the world and the time of the here as well as the hereafter, had subjugated substantial form to the standards and laws of a much longed for infinity gave rise to a new concept and content of sculptural monumentality that was not at all a return to classicism; on the contrary, it appeared to its creators as something definitely superior to the art of antiquity.[38] The artistic intentions and problems of statuary art, as founded by the spirit of the Greek genius, could only serve the new monumental free plasticity of the Middle Ages as an auxiliary means (analogous to the role played by the systems of the Greek sages in the development of medieval thought) in the solution of the tasks which they esteemed as higher than any preceding their age. Because of this attitude, the artistic goals of classical antiquity were once again fed into the main stream of development of European art. In time, as the original connecting ties began to loosen and to be replaced by other forms more nearly approximating their own nature, the artistic goals were able to develop a relative independence; in a sense they once more approached their classical significance, and indeed even surpassed their former importance in the execution of formal accomplishments without, however, ever really returning to their original position. The monumentally permanent could no longer be represented, to the degree that it had been in classical art, as objectively and substantially embodied extrinsic to man's intellectual position, for ultimately man learned to derive it from the ideal knowledge of relationships which surpass individual concrete objects and thus to refer it to the interior life of the human being. This process of transference had already been demanded, at least in theory, in the idealistic speculation of Greek philosophy, but it only became a permanent, spiritual possession of all minkind when it was realized on the basis of the Christian idealistic *Weltanschauung* that sought to embrace every value inherent in human life.

One is able to observe similar circumstances in the representation of the relationship of the figures to their spatial surroundings. There are three intrinsically related characteristics that predominate and are especially observable in medieval paintings. In comparison to the hestitant irregularity of the previous levels of style, vacillating between complete dissolution of classical forms on the one hand, approximation thereof on the other, the reproduction of spatial scenery was considerably more unified and regulated; moreover it exhibited far greater fidelity to nature in individual details as well as being more organic in the combination of these factors. This progress was, however, in no sense conjoined with a more logically consistent artistic construction or with a stronger spatial effect of the natural scene corresponding to a represented situation! On the contrary, every effort was made to exclude wheresoever possible all spatial depth within the picture so that the figures and the complex of buildings, serving as a type of scenic coulisse, seem to cling to one another; the latter often formed only an architectonically organized framework for the figural composition and hence lent to the painting the character of a surface decoration utterly devoid of the reproduction of spatial depth.

This does not mean, however, that early Gothic painting and sculpture were devoid of all spatial effect. This is not so at all. Rather the relationship of the figures to space was of a nature different from that employed in either classical or modern art and it is only in terms of the latter that we are accustomed to judge spatial reproduction. One of the major characteristics of early Gothic art was the endeavor to develop the composition out of the picture surface and not into it, as one is apt to do.[39] The figures, at any rate those which are the most important ones in the represented event, are generally not placed on the horizontal plane of a section of ground extending to the depth of the background, but stand rather on the outermost edge of the picture and frequently intersect the inner frame of the pictorial limits. Hence they seem to be ranged not behind but in front of the surface of the picture, to be circumscribed by the scene depicted, as if they would pursue a power which thrusts them toward the viewer from out of the picture's depth, and to be pressed from behind by the objects surrounding them. Under these circumstances can one speak at all of picture-depth?

A second characteristic of Gothic pictorial creation need also be mentioned, namely the tapestry-like background which regularly forms an integral part of the depicted arrangement of the figures. It is certainly not to be interpreted naturalistically as some form of rounding off of inner space, since it is applied even in cases of landscape scenery or as a type of foil for the illusion of atmospheric phenomena. Thus it signifies hardly anything other than it actually is, namely an ornamentally embellished surface before which the figures stand, united spatially in a manner similar to the relationship between Gothic statues and the facade which they adorn. As a comparison one might perhaps refer to Correggio's "Fathers of the Church" with their strong Baroque dissidence, appearing as they do to hover within the space enclosed by the walls of the church; yet in Gothic art and architecture it was not a matter of reproducing a solitary, wondrously visionary event, as it was with Correggio and his successors. Rather it was an endeavor to visualize a generalized composition based upon a subservience to established norms whose meaning cannot be dubious if one considers its origins as well as its agreement with similar phenomena in the sculpture of the time.

These origins are to be sought in late classical art, among whose most important innovations, according to Alois Riegl (q.v.), are to be reckoned "an isolation of the forms in their three-dimensional spatial enclosure [German original: *vollräumigen Abgeschlossenheit*] with reference to the base plane and the resultant emancipation of the intervals." The same is indeed true for the relationship of the Gothic figures to the "ground" from which they free themselves and constitute a spatial stratum between themselves and the background to give the impression of a free spatial envelopment of the three-dimensional form. Even though the roots of the Gothic spatial composition can doubtlessly be traced back to this fundamental transformation, the composition is not to be interpreted only as a perpetuation of early-Christian principles.

It is also necessary to discuss the differences. In late Roman art the development of spatial representation was based on the transformation of the cubistic three-dimensional form into values which correspond to the transitory phenomenon in space and as such were placed in relationship to the optical values of the free space surrounding them. Anything measurable or tangible or in any manner referable to cubistic suppression of space lost its power and force and was replaced by optical appearance, namely the dissolution of forms into color values or light and shade and into lines, signifying not a limitation of form but rather an illusion of space, which naturally resulted in the inclusion in the representation of even the relationship to the materially unlimited space surrounding the figures as well as the relationship to the spatial zone in which these figures were situated. The figures detach themselves from the background in an almost insubstantial, etherealized fashion and arrange themselves wherever they represent conceptual units into an ideal visual plane in which like a series of parallel visual phantoms they are brought into relief vis-à-vis an ideal spatial zone, likewise represented as an optical impression.

In this manner space became an ideal background staging [German original: *Hintergrundsfolie*], the expression of a depth-orientation which was not defined by a closed spatial area but was rather to appear as an abstract movement of depth within infinite space, into which figures are so placed that, by momentarily retarding the movement itself, they arrest the viewer's gaze in a dreamlike, incorporeal and yet at the same time animated abruptness and immediacy, and thus focus the viewer's attention in the desired direction. Spatial milieu played a similar role in late classical art where its value lay in its function as an "interval" between the individual figures. There too it represents primarily the framework of the form and as such a separating element. Inasmuch as it becomes an independent aesthetic factor, its function appears as coordinated with that of material form and leads directly to that rhythmic interchange of form and space, light and shadow, so characteristic of early Christian art, which fashioned cubistic form as surface and this latter in turn as the mirror of a movement of space and form, either specifically directed or radiating in every direction.

Thus it is that the progress of Gothic art in reproducing space, as opposed to its classical models, consisted principally in its technique of transforming spatial factors from attributes of a locally defined spatial relationship (in an objective sense) into a universally artistic means of expression which, gradually stripped of its originally naturalistic significance, increasingly served in the new Christian art to dissolve the material consistency and mechanistic anchoring of bodies and individual forms in their material spatial reconstruction and substituted for the previous fixity of the forms within an individualized spatial ambience a universally spatial effect which was then made to alternate with abstract spatial values. A means was thereby acquired with which to subordinate in pictorial and sculptural representations everything affixed to corporeal being or the life of the senses to the new psychocentric interpretation which, proceeding from the faith in a metaphysical relationship of things, had to strive even in art for an abstract and supranatural validity [German original: *Gesetzmässigkeit*] and importance founded on antimaterial bases.

It is clear that this process of rendering free space accessible, which of itself is the integrating reverse side of every formal creation, should not be confused with the naturalistic demand of contemporary art to represent every object as a partial phenomenon of a section of space. The fundamental basis of this modern principle was created, however, in the age of the great spiritual revolutions which bridge the gap between classical antiquity and the Middle Ages and in this way opened to art in the fullest sense of the word a new avenue of development along which it could proceed from a primitive stage to new possibilities and accomplishments, as previously archaic Greek art had done vis-à-vis older oriental art, and could completely reject the degree of perfection already attained. As far as the Middle Ages were concerned, these new possibilities and accomplishments certainly did not consist in an approximation of nature but in a universal expansion of the new artistic function of space, the history of which can afford a deep insight into the nature and development of medieval art.

To perceive at a glance the road of development which led from these basic principles to their perfection in Gothic art, a return to the monumental sculpture of the Gothic period would prove to be highly advantageous. A basic innovation is to be noted here in that the figures were no longer analyzed in terms of a system of optical form or spatial allusions, a system which, tending to veil their materiality, sought to reproduce these figures in shadowed depths and brilliant accentuations or in neutral surfaces and disembodied lines, whose effect was to be achieved in an antimaterial reflection of a spatial event. Therefore this system regrouped these figures in a concentrated form and drew upon these various elements without taking into consideration any fidelity to nature, a process demanded by the artistic play or more precisely by a supernatural creed. The figures were now conceived as cubistic bodies that as such were to produce an effect in their relationship to space. The specific arrangement of the figures, which was as frontal as possible, ran parallel in a spatial recession to the background surface (an arrangement having nothing whatever to do with either classical plastic relief or with the classical system of isolating statues and causing each to rest upon itself alone); this arrangement, I repeat, bespeaks its origin in the compositional principle of placing figures in a visual plane parallel to the vertical intersection of an ideal spatial background—a principle which originated in late classical art and remained effective throughout the entire Middle Ages. Now, however, the figures in their total tangible plastic disposition stand materially *in front of* the facade or any other wall from which they are *actually* separated by a spatial stratum. Hence it is no longer a matter of a general, ideal concept of space, as it was in late classical or early medieval art; the main emphasis has been shifted to a real, three-dimensional space in which cubistic bodies can expand and spatial events occur, a space which above all appears even to the viewer in that multifarious relativity characteristic of an individual perception of a real section of space.

It is here that the developmental lines of Romanesque art converge, an art in which to a greater or lesser degree materiality and concrete space as well as their tranquil steadfastness and free spatial evolution began to play a new role and strove for a stronger objectivizing [German original: *Objektivisieren*] of the three-dimensional function of bodies. This new emphasis on the three dimensionality of space had to result in part in a new approximation of classical art, or rather its Christianized counterpart, Byzantine art.[40] Classical fidelity to nature and perfection of form remained as usual beyond the main interests of art, although the specific problems of plastic form, namely the sculptured curvature and arching of the human body, as observed in older classical works of art and more faithfully preserved by the newly Hellenized late classical art of Byzantium—basic motifs which were appropriate for illustrating figures as an articulated and animated unity within a compact area—gradually assumed again their importance as vivifying factors, but this time in Romanesque sculpture and painting and under new presuppositions and various new developmental aspects.[41] One of the major results of this re-emphasis on bodily form was the influence it brought to bear on the development of the figural composition itself, for it caused the figures within the framework of traditional models to evolve ever more and more out of the schemata of spatial phenomena and into the reproduction of tangible corporeality and full spatiality.

With respect to this development, however, another factor must also be considered. The transformation described above was *not* connected with a detachment of the new formal compositions and the problems upon which they were based form the higher complex of spatial values which since the time of Imperial

Rome had become the dominant force in artistic creation. This concept of a complex of spatial values is not to be understood in terms of the residue of the reproduction of a naturalistic scenery which was limited to occasional objective allusions or was forced to accommodate itself to a higher compositional unity. Spatial subordination consisted rather in an ideal spatial relationship which, encompassing every detail, determined their artistic goals, a subordination opposed to which, therefore, even the new conception of form [German original: *Formenbildung*], based on elements of tangible substantiality and space suppression, has remained unclassical, a basically dependent coefficient. It would never have occurred to an artist of the Romanesque period, merely by way of homage to a principle of subordination, to disturb the relationship between form, space and spatial limitation, between static forces and rhythmic movement in space or between dead mass and the flow of spiritualized order and meaning which both forms and rises above it. These relationships were indeed the deepest meaning and purpose of Romanesque art.

Furthermore a metamorphosis similar to that which effected the creation of figures occurred also within spatial art itself, whereby tectonic and plastic elements and forms acquired a modified significance with respect to the entire spatial configuration, space itself and its limitation. This transformation, with regard to both space and its limitation, in conjunction, therefore, with a large unified spatial construction of greater proportions than were previously possible, was effected by substituting an objective, substantially spatial existence and effect for the former illusion of space. The pillars of a Romanesque church are not only elements of a rhythmic line of movement but are to no less a degree heavy, massive bodies which awaken the notion of voluminous stance and expansion within real space. Walls were divided into traves by means of which the endeavor to divide the composition into cubistically effective entities is transferred even to the limitation of space, or to the background plane which up until then had been a mere smoothly flowing coulisse, indeed, to a certain extent even to delimited space itself, which having been transformed from an indefinite ideal space into a system of spatial unities (at the base of which lay the idea of a measurable section of space) was to prove effective by means of its qualities as a *body* and not those of some ill-defined *area*.[42]

In Gothic art and architecture the most radical consequences were drawn from this transformation; moreover these consequences signify at the same time a break with the past and the beginning of a new development. Ideally speaking, the limiting wall disappears, i.e., ceases to be an aesthetic means and is replaced as far as possible by plastic bodies and free space. The barriers between the exterior world and the interior stage of religious and artistic events (which were really enacted as a spatial occurrence) and spiritual experiences—this interior world which sought to shun everything considered to be mundanely irrelevant—these barriers, I repeat, between an ideal and a real space collapsed and simultaneously nullified as it were the entire ingenious play which in Romanesque art had converted the basic architectural plan of the basilicas of that time into a closed system of geometric space-schemata.

Similar to the columns in early Christian buildings, the pillars in Gothic cathedrals are placed in rows one after another in an uninterrupted rhythmic sequence of tectonic units and thus give the appearance that Christian art in this respect was again approaching its point of origin. And yet what a great expanse of time and change lay between them! For the artistic determination and form of these Gothically peristylar systems (if one may name them thus!) did not arise from the relationship to a given, limited ideal area of space, detached from everything else. They were bound rather to infinite, universal free space in its real dimensions and extension, and with its a priori unlimited standards which rendered all else relative. There they grew in miraculous power and order from the earth into distant heights

Sainte-Chapelle, interior; statues of the Apostles. *Courtesy Giraudon, Paris.*

or expanded into remote depths; and if at times these emanations of material finitude within the eternal, boundless world of space incline toward one another, thus to form mighty halls, or unite in order to fix the limits of the house of God, that place wherein consciousness can soar aloft into the sphere of the purely spiritual, and thus ward off everything profane as from a holy grove, they do so not to establish an irrevocably delimiting seclusion which separates with an unbridgeable chasm incompatible and incomparable worlds. For Gothic art is not based on the principle of antithesis; it rests rather upon the concept of union, and that which it encloses (without isolating it) is a section of the infinite universe, which was to be transformed into an artistic medium, a source of artistic sensation and significance, by filling it with relationships of a transcendent legitimacy [German original: *Gesetzmässigkeit*] within the area of sense perception. The following stages in the medieval development of the relationship between formal and spatial composition thus resulted:

1. In Christian antiquity and in the early stages of the Middle Ages: abstract, spiritual combination and movement of dematerialized forms within ideal spatial ambience.

2. In Romanesque art: arrangement of coordinated cubistic forms and ideal, although cubistically conceived, bodies in an abstract compositional scheme.

3. In Gothic art: ideal union of cubistic forms in a real section of infinite space.

Thus as a direct consequence of this remarkable process, the first step toward unlocking the natural, all-embracing universe had been taken—the first step toward that view which dominates the modern world, namely that concept which sees in the universe the highest form of unity opposed to which all individual beings or natural phenomena are only partial aspects of experience. It is indeed unnecessary to describe what horizons this new position rendered accessible to artistic contemplation and the spiritual life of man: from the discovery of the majesty of a "view from Mont Ventoux with its breath-taking power over the soul" to the conquest of geocentrism or the gospel of that *Weltanschauung* for which the eternal natural processes in the universe signify the origin of all forms of life, the investigation of which will yield the sure path to knowledge along which man must travel in his endeavor to penetrate the mysteries of this universe. The end result effected a truly spiritual edification. Nevertheless it does seem important to me to re-emphasize that the roots of this development as well as its speculative origins are to be found in the transcendental relationship of the Middle Ages to the eternal, infinite universe, the necessary complement to the infinite effective action of God.

To return once again to the point of departure of this study —it was a union of plastic and tectonic forms within an unlimited, real free space, oriented toward the viewer that served as the basis for the spatial creations of Gothic sculpture. Considered from this point of view, many of their characteristics are more readily clarified, e.g., the deeper meaning behind the efforts to cast the figures into the depth of the material itself as though forming them within a spatial volume, an artistic technique that dominated not only Gothic sculpture but one which was applied again and again whenever the demands of the moment necessitated an intensified and, therefore, more pregnant, artistic expression of full, spatial effect. Even the new artistic relationships of the statues to the buildings which they adorned become more intelligible when viewed in this perspective. The walls before which the statues stand, if they have any independent validity at all, are organized as far as possible in such a manner that the motifs of their arrangement are in no way determined by the proportions of the statues themselves; rather they serve for the most part in their disproportionate relationship to the statuary in the same capacity as the background scenery in medieval painting; the proportions of the statuary, however, do harmonize with the pervading, free spatial disposition of the building as a whole.

The background walls were there not to serve as a relief plane or definitive architectonic framework, but were rather to function as a neutral background coulisse which, inasmuch as it could not be entirely avoided, was artistically not more than a spatial interval-element that would nonetheless cause the desired spatial connection and effect of the statues to appear all the more effectively. In fulfilling this intermediary function, *mutatis mutandis*, the walls themselves were not to appear, from the vantage point of the viewer, as a completely impregnable resistance force in the path of the trajected depth projection, but were to play a role (albeit not in any naturalistic sense) analogous to the middle-ground figures in later constructions based upon the principle of perspective. However wherever feasible, walls were completely dispensed with, by either placing individual figures within some type of niche, or more frequently, as in the case of reliefs, by casting the entire figural composition into the wall itself as onto a stage whose walls seem to disappear in shadows. The artist would thus place his whole composition in an actual, apparently unlimited spatial area, an area which was artistically one with the representation itself. By means of this simple technique the basically new concatenation of art and reality in its elementary, idealistically conditioned origins was most drastically illustrated *in concreto* and it represented not only spirit but also the matter from which it proceeds, that matter which was to become the cradle of a new, artistically oriented interpretation of nature.

It is only if one bears the foregoing considerations in mind that the relationship between form and space in early Gothic painting becomes intelligible. The background, and for the most part the framework of the representation, was of a decidedly secondary importance. This style of painting strove primarily to emphasize the free spatiality of the figures and to insert a spatial stratum between them and the background while the figures themselves, with respect to the treatment and patterning of their color, sought neither to express a real spatial limitation nor an

Chartres Cathedral; "La Belle Verrière." *Courtesy Foto Monuments historiques, Paris.*

intimation of an ideal space, as they had done in early Christian art. In the confrontation of their real relationship to space, i.e., the free union of three-dimensional bodies in a section of the infinite universe, the background elements remain what they materially are, namely a surface to be painted upon, a wall or a sheet of parchment, all of which may at times be decorously adorned with gold and other glorious colors, but at all times decorated in such a manner that no doubt might arise concerning their true character—they are and remain a surface area materially requisite for the execution of the work of art but in essence secondary to the desired creation and union of objects in space.

The proof for this interpretation is so remarkable and convincing that another proof cannot be conceived. The most truly representative creation of the development of painting in the transition from the Romanesque period to the Gothic as well as the purest essence of the latter's pictorial goals were the famed stained-glass windows of the medieval cathedrals. That this diffident, difficult and unusual type of painting attained such a great importance and perfection is explainable, in the final analysis, to the fact that in most respects it corresponded, as no other style, to what was primarily demanded of painting *qua* art. The huge Gothic stained-glass windows form immense walls (which are no walls at all) circumscribing the interior area of the churches and thereby simultaneously establishing an immediate connection with infinite space. The union is mediated by an innovation not less significant than the conquest of free space itself, namely natural, falling light which, by the fact that it must penetrate the colored panes of glass, is itself transformed into various shades of color and seems, therefore, to radiate with a mystically gleaming force from the very figures in the windows. Having been transcribed most forcibly (even with respect to contours and surfaces) into that monumental ideality, that conceptual clarity, perfection and harmony that was the Gothic ideal of the personification of the Divine, these figures step forth from out of that twilight zone which obliterates all boundaries, seem to approach from distant regions like heavenly guests and radiate "like nothing before seen." They appear as messengers of temporal and spatial infinity, a veritable miracle of spiritual, supernatural "transfiguration" whose organs of communication are the natural phenomena of real, unlimited space and the light which floods and penetrates its every recess.

The following quotation is excerpted from a study of Julius Lange (q.v.) to whom man is indebted for a brilliant characterization of medieval stained-glass painting.

> In the entire visible world there is hardly a more powerful mood-impression than that experienced within one of the Gothic cathedrals just as the sun is setting. Everything within the cathedral interior shimmers indistinctly in the growing dusk and the eye can see nothing beyond those clear, glimmering figures which hover overhead to the west in stern solemn rows or in mystic combinations of lines as the burning evening sun falls across them. There the sensation of fire permeates all, and the colors sing out, rejoicing and sobbing. In truth, this is a different world.[43]

This other world, one might add, which draws souls upward into its sphere, also gave to immediate sensible experience a new artistic content, and although Lange rightfully emphasizes the fact that the genius of Gothic stained-glass art consisted in its ability to aid "the man of the Middle Ages to find a natural means of producing an impression of the supernatural, a means based upon the prevailing spiritual orientation of the times," one would further note that in a sense the reverse was also true, for the new natural coefficients of this apotheosis effected by man's union with those most sublime elements (a view of which, according to the medieval mind, might be allotted the human eye) likewise became an integral part of the impression itself and formed from that time onward a permanent part of mankind's highest spiritual goods.

As transcendental conditionality receded into the background, this new artistic content was forced more and more to rely on its own initiative. The tangible miracle which art is able to reveal to man sought its realization with greater persistency in wholly new forms—the expanses of space stretching to the very bounds of the visible somewhere on the horizon and guiding man's gaze as it enfolds alike God's nature and the works of man; the magic of light enshrines earthly objects with a festive glow or a fabled veil and causes them to appear as reflections in the mirror of eternal being and life; these reflections, entangled in fine threads woven in space and removed from the forces of individual influence or self-determination, awaken the image of a dream-like stillness beyond the regions of desire and action.

It would indeed be tempting to pursue still further the creative force of medieval spiritualism which to date has received but scant consideration, and not only in the history of art; but for this study it is sufficient to have discussed them apropos the most important universal stylistic characteristics of early Gothic painting and sculpture.

Common to all of these characteristics was the indivisible union of the spiritual and formal content of works of art with subjective, psychic processes, which was indeed a legacy of all of Christian art from its very origin onward. However by incorporating natural values of being, as one shall see, this entire phenomenon received a new meaning. The words of St. Thomas Aquinas concerning "the voice of God within us which teaches us to know correctly and with certainty," were not solely the confession of a religious revelation, for around them there developed a universal epistemological system which contained seeds of the disintegration of the entire, superb Thomistic philosophic structure.

II. THE NEW RELATIONSHIP TO NATURE

EDIEVAL spiritualism whose significance for art one at the present time can only surmise rather than actually know formed the vast basis for the return to nature and the sensible world formally as well as objectively.[44] As I have already indicated, this process was based upon a new universal, spiritual compromise with finite reality that was considered to be a type of stage for the actualization of meritorious deeds; even more, it was recognized as a necessary prerequisite for the eternal life of the elect. In art this compromise was expressed by a new perspective vis-à-vis nature; it utilized an approach which no longer considered nature as something axiomatically meaningless in the interpretation of artistic tasks and goals—it was rather to be counted among the very means for the realization of these goals, although, of course, within specific limitations.

This change and its concomitant innovations are most clearly evident in the representation of the human body; here a transformation was effected whose progress, at least in its earlier stages, can be viewed more clearly in the plastic arts than in painting where traditional compositions based upon other presuppositions retained their influence for a much longer period of time. Later the situation was to be just the reverse. The concentration of interests upon supernatural truths in the early Middle Ages had as one primary result the reduction of the human body to a totally subservient role. Consequently in artistic representations the human form assumed a lifeless, rigid, almost wooden character similar to its counterpart in archaic Greek art. The stylistic progress of medieval art in sculpture as well as in painting is embodied in the austere, rigidly perpendicular figures which the medieval world inherited as a legacy from early Christian antiquity. In this form of art the figures confront the viewer face to face, are loosely united by means of various external gestures and are more narrowly bound by a certain inner spiritual potentiality shared by all. The vigorously agitated forms employed intermittently throughout the Middle Ages were likewise an inheritance from the great historical cycles of early Christian art but functioned solely as isolated vestiges of the past, just as in contemporary art Baroque motifs are still occasionally used and yet in no sense can they be said to represent the spirit of twentieth-century art.

When the later medieval spiritual orientation had begun to concentrate anew upon man as a creature of this world, the formerly rigidified human figures in art once again became alive, not however by being reduced again to their classical point of origin nor by developing in a direction similar to that pursued by the ancient Greeks but by surmounting the classical art of the Greeks which had also endeavored to wrest a stronger degree of immediate vitality from the older oriental forms of art as well as from their own archaic forms. With the Greeks, however, this revitalization rested primarily upon observation and representation of motifs of physical motion which, present in specific pictorial conceptions, were reduced to their natural essence [German original: *natürliche Gesetzmässigkeit*] and originality as well as to their organic union; at the base of these self-same

Sigmaringer from the John's Group. *Courtesy Stiftung Preussischer Kulturbesitz, Staatliche Museen, Skulpturenabteilung, Berlin-Dahlem.*

motifs lay volitional act. Thus it was that man was to be reflected in art as a spiritual being but only within the mirror of material act. In the newer Gothic art forms, however, this consideration was entirely out of the question since its whole historical development was based primarily upon an attempt to surmount the artistic materialism of classical Greek and Roman art.

Consequently even the statues or the individual figures in paintings continued to retain their wooden character for quite some time—indeed it was not until the techniques of Renaissance art had made considerable progress that this hyper-constraint began to wane in spite of the minor, isolated accomplishments that had been achieved prior to the major Renaissance advances in the representation of physical motifs of motion.[45] Some other means, therefore, must have been employed to circumvent the lifelessness, the crystalline immobility of the older medieval figures, namely a spiritual vivification. By means of the expression of the spiritual in man, be it in general as the representation of a unifying spiritual tendency or in particular as the reflection of a spiritual contact or a psychic characteristic, a new life was breathed into the dead figures. This new, postclassical naturalism proceeds, therefore, from an interpretation of man as a spiritual personality, and it is here that one encounters the fundamental factor in the new development of art—a conception which could not fail to exercise a decisive influence on man's entire relationship to all of nature. This was also a necessary consequence of the historical development of Christian art which from its very inception, as I have repeatedly affirmed, took spiritual situations and not specific actions as the basis for its statuary art, with reference either to the individual figure or the compositional groups. However in the earlier stage of this development the psychic base-element of the artistic conception was almost entirely impersonal, namely a higher spiritual force that governs everything which occurs. It is for this reason that at times an abrupt contradiction arose between the psychic event and its physical counterpart, a contradiction which of necessity must appear paradoxical and barbaric to the modern viewer who is accustomed to a reciprocal harmony of both of these factors. After the former metaphysical *Weltanschauung* had been combined with a relative recognition of earthly, physical values, the psychocentric interpretation of being continued, however, to remain as decisive as it had been for all of life's manifold relationships, among which is also to be reckoned man's relationship to nature. But a basic difference is discernible in the fact that this spiritualization was not sought exclusively in transcendental substances, interpreted as it were as a dominating force beyond the scope of natural phenomena and events, but was rather wherever possible united to these transcendentals in the form of sense perception and psychic experience.[46] The most important consequences of this development can be thus summarized.

Initially it should be noted that the first accomplishment, or the most important step toward a complete transformation of the ideality in the representation of the human being, is to be found within the historical development itself. This transformation was not based on bodily mechanics, which however had been artistically mastered to the highest degree of perfection, but rested rather in essence on spiritual priorities, primarily degrees of ethical excellence. The goal of this newer art was not the formation of ideal bodily figures through whose material beauty of form and of conformity to established norms [German original: *Gesetzmässigkeit*] the realm of the higher, more edifying verities in the course of reality, was to be artistically attained; rather its goal was spiritual individualities that were to confront the humdrum reality of daily life with the concept of an intellectually and ethically higher humanity.

However one is not to conclude that bodily beauty had been axiomatically excluded. Indeed until the period of Gothic hegemony in the arts such physical beauty had been opposed or at best had played a minor role.[47] Only the divine figures and the angels in early medieval and Romanesque art retained a shimmer of classical perfection of form. For in the mass of the figures virtually no trace of this classical perfection can be found. At the beginning of their development in the seventh and eighth centuries as well as in their final lingering vestiges in Romanesque art, the majority of these figures appear to be distorted, disproportionate, grotesque and caricatured and thereby minimize if not actually invalidate the theories of either a gradual loss of the classical canon of art or of a gradually surmounted primitivism.[48] The mummy-like character of these representations is explained by the fact that the artist of the Middle Ages sought to suppress everything which was reminiscent of bodily excellence or which would exult the cult of the body or this life. This does not imply, however, that the characteristically ugly was exaggerated as is occasionally the case in contemporary art. When everything vigorous and materially effective had been deleted from the object to be depicted in art, the old classical canon of forms was automatically transformed into a withered phantom of senile proportions. This characteristic was all the more recurring because it corresponded to the basic tendencies of the artistic interpretation striven for by the medieval artist; this became consistently more evident especially when in conjunction with new medieval solutions to formal problems (as for example in the ninth and eleventh centuries) the attempt was made to incorporate classical formal constructions as well as classical solutions into the more recently evolved medieval formulations. The early Middle Ages had ideals independent from such constructions and any traces of the glorification of the human body found in art up to approximately the twelfth century are more the vestiges of past ages or some practical formula than they are new advances in artistic technique.

Of course the very employment of strictly classical formulations does indicate an incipient transformation of values more in keeping with the progressively advancing worldy orientation of spiritual interests, a change of which the artist was doubtlessly aware. The Greek concept of beauty was reintroduced in literature and was justified by appealing to principles formulated principally by St. Augustine and the "neo-Platonic pseudo-apostle, the aesthetician among the Fathers of the Church," Dionysius the Areopagite,[49] the commentary of whose works played such an important role within the framework of the Thomistic theory of art and to whose memory and fame Dante erected an imperishable monument. The classical themes of aesthetic speculation were taken up again but to be sure were given a new content. While for St. Augustine the point of origin of all artistic ideas was the absolute transcendental beauty of God which was expressed as "the living rhythm and the purely spiritual form and unity of the enormous poem which is the world,"[50] the philosophers of the Gothic age were wont to concede to beauty a purely worldly sphere wherein, however, it was to be conjoined with the quality *honestum*, which in the words of St. Thomas Aquinas is to be interpreted as *spiritualis decor et pulchritudo*.[51] Out of this combination arose a new concept of artistic beauty and sublimity in which the materially beautiful form appears as the expression of spiritual excellence. The Gothic representations of the Virgin Mary are an image of lovely feminine grace; those of the holy knights illustrate the embodiment of noble, youthful power; the apostles and confessors of Christ are veritable forms of imperturable manliness. The holy figures were meant to be of an obvious, bodily beauty and in this respect, both in art and on aesthetic principle, a new way was opened which would lead not only to the world of the senses but over and above this to the world of classical art; this was a direction in art as tenable for the contemporary world as it was for the Middle Ages. Yet the emphasis did not rest primarily on physical characteristics, but rather strove to accentuate the spiritual properties which informed them, as for example, the charm of the tenderly sensitive woman; the will of a Christian champion, at once firm and yet resigned to the will of God, a combatant in the army of Christ to whom every form of presumption is foreign; the mild, illumined wisdom of the founders and teachers of the new humanity.

It is this union of the spiritualistic idealism of the Middle Ages with the new affirmation of mundane existence that formed the origin of the new artistic interpretation of man, a conception which I have designated as a striving after the representation of the spiritual personality and which could only lead to new presuppositions concerning the representation of the physical nature of man. By their very nature spiritual personalities demand a bodily individualization and although at first a strong degree of stylization, determined by the guiding principles of Christian ethics, can be observed in this individualization, in such schemata it is not a matter of the synthesis of the individual to a unified corporeal ideal as it had been in classical art but is rather the attempt to capture the similitude of the nature shared by each of the various individuals. Although this endeavor to objectify in art a strictly metaphysical principle may have stamped the creations of the first period of this new art with a particular conventional character, it did not result in any progressive synthesis but enhanced a progressive individualization which had already derived renewed impetus from the further development of the new spiritual-mundane organization of society in Church and State; consequently in this manner it can be said to signify the beginning of a process which even today cannot be considered concluded despite a few later reversals.

Not only the concept of personality had changed; even the relationship to the entire external world had become something quite different once an interest in this world for its own sake had been rekindled by transferring the emphasis of human speculation to those psychic phenomena which separated the Christian from the classical era. In perpetuating a transformation that had already begun with the philosophical and artistic problems of

Chartres Cathedral, south portal; St. Theodore as a knight. *Courtesy Giraudon, Paris.*

late antiquity, Christianity with its belief in salvation and its ethics based on the intentions of the will taught mankind to subordinate its interpretation of the world to the spiritual welfare of the soul and to the Christian way of life. Thus Christianity instructed man to take cognizance first and foremost of the emotional life and the religious, that is the spiritual interests of the individual. Therefore sentiments and faith, the powers of sight and thought as well as man's individually conditioned needs and experiences became the measure of his relationship to the external world which man had now begun to conceive as a projection of the spirit. This discovery of the world as a reflection of individual consciousness comprised the second fundamental accomplishment of this development of art; this reflection strove to the fore when man's vision had once again been directed to the world about him and was focused on three aspects of human life. In the representation of man the new spiritualization and introspection were expressed in a threefold manner.

1. In the representation of the psychic contact between the individual figures. For a long time psychic relationships or conflicts did not function as an independent problem of art but wherever they did evolve from the narration to be represented they were emphasized incomparably more than they had been previously and formed an integrating part of the artistic interpretation of man. By way of example one need only consider the various versions of the Visitation. Even in Romanesque art the scene was conceived in the sense of the typically classical, materially motivated grouping of individual figures; this conception was transformed in Gothic art into an almost motionless, spiritual union to be replaced somewhat later by the form of a psychic dialogue.

2. In the representation of the emotions, their expression was not only intensified, as can be observed in the figures of the various Crucifixions, but even those psychic processes, which for the first time in the history of art were conceived as something

Chartres Cathedral, north portal; "The Visitation." *Courtesy Marburg–Art Reference Bureau.*

passive—from the quiet, inwardly directed absorption into self to the most powerful emotions of joy or sorrow—had now become recognized as independent subjects of the creative imagination to be juxtaposed to the scenic plots being portrayed, or even at times to supplant them.

3. In the relationship to the external world. In the rows of statues adorning the facade of a Gothic cathedral, one can observe that the majority of the figures are in no way related to one another, but rather they range beyond any form of action over and above symbolic allusion. Nevertheless they are figures filled with an inner tension based not upon an act of the will but stemming rather from a receptive psychic process—upon the power of vision perhaps, or maybe upon the conscious awareness of impressions which unite each individual figure with the external world. Nothing can more poignantly illumine the basic difference of this newer art vis-à-vis the art of classical antiquity than can this characteristic which clarifies the old adage that it was Gothic art which freed man's vision. This is true not only with reference to what was to be portrayed but equally so in reference to the artists themselves. Since perception, that is the viewing of the world as a product of the spirit, had gained ascendancy over the former view of the world, the nature of things demanded that the relationship between art and reality be equally radically transformed. In place of an objective perfection or a projected embodiment of the highest concept of a formal proposition involving a sweeping solution to the manifold problems confronting reality *face en face* in the form of its individual manifestations, there now emerged a receptive attitude vis-à-vis the limitless multiplicity of natural forms and the phenomena of life.[52] This attitude heralded the advent of nature studies in an entirely new and formerly undreamed of meaning of the word [German original: *nie dagewesene Bedeutung des Wortes*]. Man became the center of art but in a sense totally different from that which he maintained in classical art. He was now not the object but rather the

subject of artistic truth and legitimacy. The measure of artistic values was no longer based on the norms established by the accomplishments of previous generations but rather was the direct result of newly acquired experiences and observations. Graeco-Roman classicism had endeavored to suppress as far as possible the subjective element in art; however in Gothic art this subjective factor was to form the most important point of reference in any artistic creation, not only through the relationship it bore to any metaphysical explanation of the substance and external manifestations of the created world, a relationship that dominated the initial period of development of Christian art, but of far greater import it was now to find an equally potent expression in all phases of daily life. This shift in emphasis was to exercise a powerful influence on art in a twofold manner—extensively as well as intensively. The pictorial concepts of classical art were definitely limited despite their diversity; now, however, there were to be basically no inhibiting factors since the observable world, that is the world of subjective impressions knows no limitations. Thus in the Middle Ages, *in principle* at least, the entire visible world had become for art and everything related to it a posited and solvable problem, although *in fact* the mastery of this domain was to be a gradual process not as yet completed. Although this new, more comprehensive discovery of nature was united to the love of nature inherent in the younger Germanic tribes, it must nevertheless be emphasized that in the preceding centuries neither the poetry nor the plastic arts of these peoples had offered any basis for such a union. At best, therefore, one can speak only of a disposition innate to these peoples in the face of which the actual extension of the goals and tasks of art, by means of unlimited observation of nature, was without a doubt a determined, historically conditioned experience, analogous to the rise of the empirical sciences.

In a similar manner, it would be inaccurate to attempt to explain this entire historical process which precipitated a new relationship to nature—or as one is more apt to say, the discovery of the human person and nature—as a form of self-assertion of these new peoples vis-à-vis the traditional dictates and controls of the Church over their lives or to define it in terms of a secular Renaissance movement of mankind independent of all ecclesiastical constraint. This is not the case at all since the new attitudes were definitely rooted in the Christian spiritualism of the Middle Ages without which the new interpretation of art would be just as unthinkable as are the new sciences, the new poetry, the new worldly orientated social consciousness or the new secular *joie de vivre*. To be sure, on the basis of an extremely complicated historical development, a conditional secularization of the spiritual authorities had occurred, not, however, in opposition to the religious culture of the Middle Ages but within the framework of this medieval culture. Moreover it utilized the latter's fundamental principles for its own end. The new significance of the spiritual personality of man and the new interpretation of nature as well as the decisive points of view within this re-formation itself were founded, therefore, on developmental cycles which cannot be separated from that transformation of mankind which found its expression in Christianity.

It is evident that such a change would necessitate an extensive revision [German original: *eine weitgehende Überwindung*] of traditionally accepted concepts of art. In the period preceding the High Middle Ages the themes to be portrayed were limited to specific traditional cycles, newly conceived in various manners by either extending them or reducing their scope. Nevertheless these themes continued to operate within a highly concentrated circle of pictorial concepts, an area certainly much poorer than its early Christian presuppositions. About the middle of the twelfth century these barriers disappeared and a new world of imagination was opened to art in an apparently unlimited fullness —traditional topics were reworked and revitalized embracing countless new epic and lyrical themes of both a religious and a secular nature. This topical enrichment of art was not less extensive than the similar revolution in the art of the nineteenth century vis-à-vis the Renaissance and Baroque periods; moreover the main difference was that the extension of the realm of art in the late Middle Ages was accomplished less within the area of objective observation of nature (although even here the greatest revolution had also been effected) and concentrated rather on the narrative elements to be depicted.

The fact that the whole of medieval art had a strongly literary and illustrative character has been frequently, indeed justifiably, emphasized;[53] consequently it is only natural that this specifically narrative character should be expressed in the plastic arts to the extent that the ecclesiastical and secular literary interests of the period, permeated by a fresh blossoming of the life of the imagination, were expanded and transformed. Here it is not only a matter of the necessity to provide new works with illustrations; it is rather another example of an independent parallel phenomenon. Thus the endless narratives of the stained-glass windows were in one sense an ecclesiastical reflection of the chivalric epics of knighthood. The references to cycles of literary imagery were, however, so frequent that one can observe their decisive influence not only in the representations of historical or poetic events but also in every description of life and nature as well as in the reproduction of individual objects.[54] It is certainly not pure chance that the extensive encyclopedic knowledge of the Middle Ages, for example the *Speculum* of Vincent of Beauvais, and the late medieval pictorial subject matter agree to such a great extent—a common source gave rise to both the scholastic and the contemporary objects to be represented in art.[55]

The origin of this varied pictorial enrichment of the twelfth and thirteenth centuries was not, as it had been in antiquity, either sense impressions or primary pictorial conceptions but was rather a theoretical system of knowledge, a formative process which, derived from contemporary literary sources, determined not only the course of medieval art but also the entire consequent direction of European art as a whole. Therefore in contradistinction to oriental and classical art where the area of artistic representation was limited from the very beginning to specific material relationships and artistic problems, European art acquired both an almost unlimited program and a scientifically expanding character expressed at first only in the naive extension of basic interests; yet this character later transformed the entire concept of the artistic itself.

Far more radical than the transcending of the traditional material to be reproduced by art was the conquest of the traditional view of form. Even in the most unfavorable cases this victory can be unmistakably established, even there where a representational type of long duration had been adopted and, as if it were sanctified by tradition, violently withstood any form of change, for example in the representation of the figure of Christ or the Madonna. A Romanesque representation of the Virgin Mary or of Christ (be it viewed either as a specific type or in its particulars—for example the treatment of the garments, the various forms of the bodies, the designs and pattern figures, the relationship between form and surface or between light and shadow) appears clearly to be a member of a line of development whose uninterrupted genealogical lineage can be traced back to the period of classical antiquity. This continuity is completely lost in Gothic art. Even though at times the traditional composition was retained, the various forms and technical solutions inspired by this composition were wholly new, no longer based on tradition but rather upon a new and independent interpretation of nature, which interpretation is particularly unmistakable in representations more or less independent of the older pictorial devices.

A transformation in the formal problems, that is in the "how" in the reproduction of nature, was necessarily precipitated by the disarrangement of the relationship between the artist, nature and the work of art. The decisive psychological factors

Amiens Cathedral, south portal; trumeau, "La Vierge Dorée." *Courtesy Jean Roubier, Paris.*

of subjective perception and observation also had to play a large part in the reproduction of form and all the various formal as well as spatial relationships.

Fidelity to nature no longer consisted of a knowledge of nature raised to the level of a conceptual norm or perfection of form but was rather felt to reside in the actuality of the observed phenomenon, that which was characteristic of the individual. Thus it was a completely different and new fidelity to nature that triumphed with Gothic art, a concept not only new vis-à-vis its object or even its spiritual content, but one which, stylistically new to its very last stroke, irrevocably vanquished classical art for all times despite numerous apparent reversals. The significance of the new Gothic naturalism does not lie in individual, formal or practical advances and accomplishments but rather in the fundamental fact, which was to prove so decisive for all time in the entire cultural sphere of the Western world, that in Gothic art an artistic interpretation of nature prevailed that was entirely different from its classical prototype and this situation was analogous to the position of classical nature concepts vis-à-vis their oriental forebears. A new mankind, emerging from the most violent spiritual revolutions, began to disclose nature artistically anew when viewed from their newly acquired points of view and spiritual interests. The development of postclassical art cannot be understood if this fact is not kept constantly in mind.

Indeed one might ask why this new Gothic naturalism whose influence can be observed in the postmedieval era and which one might call an individual-receptive naturalism never developed beyond certain limited initial stages, although it was of decisive significance in as far as it dealt with direct observation of nature. This can be explained from its transcendental-idealistic presuppositions described above. For above the world of the senses, above life, above the truth and joy of nature, as man understands the word, stood God's revelation, the sphere of a transcendental, religious ideality, a being that obeyed laws other than those dis-

Bamberg Cathedal, gate of Adam; view of the Apostle Peter. *Courtesy Marburg–Art Reference Bureau.*

cernible by the senses or grasped by man's reason, a being not to be ascertained by transitory, secular values alone.[56] It is this eternal and immaculate transcendental world that art is to approach and by which it lifts the viewer upward in its wake—not only by means of an ideal abstraction as in the previous periods of Christian art when body and spirit traveled their separate ways, but now rather through a union of spiritual content with a physical effect of ideal and bodily beauty, an effect to which beauty must be subordinated although it itself is both limited as well as conditioned by the content.

Thus the representation of the Virgin Mary was supposed to be more than a mere image of a beautiful woman, a humanly lovely mother; it was at the same time supposed to embody the heavenly sweetness of the Mother of God in her immortal ideality. And if the Apostles and martyrs were characterized as spiritual personalities, this characteristic with its naturalistic auxiliary means of expression was based upon the endeavor to concretize before the gaze of the viewer representatives of a metaphysically absolute, eternal and holy community. This artistic endeavor did not strive solely to realize didactic aims (a fact so frequently and yet one-sidedly pointed out); nor did it merely instruct man in the ways of the church by means of a painted or sculptured theology. On the contrary it strove to no less a degree to effect formations of the imagination in which anthropomorphic religious conceptions could be condensed as pictorial figures of the ideal as they had once been depicted in the art of Greece.

They appear less new to modern man than do the Grecian figures because they were not iconographically new as were the latter, but were for the most part based upon old, and in many ways antique, devices. And yet they were just as new as the new interpretation of nature! They derived from a concept of ideality basically different whose point of departure was no longer the metaphysical projection of sense experience as it had been in Greek art; here the reverse was true, for the general significance of the artistic results of medieval art was measured by their relationship to transcendental spiritual values. How infrequently has the epoch-making importance of this fact been considered! What a wealth of new horizons, of infinitely new possibilities of artistic conception and effect was contained in this transposed view of art which conceived the physical form in art as the adequate expression of abstract psychic processes, a form both subordinated to these processes and at the same time deriving its ideality from them. Classical art could attain its greatest flowering and its profoundest influence on life by objectifying bodily and cosmic conformity to basic laws, or beauty or harmony within specific creations of the imagination. And yet within this physical objectivity lay also a limitation which sooner or later could only effect an end to the rise of this same classical art. On the other hand an equal danger was concealed in the pure spiritualism of late classical and early medieval art, that is the danger of ultimately losing every possibility of the progress rooted in physical experience or in the perception and practical knowledge of life. In contrast to these two systems of artistic idealism, the late Middle Ages offered a third one wherein objective reality and the beauty of material form were raised to the level of an adaptable expression of transcendentally spiritual values or the universal and individual struggle for ideal, ethical progress of mankind.

Just as the new naturalism had derived from the basic spiritualizing of all relationships of life so also a new secularly idealistic orientation of art arose from this same source, namely a new relationship of art to the ideas and emotions which move humanity. A line of development was thus established whose ultimate result was that the product of artistic creation, without losing its relationships to physical life, was hereafter to participate, to a far greater degree than it had in earlier periods of art, in great spiritual movements and to derive its source of transformation and rejuvenation from these very movements as well as from nature. This form of immediate participation ranged from the overpowering pathos of new universal ideals of mankind as a whole down to the silent confession of a subjective experience of an individual soul.

In Gothic art the primary concern was only the establishment of a link uniting the artistic values of worldly existence with the transcendental world order, or more specifically a bond between worldly beauty and the ideals of a Christian life. In this union, however, lay a further source for the transformation of old Christian pictorial base-types—the ancestral line of those personifications of a spiritualized beauty combined with either a depth of feeling or with certain ethical merits. In a sense analogous to the idols of bodily perfection prevalent in the art of the ancients, although operating under modified presuppositions and in conjunction with these classical modes of perfection, these base-types exercised a repeated influence on the idealizing portrayal of man in all subsequent periods of art. In Gothic art, however, they became as were the prefigurative incunabula of a spiritualized concept of beauty which was to play so great a role in contemporary ecclesiastical and secular poetry. Only thus is it explicable that one still encounters these base-types objectively limited in a period where there certainly can be no discussion of a timidity in the representation of nature.

And yet it was not only a matter of new ideal-types. Everywhere one can observe the genesis of a new interpretation of beauty in which, vis-à-vis classical art, a new standard had been established; however the interpretation effected was not only in reference to the spiritual elements of beauty but to its physical aspects as well. Although forms expressive of power and energy had not completely vanished, a striving for subtle delicacy and graceful lightness began with increased frequency to replace the Hellenistic figures composed in the style of the symmetrical harmony of a systematic physical culture as well as the massive, thick-set human forms elicited by the Roman sense of might or the plump figures resulting from the early medieval use of every aspect

Chartres Cathedral, north portal details. *Courtesy Giraudon, Paris.*

of bodily beauty. Irrespective of the various transformations this striving underwent between the twelfth and sixteenth centuries, it constantly preserved its connection with an ideality for which edifying emotions and an altruistic disposition as well as patterns of life based upon spiritual brotherhood, spiritual excellences, asceticism and an inner sense of subjectivity were far more important than bodily perfection and individual or public consciousness of power.

In this strong dependence upon spiritual content there lay at the same time, however, a certain fluctuation, an alternating approach to nature and then withdrawal from reality, an oscillation wholly unknown to the consistent development of classical art with its objective problems. The great realists who executed the north portal of Chartres[57] are hardly a generation younger than the masters in Moissac, Vézelay or Souillac who "created those abstruse figures born of hatred and anger, denying as nothing else in all the world the classical beauty of supple movement and the heathen cult of the hero, those forms rattling like skeletons beneath their outer garments, reflecting as it were what the hollow-eyed inmates of the medieval monasteries yearned to become: a pure soul annealed in the fire of mystic ecstasy, a spirit united to a body only to the same extent that a fragrance adheres to the ash particles of burned incense, a soul humbled in humility and borne yet aloft in yearning, which, while lying prone upon the floor like a broken reed crushed by a storm, still casts its gaze heavenward as a lily lifts its calyx."[58] In Bamberg the mighty spiritual pathos of the prophets of the St. Georg choir—a masterpiece of sculpture that might be described as the first part of a trilogy of powerful representations of pre-Christian prophetic figures, a trilogy whose second part is formed by the prophets and sibyls of Giovanni in Pistoia, the third part of which ("large things cast their shadow before them") encompasses the divine figures of the Sistine Chapel—was succeeded by the subtle epic quality of an art which, presiding beyond all spiritual conflicts,

Bamberg Cathedral, St. Georg Choir; Prophet Jonas. *Courtesy Marburg–Art Reference Bureau.*

created its harmonically noble forms out of the comforting assurance flowing from a joyful consciousness of God's presence.

And yet the inverse is also evident, for the almost brutally lifelike portraits of the founders of the religious houses in Naumburg were produced hardly more than a generation after the creation of Lettner's sculptured figures in Wechselburg and Halberstadt,[59] forms lyrically transported through pain and self-surrender in the being God. This prelude to a great mobility of spiritual content was based not only on the opposition between schools of thought and artists' studies but arose to no less a degree from the greater and more immediate dependence of artistic creation upon everything which moved the spiritual life of the age; moreover this dependence was greater and more immediate when compared to the relationship between life and art in classical antiquity, but it necessarily resulted from the evaluation of all things from the point of view of the exigencies of the life of the soul. This evaluation was peculiar to Christian art because of its basic character.

From these same sources, however, flows the astonishing wealth of imagination in Gothic art, that restless search for innovation in the invention of motifs which are not only to contain new impressions of nature but which are continuously to nourish the imagination. How basically different from the limitation of the classical spirit which "could find rest and satisfaction in the furrows of its triglyph" was "this strange joy of the new art in creating again and again new dream-like formations, in inventing forms which had the advantage of not only being new but also of bearing within themselves the germ of perpetual innovations."[60] The epoch of great imaginative art that according to Dilthey extends from the middle of the fourteenth century to the middle of the seventeenth century was actually introduced earlier through Gothic art.

Just like Peter Bruegel's peasant scenes, Rabelais' or Caravaggio's works, the series of Northern genre-painters, in word

Pistoia Cathedral, chancel; Prophet Jeremiah, by Giovanni Pisano.
Courtesy Fratelli Alinari, Florence.

or picture, are rooted in Gothic naturalism; and thus are spun out connecting threads uniting the Gothic world of the imagination and Dürer's "Apocalypse," Bosch's ghost stories, Altdorfer's idyls, Rembrandt's ghetto fairy tales, the spirit world of *Macbeth* and *A Midsummer Night's Dream* or the figures in which Spain's greatest poet raised the phantasmagoria of the imagination itself in the reflected image of an overpowering irony to the very subject matter of his own creation. And indeed it is not simply a matter of a continuation of the Gothic! Radical revolutions in spiritual interests, revolutions which I shall discuss later, lie between these varied epochs. It was, however, of decisive significance for the development of the new art that in the Gothic period the tremendous spiritual activity which flowed from the double source of a dying as well as a newly arising culture was diverted to the area of an artistic interpretation of nature and life, for inasmuch as this intellectual fermentation stood before the gateway of the medieval world-regeneration it was bound on the other hand with the remains of the classical objective reconstruction of the physical world in art, and yet on the other hand it was at one with the initial attempts to overcome this classical, this objective bias and thus to attain a world image founded on subjective perception and conviction.

The vernal stages of the imagination's undisputed sway were limited, as were all the other new methods in Gothic art, by the transcendental presuppositions from which these stages had developed. Thus I have arrived once again at the point of departure of this study—namely those stylistic characteristics of Gothic art which, anchored in a basically idealistic *Weltanschauung*, had set a priori a specific limitation to each form of imitation of nature and thus to any enrichment of art.

III. THE NEW RELATIONSHIP TO ART

HE inner development of medieval art resulted in a division, not necessarily between naturalism and antinaturalism, but rather a dissension between what is known by means of concepts and what is experienced by means of subjective observation. This discord was based upon a fundamental question or philosophic position which occupied the entire Middle Ages in every sphere of intellectual and spiritual endeavor and which was given formal expression in the "conflict of universals." The fundamental problems of the conflict that had been protracted for centuries and that in the Middle Ages played a role analogous to that enjoyed in modern philosophy by the critique of experience were a legacy from antiquity, inherited by the Middle Ages principally in a neo-Platonic version. Its position vis à vis the general intellectual life was, however, far different in the medieval world than it had been in classical Greece or Rome. Because of their most intimate connection with the profoundest secrets and teachings of the Christian *Weltanschauung*, these basic problems were thrust out of the sphere of theoretical epistemological systems, established for their own sake, into the focus of the total relationship of man to being; thus to a far greater extent than in classical antiquity they could and had to assert themselves directly in all the spiritual relationships of man to his milieu.

Through this shift of emphasis from epistemology to ethics, the inner antithesis in the possibilities of artistic or scientific investigation of nature was not only clearly grasped and formulated for the first time, but was also practically applied in contrast to the naive objectivism of Greek art and scientific observation. In this manner, namely through the transference of the dualistic religious and philosophic explanation of the world to the area of the physically perceptible and intellectually fathomable, was that duplicity of epistemological systems elaborated. From this elaboration emerged two primary factors: 1) the scientific progress of succeeding ages, and 2) artistic advances which resulted from an analogously greater separation of idealistically generalizing and naturalistically subjectivizing aspects. It is most remarkable how much the conflict between the realists (for whom ideas were the most real being—"the more perfect something is, the more being it possesses"—while to the physical individual object they attributed only an attenuated and completely dependent form of existence) and the nominalists (for whom the universals represented only designations, sounds and symbols, *flatus vocis* for a multiplicity of substances, and for whom the truly real was recognized only in the unique concrete object, that existent form founded solely on individual sense experience)[61] contributes by way of commentary to what had begun to be effected in art as in all phases of life since the twelfth century when circumstances forced a compromise with the realities of this world.[62] Is not Abelard's well-known formula, through which the conflict attained a temporary settlement, somewhat like a blueprint of that fusion of the transcendental world view and its secular counterpart that one can observe in Gothic art? The dialectical solution of the great philosopher could not permanently remove the actual opposition any more than could the new "style." But to the extent that the mass of knowledge, having finally gained entrance through this partially opened door and having been based on subjective observation, experience and conviction, began to flood the European intellectual life, to this extent did the bifurcation of the ways, the contradiction between Gothic idealism and naturalism, have to come to light; moreover this dichotomy became sharper and more pressing from generation to generation.

From its very beginning Gothic art split in two directions, less exteriorly than interiorly, somewhat as individual sciences have gradually branched off from their common metaphysical basis: on the one hand the idealistic, on the other the naturalistic. Although both are interwoven, it is not difficult at any time to separate these disparate tendencies. In addition to representations which unite the new interpretation of nature and observation with the metaphysical basis of medieval art and the form-selection conditioned by it, one finds those which, free of all tendencies toward idealization, represent only unique reality. The expansion of the objects to be represented continues in this direction. In addition to new epic cycles, more and more frequently portrayals were forthcoming (especially where the artistic imagination could drop all secondary considerations) in which the reproduction of the simple, observed content of nature or the artist's milieu, a section of life, had displaced all transcendental, teleological interests. The heroic in every sense of the word yielded to an objective realism; the strictly generic gained in importance and even the biblical narratives—and it is clearly evident that the historical tales of classical and national literatures shared the same fate—were transferred in every detail to a contemporary setting and were thereby divested of their historical character in favor of a naturalistic, perceptual representation.

The same process can also be observed with reference to formal solutions. Already in the thirteenth century, one can find works of art which seem to reflect the most advanced stages of the naturalism of following eras. These art works apparently originated in the endeavor to capture whatever was actually unique in any subject, its essential portrait-quality, its reality down to the very last detail.

IDEALISM AND NATURALISM IN GOTHIC ART

Thus, at least in principle, that extremely individualizing fidelity to nature, that artistic pantheism, which, although it has tended to vacillate between the poles of extreme importance and complete insignificance, must without a doubt be enumerated among the most obvious characteristics in the development of postmedieval art. This artistic pantheism was derived directly from the naturalistic components of Gothic art which did not seek those permanent characteristics common to all men, the normative element of a phenomenon, but those which strove rather to capture those particular aspects of an object which served as the basis for that individuality differentiating it from all other things. It might also be justifiably maintained that this subjective, pantheistic tendency is not only one of the dominant characteristics of modern art but constitutes as well one of the most difficult problems in the explanation of its historical development since such a tendency was unknown to all previous periods of art. The "dry naturalism" of Augustan art, which one might tend to consider an analogous spirit in art if not a direct source for Gothic naturalism, was apparently frought with similar efforts; actually, however, the naturalistic endeavors in this art constituted little more than a relative extension of its objective goals based wholly on the old normative efforts of classical art. On the other hand, the endeavor to overcome *every* norm must be considered decisive in the Gothic artistic current here under discussion.

How was it possible that within the framework of a primarily idealistic art this extreme empirical anti-idealism (if I might be permitted to use the word) was able to arise, a philosophic position so fateful for the future of art, based as it was on the subjective aspects of reality? Undoubtedly the explanation lies fundamentally in the special character of Gothic idealism which had opened the door for a more accurate observation of nature, without—at least in the beginning—considering nature to be the sole source of a higher spiritual and artistic subservience to established laws (*Gesetzmässigkeit*) as in classical antiquity where physical reality had been the measure of all things. This source of conformity to accepted norms was sought in a realm beyond the limits of transitory nature, in suprarational relationships, opposed to which the phenomena of the visible world were but subordinated elements embodying not the permanent nor eternal nor normative aspects of reality but on the contrary only the unique, perishable and infinitely manifold mutations of being. Of themselves somewhat insignificant, these facts did find individual justification in the great idealistic system of the late medieval spiritual culture, *ad maiorem Dei gloriam*, as *testimonia* and exemplifications of the supernatural by means of the physical—a concrete revelation of the being of God in the most minute of His works.[63] Thus the transcendental idealism of the Middle Ages in its union with secular values leads directly to extreme naturalism; later in the Renaissance and post-Renaissance periods the very reverse was true, for out of this naturalism developed a new anthropological and cosmic idealism in conjunction with a partial return to classical antiquity.

"I cannot escape the spirits whom I have summoned. . . ." Once the Middle Ages had bridged the chasm between a *Weltanschauung* anchored in the eternal verities of the beyond and one which admitted, though at first only conditionally, the intrinsic value of mundane objects, it was inevitable that in various ways, but above all, through the inner dialectic of the observations and experiences inherent in such a philosophic position, the world view rooted in these same observations and experiences would move further and further away from its initial metaphysical presuppositions. This decidedly internal process of secularizing man's entire *Weltanschauung* can be observed everywhere from the second half of the twelfth century onward. The latent stoic elements in Christianity, and with them the belief in the rights of nature, were given new meaning and significance by means of a bisection of philosophic thought, a division of truth and knowledge which provisionally, in spite of all attempts at reconciliation, was often at least theoretically emphasized. The theory of St. Thomas Aquinas, namely that the good is also contained within man's reason—an old idea, basically Socratic in origin—would in its new application likewise have to lead to a certain loosening of intellectualism from its general transcendental conditionality. But above all it was the Aristotelian concept of natural, organic evolution—a concept reintroduced into the spiritual life of the Occident via the circuitous route of Arabic and Jewish literature—which, no matter how much it was assimilated in its Thomistic form into the unified ecclesiastical culture, contributed infinitely to investing human knowledge and research with an esoteric content independent of divine revelation.[64]

In all of these phenomena, as well as in many other similar ones, there lies far more than the "history of religious enlightenment in the Middle Ages," a development which the nineteenth century sought to find in them. In the evolution of the human spirit they signify rather the beginnings of a new stage of growth whose fundamental characteristic lay in the fact that knowledge, based on observation and rational demonstrability, became an independent field of spiritual activity and an end unto itself, a discipline subject to its own laws. It was not a matter of the revivification of classical, metaphysical logic; what arose out of the medieval *Weltanschauung* for which the metaphysical verities were either really or *pro foro externo* beside the point, i.e., what the thinkers of the school of Chartres and Duns Scotus, the Averroists and Roger Bacon had founded, at first as it were in a small corner of the towering spiritual cosmic structure of the Middle Ages, was something entirely new: the theory of a double standard of truth, both conditioned by the strange complications of medieval spiritualism and yet a reflection of the dualistic relationship of man vis-à-vis nature was the cradle of a new autonomous science independent of all a priori explanations of man and the world he inhabits.

ONE HUNDRED TEN

This development was supported by various Arabic influences to which, however, in contrast to current opinion, I would attribute only a secondary role. The compromise with philosophically abstract thought was a position peculiar to occidental Christianity and had been reached in Islam to a far less degree; and thus in Islamic culture religious speculation was again invested with its original prophetic character and the classical legacy inherited from ancient Greece, an inheritance certainly no less extensive here than in European culture, was to lead a life of its own and to be separated from specifically religious thought and emotions. As Wilhelm Windelband has already pointed out,[65] it is characteristic that the bearers of Arabic science in the Middle Ages were doctors and not clerics and that this science bequeathed to future generations far more practical knowledge inherited from classical antiquity than did its sister science in Europe. In the interpretation of the goals and tasks of science, however, Arabic science like Arabic art moved further and further away from its classical basis. The Greek conception of science as an anthropological philosophy of nature which sought to explain the world of the senses in terms of metaphysical systems was united in Christian antiquity with the pure religiosity emanating from the Orient; thus science acquired a new significance in the further spiritual development of mankind.

Among the Semitic peoples of the Middle Ages, however, this conception played only a minor role and yielded increasingly in the face of a mystical and cabbalistic interpretation of the varied interrelationships of life. On the other hand the Arabs and Jews preserved not only the sum total of scholarly material, that is the concrete scientific knowledge of antiquity, far more immediately and completely than the monasteries of Europe had done, but also the fragments of Aristotle's epistemological positivism which had been almost totally repressed by the ethical and transcendental idealism of the early Middle Ages. The Semitic scholars both preserved these aspects of classical culture and expanded them still further through their practically applied investigations and explorations of nature. From about the end of the twelfth century these treasures began to flow into the body of cultural and scientific possessions of the Christian peoples. Without the development discussed above, this certainly would not have been possible, for it was this very evolution that raised nature and its laws and the various aspects of conformity to these norms as well as the secular history of mankind to the level of an area of knowledge relatively independent of the problems of Divine Revelation. All things considered, it was not unimportant that Western Europe obtained a wealth of new scientific data in this particular manner.

Indeed its significance in Europe changed rather soon. Whereas in the East natural scientific, astronomical, chemical, medical and mathematical studies represented a series of more or less unrelated disciplines, each subject to the whims of chance, in the West they could be further developed in a far more unified and consistent manner since the orientation of occidental thought had incorporated subjective experience into its total *Weltan-schauung* and, in conjunction with the entire intellectualism of the post-Thomistic era, this subjective experience became not only an independent nucleus of intellectual activity but at the same time it was transformed into a unified and conscious logic in a new sense of the word. Since theology could not follow the newly acquired scientific knowledge and the antithesis was still not felt to be decisive for either of the two paths leading to truth and spiritual edification, a separation of viewpoints was effected —theoretically at first by Duns Scotus, practically by Roger Bacon;[66] in the time to come the newly revived nominalism by its very nature would have to terminate in the consideration of nature as the sole object of science. Thus the boldest questions and accumulated data, all standing in sharpest opposition to ecclesiastical dogma, were discussed *secundum rationem*, whereby man's religious conscience was assuaged with the reservation that *secundum finem* such seemingly heretical ideas naturally must be considered inconsequential.[67]

ONE HUNDRED TWELVE

I have dealt somewhat at length with the origins of this new dualistic separation of the investigations of nature and man from the consciousness of God's presence because it corresponds to something one can observe in contemporary art, namely an opposition on the one hand of an observation of nature, immediate and totally free of all directional presuppositions, and on the other hand an ideal style surpassing everything strictly mundane.

From the Middle Ages onward a type of mathematical relationship seems to function between art and science, an equation of sorts in which the significance of descriptive naturalism (corresponding in principle to the nominalistic interpretation of Gothic art) vis-à-vis the general position of art rises or falls with the significance of the positive sciences within the general European intellectual life. With the victory of the sciences in the course of the nineteenth century, this equational relationship apparently attained its zenith.

And yet these circumstances cannot adequately explain the great transformation that began to take place in the significance of an absolute fidelity to nature within the total construct of artistic creation, a change that began about the middle of the fourteenth century and which in the first half of the fifteenth century resulted in a complete disarrangement of the relationship of the two major tendencies in Gothic art. In all the residues of the medieval conception of art and nature (alluded to in a most perceptive manner by Ernst Heidrich [q.v.]),[68] one encounters, unexpectedly and forcefully, a total revaluation of all values of existence, for example in the pictures of Jan van Eyck; and only an historical prejudice could doubt the fact that at the same time in Italy—in Masaccio's paintings or Donatello's statues—the trends in art and philosophic orientation involved much more than a mere continuation of medieval lines of development.

In a later study I will attempt to explain exactly what the particular problems were that formed the nucleus of the transformation from medieval to Renaissance art in Italy;[69] for the present, however, I will center my attention upon one pivotal fact, namely that in the North as well as in Italy the essential factor in this transformation was the attainment of complete independence by art vis-à-vis every form of transcendental subservience to established norms [German original: *Gesetzmässigkeit*]. The stylistic presuppositions of this transformation, a change which will have to be clarified in greater detail, were, as I attempted to illustrate in another connection, contained in Gothic naturalism; and yet another question remains as to how this naturalistic direction could attain a complete ascendency over the artistic dualism of the Middle Ages. For although a particular sense of reality, which must be counted among the most important developmental factors in postmedieval art, was already collaterally present with the general advancement in direct observation of nature, as a special strain in the Gothic art of the thirteenth and fourteenth centuries, it nevertheless possessed only a secondary significance within the total picture of artistic creation until the end of the fourteenth century; it was analogous to the position maintained by the new and contemporary scientific endeavors vis-à-vis the total view of life common to the age. However it was precisely in the historical peculiarity of this union of the two basic tendencies in Gothic art that its insolubility seemed to be contained. Even though the new conception of nature was still conditioned by medieval standards of perfection, the bonds uniting medieval and postmedieval art and aesthetics would hardly have been loosened as quickly as they were—in other areas of cultural life medieval influence can be observed far beyond the dawn of the Renaissance—had not a new concept of the work of art itself been associated with the causes discussed earlier, a concept which at first did not range entirely beyond all medieval constraints but nevertheless one that did signify something new and independent in contrast to them. Southern Europe was the birthplace of this concept.

The essence of the whole problem in the visual arts might become clearer if one compares it to the parallel development in literature. The literature of the Middle Ages was like their art completely subject to a firm transcendental order, a metaphysical kingdom of abstract substances.[70] In poetry and in history no relationships to the sensual world, to human life and experience, existed that did not somehow derive their origins and their limits from the supernatural, spiritualistic idealism of the medieval, Christian *Weltanschauung*, beyond which limits no poetical or historical importance existed. It was not from the sensual life of man nor the emotions rooted in this physical existence nor from the causal interconnections of material events that the spirit proceeded to a higher poetical and historical consciousness; rather the reverse was true, for the belief in the omnipotence and the singular value of metaphysical, spiritual forces was the point of departure of poetic creation and historical consideration, or more specifically the new poetical and historical discovery of the world and the history of mankind. Wherever the Middle Ages sought to surpass annalistic raw material in its local, temporal and social limitation,[71] the result was inevitably an attempt to arrange into a system of supramaterial points of view the events comprising this very raw material in legend, epic or in universal, historical narration. In a sense other than that stated by Joseph Bédier (q.v.), the *chansons de geste* are to be traced back to the religious spiritualism of the Middle Ages;[72] similarly derived were the ecclesiastical counterpart of these *chansons de geste*, namely the great legendary poems and world chronicles, the purest expression of medieval historical conceptions, all of which signify enormous progress in the direction of an ideally unified history of mankind.

The Gothic cathedrals, those magnificent epics in stone, more nearly approximate Dante's *Commedia Divina* in artistic conception and intellectual construction than do all the various works which are generally considered to be the literary rudiments of this, the greatest poetic masterpiece of the Middle Ages. In these cathedrals everything of significance to contemporary mankind in his past, present and future was inserted into a framework of spiritual unity which victoriously conquered the world of the senses and which was based upon direct relationships to the world of the transcendental; from this unity the most profound artistic meaning was derived. However even in the most important sources of the profane content of the *dulce stil nuovo*, a similar dependent relationship preponderated since, as Edward Wechsler (q.v.) so convincingly proved not so long ago, the concept "Minne," upon which the new style was based, must be considered as a transference of the spiritual relationship between God and man to a reverence for womanhood,[73] whereby for the first time eroticism was introduced into the intellectual development of mankind as a purely spiritual force totally detached from anything sensual. A phenomenon corresponding to this origin can be seen in Dante when Amor appears in the form of an angel with white flowing robes.[74]

Thus in art as well as in literature, the new relationship to the world was constrained by the spiritual and transcendental idealism of the medieval religious explanation of earthly existence whereby in a manner analogous to the plastic arts, a certain conditioned independence of poetic and historical motifs and problems contained within the values of a life oriented toward mundane goals resulted by means of this transference to only earthy limited areas of the poetic imagination and a life of feeling. Within the context of these general European relationships, a special development began in Italy in its literature and in its art.

In order to comprehend this newly acquired independence, its territorial presuppositions as well as its date of origin must be considered. Although Italy had produced the greatest organizer, the greatest thinker and the greatest poet of the medieval compromise between the natural and the divine law, the ideals contained therein and its inherent unification of the spiritual (and material) culture attained an influence there less universal and decisive than north of the Alps. Italy likewise took only a small

"The Lamentation," by Giotto; from the Arena Chapel at Padua.
Courtesy Fratelli Alinari, Florence.

and indirect part in the development of medieval theology[75] and epistemology, and the interpretation of man's ethical and public duties derived from these disciplines. In like measure the creation of the new anticlassical Gothic art found no responsive echo in the Italian peninsula. Therefore from the point of view of Gothic art, but more especially in the age of its forceful growth between the eleventh and fourteenth centuries, Italian art can be viewed generally as something stunted and backward. Like the Semitic peoples, the Italians, however, preserved much of the practical knowledge of antiquity, potent remains of a formal culture independent of the metaphysical ideals which permeated everything in Northern Europe; this culture's influence can be observed in widely divergent aspects of European life: in the continuation, although in a very attenuated form, of a secular education based upon the last direct radiation of the late classical rhetorical formative ideal, a classical education unaffected by Christianity; in the significance of the old concepts of law and in the preference for legal studies in general; in an economically sober and practical sensibility so far removed from the inner emotionalism of the medieval citizen of Northern Europe; and, not least of all, in the Italian art which appears in a far different light if judged not according to the standards of Northern Gothic art but rather by its own methods and goals. All of these factors attained a new meaning and value, as did the residual elements of classical science, when the avenues of knowledge based upon reason and perception as well as upon revelation began to develop independently within the *Weltanschauung* of the late Middle Ages in the manner described above.

From this process of growth resulted consequences (vis-à-vis the position of art) of which the greatest philosopher of the medieval spiritual dualism had remarkably enough already been aware before they had exercised a decisive influence upon the development of art. In a most brilliant manner, Thomas Aquinas had drawn a sharp conceptual line between the content of religiously moral and artistic striving and posited that although the ethically good and the artistically beautiful are identical *in sub-jecto* or in their concrete content, conceptually—*in ratione*—they differ according to their purpose and effect, since the good is to be interpreted as *recta ratio agibilium*, that is a virtuous life and manner of acting related directly to the highest and ultimate determination of man; art on the other hand must be viewed as based upon *recta ratio factibilium*, laws of formation, whereby the beautiful emanates from purely formal elements (*in ratione formali*).[76]

In this distinction, based to a certain extent on Aristotle, and yet at the same time far surpassing him because of the entirely new situation developed in the Christian spiritual life, a program was contained which in its progressing execution would have to lead to a complete separation of the religious and the artistic view of the world. And at the same time, given the reasons discussed above, it was a program for whose goals the Italian heirs of the classical tradition were particularly suited.

Thus through the general development of the European intellectual life in the course of the thirteenth century, a situation ensued that enabled Italian literature and art to attain an independent significance and intensive expansion, in a sense precisely because of the superstitions which until that time had effected their retardation. And not only did Italian art flourish in the cultural centers of Italy itself, but it soon exercised a tremendous influence on all occidental art.

However one must not tarry at the first beginnings of this transformation in literary production, but rather should be concerned with its first great results. In the poems and prose works of Petrarch, the *patris poeseos*, one encounters the artistic form that in the early Middle Ages had absolutely no independent task and importance vis-à-vis the universally spiritual or concretely objective meaningfulness whose correlative it was. Although this artistic form was always more or less typical, at first in a purely external but nevertheless decisive manner, it constituted the real purpose and meaning of artistic creation. To the two worlds dominated by the will, the emotions and the thought of medieval man, to this world of a limited earthly life and an eternal existence in the beyond, a third was associated, that of artistic conception. This latter world obeyed its own laws and discovered within itself its tasks and goals and standards; in addition it was a world which henceforth elevated the poet to the level of *Vates* and author and bestowed upon him a nobility of no less significance than that offered by the State or the Church.[77] How sharp the distinction between his newly acquired position and his role during the Middle Ages when the vocation of poet was the prerogative of clerics or wandering minstrels.

In art as well, this transformation had become a reality. Much earlier in Italian art, as far back as the twelfth century, architectonic, plastic and even pictorial form had attained a certain independent existence based on artistically autonomous interests.[78] The autonomous work of art, this third intellectual world power of the late Middle Ages, appears completely clear and fully developed in the paintings of Giotto. Their basic task, namely to narrate the life of Christ, the Virgin Mary and the saints, was to be sure old, almost as old as Christianity itself; the way and manner utilized by Giotto to fulfill this task, however, was new and fundamentally different from everything which previous art had created in its attempt to portray like themes that differed from both the naturalistic as well as from the idealistic points of view of the Middle Ages. As Friedrich Rintelen (q.v.) correctly emphasized in his beautiful study of Giotto,[79] the most important factor in this transformation was not the progress made in the observation of nature, as great as this progress was. For the holy stories so wondrously retold by Giotto appear in his works not as realistic descriptions of life but rather transformed into an heroic idealized style which in many respects consciously deviates from an exhausting fidelity to nature.

"Crucifixion," by Giotto; from the Arena Chapel at Padua. *Courtesy European Art Color Slide Co., New York.*

This idealized style was, however, not the emanation of an irrational supranaturalness as in Gothic art but was an artistic paraphrase and transfiguration, a monumentalization of sensual reality such as classical art had striven to attain. And yet at the same time this style was fundamentally different from the classical interpretation. In the classical period, pictorial concepts and formal accomplishments of art developed within the framework of an indissolvable union with myth and nature personified and idealized in the figure of the hero, so that the further development of art was at the same time the further developments of its artistically objectified religious content and the interpretation of nature contained within it. With the ascendance of the spiritual content and the complete subordination of formal solutions in Christian art, this relationship changed. A further transformation resulted in Italy where art, with respect to its formal goals vis-à-vis nature as well as religion, began to constitute an independent third entity, a world unto itself in which the imagination created its own values.[80] Art like science became not only the expression of a *Weltanschauung* but also an independent source thereof, free of all metaphysical presuppositions.

The belief in permanent principles of art is to be counted among the causes of the prevailing uncertainty and confusion in the critical examination of works of art from earlier periods, works which arose amid other general historical presuppositions. This belief was based upon the assumption that, no matter how often the goals and technical skills of art might change, the concept of a work of art can nevertheless be considered something which on principle is constant and immutable. Nothing, however, is more false and more unhistorical than such an assumption, for the concept of the work of art and of the artistic has in the course of its historical development undergone the most diverse transformations even with respect to its most fundamental presuppositions and is at all times a temporally and culturally defined and variable result of the general evolution of

ONE HUNDRED TWENTY-TWO

mankind. What was understood by the term art and what was sought in it and demanded of it varied in the old oriental, in the classical, in the medieval and in the contemporary European intellectual worlds—to say nothing of other cultural milieus— just as much as did the conceptions of religion, morality, history or the sciences. Only on the basis of a clear knowledge of the historical particularities of the underlying principles in various times and places, individualities conditioned by these circumstances, can the way to an historical understanding of the artistic phenomena of by-gone periods be found. This comprehension would necessarily rise above nebulous preconceptions of art per se.

The autonomous position of art within the framework of the forces dominating human existence appears today so self-evident that one generally tends to forget the relatively late development of this position which, after extensive preliminaries, attained its ultimate form only in the Italian art at the turn of thirteenth and fourteenth centuries. Every one of Giotto's paintings is a world unto itself in which the directive power of supernatural forces is expressed only in the events depicted, a pictorial universe, however, which follows its own laws in the artistic reconstruction of these events. And it is these laws that determine the artistic significance of the figures, their invention, their arrangement and their spatial position and union. In contrast to the attitude of the classical artists, this newer artistic subservience to established canons, independent of metaphysical relationships, is not considered to be based solely on laws inherent in the objects themselves, in their material beauty and causality; rather it is based to a far greater extent than ever before on the conjunction of these objective aspects with subjective, artistic judgment; they represent the individual artistic act of creation in the paraphrase of a material situation, a creative act determined by artistic demands. In other words, the fundamental subjectivism of Christian art was now transferred to autonomous artistic problems. Up until this time the realm of artistic values had reflected subjective faith in revelation and subjective observation; from the thirteenth century onward this same set of values underwent a process of revision whereby art now mirrored man's subjective imagination based only on its own power; in the ensuing confrontation of art with reality and supernatural verities, the artistic personality in literature as well as in the plastic arts acquired a new significance.

This new concept of the artistic necessarily contained, however, a new conceptualization of artistic truth and vivification as well as an ideality henceforth specifically artistic. Both of these aspects were incomparably more firmly wedded than the ideas of the ideal and the natural had been in the art of the preceding Gothic era.

To be sure, the progress of Giottoesque art, even in the direction of that Gothic fidelity to nature based on observation of the individual form of isolated objects, was considerable and diverse; of greater importance was the new inner unity of the representation to which the former consideration of fidelity to detail had to be subordinated and in which a new interpretation of natural relationships was implicitly contained. It is not difficult to find examples in contemporary miniatures, frescoes or plastic decorations north of the Alps in which concrete reality is represented far more accurately than in Giotto's rocks and miniature trees or his generalized architectural constructions. By the same token, however, in Giotto's paintings everything gains a new artistic power of convincing and an actuality with only a tentative bearing upon reality. To his contemporaries it must have seemed like a magic game as the great artist unrolled before their eyes, in the guise of old holy legends, a state of being and a manner of action in which, out of the raw material of sensual experience, forms and interdependencies were created which, vis-à-vis the accidental qualities of daily reality, must have appeared as the revelation of undreamed of and yet typical truths and relationships forming the basis of physical perception.

It was these same truths and relationships which also made it possible to transform the legend into the sphere of a more penetrating and clearer reproduction of the formal powers dominating nature and their causal unifying norms. It was also thus that observation in the invention, plastic effect and compositional significance of the figures, as well as in their interweaving within the represented space was assimilated into a natural, normative and artistic subservience to established laws. This subservience was no longer a reflection of transcendental presuppositions but one having its source in a sensual experiencing of life. New and more universal categories of truth and formal systems of values were made manifest to the artistic view derived from this experience sooner than to the speculative mind. In the classical period and in the periods following, dominated as they were by the classical influence, these new truths and systems of value evolved as a criterion for mundane actuality. Yet at the same time they were effected as an expression of the personal struggle for an artistic mastery over the visible world and not least of all as the way to a formal meaningfulness in which the artist as creator, independent of the most profound secrets of ecclesiastical revelation, could clothe the divine and the human content of these holy tales through the free play of his imagination and through his art, rooted in earthly sensual life.

In the new art, therefore, a twofold progress is discernible.

1. General problems and norms of the reproduction and paraphrase of nature won independent significance and became the most important content of the specifically artistic endeavor and success.

2. In its autonomously artistic and easily perceptible subservience to established laws a new point of departure for artistic idealization and monumentalization was found. Thus, for example, the spatial unity [German original: *Raumzusammenschluss*] as the basic form of natural spatial relationships and as such also one of the most important characteristics of the fidelity

to nature in pictorial representation became an indispensable requisite of every pictorial composition. At the same time, however, through a free adaptation of this unity of space to the closed effect of the picture, concentrated and balanced in surfaces and free space, this new basic form became the principal means of awakening within the viewer the impression of a clarifyingly liberating and edifying artistic solution. The same is true of the new ideal-types in which the formalism of the Middle Ages was complemented by conscious artistic precepts; in like measure medieval idealism, based upon universal spiritual aspects and the conceptions of beauty corresponding to these aspects, was expanded by a new concept of idealism rooted in purely formal aspects, in addition the concepts of size, style and artistic superiority were derived from them. This consciousness and open avowal of the autonomous play of the imagination, envisaged as the real independent goal of art, contained within itself that transformation which, to authors of the fifteenth and sixteenth centuries who lived to experience its consequences, must have seemed to be the regeneration of art and the return to true doctrine, the rules of art which had been lost during the Middle Ages. Ghiberti stated the matter clearly and decisively when he wrote: "Cominciò l'arte della pictura a sormontare in Etruria in una villa allato alla città di Firenze" ("The art of painting began to flourish in Etruria in a village near Florence"). There is no possible doubt about the validity of this statement. Considering the innumerable older documents, which certainly were not unknown to Ghiberti, these words would be unintelligible if it were not for an entirely new concept of painting.

Like Petrarch's theory of the nature of literature, Ghiberti's theory of painting did not remain without influence north of the Alps. It can be observed in various effects, some consecutive, some simultaneous. In conjunction with iconographic and individual formal borrowings, one can observe an approximation of the new Italian principles of pictorial invention in which at first a strong displacement was realized in both idealistic as well as naturalistic relationships in favor of the independent significance of formal points of view.

With the new Italian norms of representation, new concepts of formal perfection and beauty were doubtlessly united along with the initial beginnings of an inner-worldly Platonic ideality which even north of the Alps had begun to exercise an influence. Thus, for example, it is not difficult to observe the influence of the Giottoesque and Siennese ideal types in the portrayals of the Madonna which were so popular, and which were united as they were by the expanding cult of Mary (a sign of the transformation is also evident in this cult itself). Its precept of beauty, imitative of a classical prototype, united with those conceptions of grace and charm that developed within the framework of the ecclesiastical art of the Middle Ages, became the point of departure even in the North for a concept of beauty in which the emphasis was transferred from a religious to a purely artistic ideality. Thus in such Madonnas or similar representations of the saints, a human ideal began to dominate art north of the Alps for the first time since the classical age; this ideal elevated harmony and grace of forms above all other considerations and united them with a stronger emphasis on psychic characteristics (thanks to the preceding medieval development vis-à-vis antiquity), not only as mundane exemplifications of divine truths but for their own sake as the expression of a purely artistic joy in humanity and the earthly excellences treasured in it.

Formal goals acquired a new significance and prestige, but not only in such preludes to the later strivings for a classical style, whose reflection can be observed in the oldest "humanistic" literature north of the Alps; this tendency is discernible in the framework of the old Gothic world of forms as well. The Gothic delight in lives, the graceful hovering or pathetic rustling of Gothic motion, the ever-richer, more artistic life of plastic forms and constructions intensified even to Baroque excess, the effects of the joyously flowery or ostentatiously resplendent color of the paintings as well as the rhythm, spatial effect and decoration in architecture began to develop a greater independence and a general artistic significance over and above the medieval concept of an ideal unity. In addition to the ideal types originating in Italy, new Nordic types also arose in which abstraction and generalization as well as the conceptions of individual excellences inherent in such types were based less on an a priori limitation of the representation by means of a Christian subjective and metaphysically conditioned interpretation of personality than they were on formal aspects.

And just as the inner dialectic of the new theses and points of view in the contemporary theological and philosophical thought began to become more and more effective, as opposed to the unified and authoritatively absolute religious ideas of the Middle Ages, in like measure one can also speak of a similar dialectic in art, a dialectic of lines, forms, types and problems, which was not entirely able to destroy the great spiritual unity of medieval art but did, nevertheless, weaken it and thereby paved the way for a new position of art within the general framework of cultural life. It is characteristic that north of the Alps this development in art, akin to the parallel development in literature, was at first linked with personal insight, a higher degree of intellectual formation and a special connoisseurship; this was being first observed in paintings or statuary that had no firm relationship with the vast legacy of Gothic art, namely panel paintings, miniatures or individual statues which, in a time when architectonic sculpturing and painting was still developing along the paths of transcendental Gothic idealism, were created for connoisseurs who commissioned them or perhaps they were already executed, without a direct commission, simply as works of an artistic credo based upon the new specifically artistic subservience to law.[81] It is hardly mere chance that from that time to the present day the further development of the plastic arts proceeded far more from mobile works of art than from their monumental counterparts related to architectural construction; only the art of the Counter-Reformation is an exception to this general rule, but here as in so many respects the art of this period approximates its Gothic antecedent.

The most important aspect was then that this autonomy was transferred not only to generally formal problems but also to the representation of nature and even to older Gothic naturalism. One has heard how, in connection with the position of Christian man to the sensually perceivable world in the later Middle Ages, a new interpretation of the truth of nature as a reflection of the individual phenomenon in subjective observation arose that corresponded to the psychocentrism upon which this position was based. This new interpretation was at first conditioned and delimited by a supernatural subservience to law to which all worldly phenomena were bound. One has also learned how this nominalistic naturalism, corresponding to the theories of a double truth, gradually became an important source for the enrichment of the contents and formal aspects of art, knowledge and general *Weltanschauung*. I have further indicated how in the general spiritual life of the times a parallel development was not evoked but was indeed promoted by the appropriation of the residual positivistic factual knowledge about nature which had been preserved as a classical heritage in the scientific literature of the Semitic peoples. Through this process, in which the positive sciences began to be contrived as an organon for understanding man and the world surrounding him, namely a body of knowledge independent of philosophy and theology, the close union between the new direct observation of nature and the great medieval system explaining the world and its existence must naturally also have been weakened in art.

At this time the new concept of an autonomous work of art began to exert an influence in Northern Europe and models, whose inner structure was independent of that system, were imitated. Here one can observe a most remarkable and instructive state of affairs, equally applicable to similar phenomena of later periods. Although at times the Northern artists of the fourteenth century rather faithfully followed their Italian models in their new naturalistic accomplishments, as did the later *Romanisten* artists of the Northern Renaissance, one almost never encounters the borrowings in that particular application and form which in Italy had formed their most important characteristic. While in Italy both were conditioned by means of an artistic microcosmos whose connection with reality was derived as it were from a free theatrical framework determined by the demands of universal artistic truth and internal logic, and from this closed reciprocal relationship between pictorial unity and all of its parts both had also derived their meaning and form, their truth and their beauty; in Northern Europe the new borrowed forms and norms of pictorial invention, in contrast to their artistic origin, were united to motifs which had developed out of the old Gothic striving for a reproduction of individual reality.

It is even more remarkable, however, that the Italian compositional schemata in Northern Europe were intermingled not only with traces of the subjective naturalism of Northern Gothic but were also one-sidedly conceived as a whole only from the point of view of the observation of nature. Thus, for example, the consistently uniform rendering of space, which under the influence of classical art was introduced into Italian painting as a requisite of that higher artistic subservience to law to go beyond a simple imitation of nature, was interpreted north of the Alps above all as an advance in the reproduction of subjective observation which could now also be extended to include the natural relationships of the figures among themselves as well as the space encompassing them. Therefore what in Italy was meant to provide the artistic reconstruction of a landscape or an inner space, conditioned by the desired total effect of the compositional invention, in Northern Europe quickly assumed the character of a portrayal of a specific sector of infinite space. Jacob Burck-hardt's (q.v.) seemingly paradoxical statement that without Giotto, Jan Steen would have been different than he was and pre-sumably less important,[82] can also be applicable in this respect and extended to include all of the landscape painting of the Low Countries, complemented as it were by reference to classical art. From the standpoint of the general development of intellectual life, however, it is of the greatest interest to become aware of the cycle by means of which that interpretation and invention of painting (for which one is indebted to the spirit of classical Greek culture and its struggle for an artistic and scientific ob-jectification of the world) penetrated into Northern Europe, de-toured so to speak through the Italian efforts to achieve a formal and autonomous artistic perfection; and one should also be cog-nizant of how once there it adapted itself to the relationship be-tween man and nature as developed by the European peoples during the Middle Ages and thus became the point of departure of a new discovery of the world and its scenic beauty and poetry within the mirror of subjective consciousness.

At first, to be sure, as I have already stated, it was only a matter of certain stereotyped patterns of real relationships which had replaced the Gothic supernatural union of phenomena and, like the latter, had been combined with naturalistic observations. Herein lay a new step forward, but also a new problem!

The progress consisted in the fact that just as in Italy formal beauty and subservience to law had become an artistic end unto itself, a characteristic of a great work of art, so now in Northern Europe the greatest possible fidelity to nature, based upon sub-jective observation, became an end forming its own object. It is not a new interest in nature which distinguishes the older art from the works of the new "realistic" trend of the fourteenth century—for example, the portrait statue of Charles V, the busts of the master of the royal family in Prague, the monument of Bishop Albrecht von Beichlingen in Erfurt or similar works—it is

rather the conscious study of nature, the struggle first and foremost to enable art to reproduce in a constantly ascending degree
the reality perceived in any specific model without taking into
consideration all the other points of view. What until then had
been but one of the means of expression of medieval dualism
was transformed into an independent goal, the most important
task of artistic progress, opposed to which everything else had
to recede into the background. This is the very same path taken
almost contemporaneously in epistemology by the neonominal-
ists and terminists Durand (q.v.), William of Ockham and John
Buridan (q.v.) when they attempted theoretically to reduce all
knowledge and all truth, attainable by man by means of his own
power, to isolated data of sense experience. "Science is concerned
with external phenomena and since in the world of reality there
are no universals, knowledge cannot have its origin in the universal but only in the particular"—this in essence is the teaching of
Ockham, the great precursor of Bacon and Spinoza; these theories can likewise serve as a commentary on what soon thereafter
became a fait accompli primarily in France, the actual ideal center of these new epistemological theories.

Although the transition to these new forms was neither sudden nor were the forms themselves completely independent of
the past, everything which art had acquired by way of perception of reality since it began to create anew directly from nature
was given a new meaning and became the real aesthetic factor
for whose further development and enrichment artists everywhere were striving in incalculable numbers of individual artistic
experiments. For this reason these attempts gradually penetrated
and to a vast extent dissolved the "style" of Gothic representation of form, the expression of an idealistic convention, by their
more faithful imitation of individual objectivity; in like measure
they also gradually destroyed the former compositional unities,
interweaving them with an abundance of factual observations.
This was analogous to the process of artistic transition in the

Church of the Celestines; Charles V of Anjou. *Courtesy Giraudon, Paris.*

eighteenth and nineteenth centuries when the great imaginative constructs of the Baroque age were gradually altered or dissolved by the new demands of a meaningfulness rooted in secular life, its ideas and its historical values on the one hand, or on the other hand by a new wave of naturalistic goals in the reproduction of nature and the phenomena of life.

Although this development in the fourteenth century might appear to have been a gentle and hardly noticeable transition, it was, nevertheless, the point of departure for an unavoidable revaluation of all values in art. The observation of nature was transformed from a supplementary corollary into the roots and the most principal goal, the alpha and the omega, of artistic creation, a fact which encompasses infinitely more than a mere formal reorientation of art. Furthermore this movement signifies nothing less than the expression of the first artistic manifestations of a new period in the history of the spiritual development of mankind which was to distinguish itself from all preceding periods by the fact that the human spirit had begun to seek the point of departure for artistic truth and elevation above the commonplace realities of daily life in the self-assurance of observation. This was new:

1. vis-à-vis the Middle Ages, because, through this identification of observation and art, the artistically signficant was no longer sought in a subordination of real phenomena to a supernatural order and determination of human existence but only in reality itself;

2. vis-à-vis classical art it was also new inasmuch as this transition was not a matter of an objectification of the universal in the Socratic sense or in the variation of the phenomena of the conceptually constant; it was rather a striving toward the most extensive formation of the ability to transform the phenomena of nature and life into a permanent spiritual possession and an enrichment of man's total *Weltanschauung* by means of the most intensive comprehension of and representative mastery over their

individual characteristics and peculiarities; the whole was predicated upon the transference of the Augustinian precept *in interiore homine habitat veritas* (truth dwells within the souls of men) to the relationship of man to the physical world.

This movement resulted at first almost everywhere within the whole range of European art in a wavering and searching that might be designated as a period of Storm and Stress consisting of a remarkable mixture of old and new elements. The characteristic feature of this transitional art, whose aftereffects continued to be felt for a long time within individual peoples, schools and masters, lay in the fact that although all the individual motifs and forms were developed into a portraitlike reproduction of nature in its individual form, physical qualities and color phenomenon (one can find completely "modern landscapes," "exact architectural drawings," "lifelike portraits") and that although the new naturalistic demands and accomplishments attained the ascendancy, both quantitatively and qualitatively, effectual inferences stemming from the demand for an unconditional imitation of nature were, however, not drawn.

The will to open unto art the total range of the splendors of the physical world and its inexhaustible multiplicity became the dominant force of artistic endeavor. And yet how was this will to make itself felt in the problems of the general pictorial composition? Analogous to the protracted aftereffects of Baroque patterns in the realistic descriptions of life and landscape studies of the preceding century, one will find everywhere at the beginning of the new "naturalistic" painting north of the Alps, as it were at the basis of the representation of reality, both an addition to nature observations reminiscent of medieval techniques and only incidentally corresponding to experience and soaring Gothic figures, older ideal compositions conceived in the style of Giotto. This is so not because the artists were "clumsy," but because it was precisely here that the basically most difficult problem lay, namely how was the new interpretation and demand

for fidelity to nature, having developed out of Christian subjectivism, and, once of age, desirous of controlling the totality of
artistic creation, to be expressed in representational aspects that
would surpass individual, objectively isolated nature studies! An
accumulation of individual observations of nature, as are to be
found in works of this transitional period, no matter how intensive and extensive they might be, could not alone produce the
solution for which neither the old idealistic compositional abstractions of Gothic art nor the newer compositional schema of
Giottoesque painting could be of importance.

The idealistic abstractions of the Middle Ages formed an
a priori and harsh contradiction to any natural conditionality:
implicit in this concept was a dependence on nature which earlier
was not only not considered to be a disruptive influence but was
on the contrary striven after and which now had to be experienced as an unbearable contradiction; this was somewhat akin to
the contemporary problem posed by the Ockhamists concerning
the incompatibility of empirical knowledge and faith, a problem
expressly raised for the first time in the history of humanity. The
latter schemata were indeed based on real being, but they had
transformed it into a free artistic paraphrase which also found
itself in opposition to the basic principle of the new interpretation of fidelity to nature. Thus a conflict arose which dominated
the artistic development around the turn of the fourteenth and
fifteenth centuries in Northern Europe as well as in the South.
This conflict concentrated within itself the most important
problem of the time and out of which simultaneously, but
along different lines, a new art arose both north and south of the
Alps.

I will consider within a different context the Italian solution
to the conflict in which Florence played the dominant role. In
the North, however, it was the painting of the Low Countries to
which the historic mission was entrusted to lead art along a new
path and thus extricate it from the contradictions of its various
motivating spiritual forces.

It is certainly not mere chance that this transformation, which in the field of art signifies an epoch in man's *Weltanschauung*, can be linked with the name of a great artist, with the first pioneering personality of Northern art clearly comprehensible in its individual significance. The life's work of Jan van Eyck will appear in this connection in a new light. The perception of nature embodied in his pictures was not new, and much of what appears in his works as a miracle, because of the maturity he had attained, has a pedigree extending far back in time. Therefore it is also self-evident that many of the characteristics and stylistic peculiarities of his works can be considered to be the expression of the general progress of his time and his homeland, a degree of progress attained by his Dutch contemporaries quite independent of him. His originality and his merit lie, however, in the boldness with which he drew new pioneering consequences from the transformed presuppositions of art and confronted inherited traditions with them as the only valid principle. This is expressed most articulately in his tremendous simplification of composition. Paintings in the style of Giotto have rightly been classified as epic and compared with Dante's *Commedia Divina;* thereby their narrative content is emphasized and is shared to a certain extent with the entire contemporary Gothic art. The pictures in manuscripts, the stained-glass paintings, the tapestry-work or frescoes that adorned the walls in the fourteenth century are all comparable to theatrical productions with innumerable *dramatis personnae* and a narrative content. Indeed representative reproductions with only a few figures were not wholly lacking, but they were, nevertheless, an exception, for the general endeavor was unmistakably bent upon forming the figural composition as rich and as mobile, as varied and interesting in content as possible. In addition to this is the fact that, with the ascendancy of naturalistic endeavors, nature observations were also depicted in sequence form with the greatest possible abundance, analogous in a way to a picture-book; thus the "Adoration of the Lamb" in Ghent—*totius orbis comprehensio*—was indeed a procession of the heavenly host and the representatives of all the social classes within an ideal landscape, abounding in figures and the splendors of nature.

In contrast to these, all the works of Jan van Eyck[83] are of a compositional restriction which could almost be conceived as an impoverishment were it not clear that they were so because the artist intended them to be thus and that this very restriction also brought to art a new internal wealth. Especially unmistakable is the progress in the interpretation of the pictorial problems expressed in his paintings where the composition could be limited to a solitary figure, as for example in his portraits or in the two naked forms from whence in the sixteenth century was derived the name of the shrine in Ghent. It was not the striving after the individual likeness nor the study of nudity alone which formed the new element in his works—prior to his paintings there were numerous attempts at such simplification—the essence of his originality lay rather in the determination with which the artist raised the study of nudity, or the fidelity of the portrait to its subject, to the level of the exclusive content of reproduction. A nature study in a modern sense of the word—a section of reality as it is offered to observation in its individuality—became for the first time in these paintings essentially synonymous with pictorial invention! In other words, it was a conscious renunciation of everything situated beyond immediate physical perception and of the detachment of perception from all metaphysical or empirical relationships and norms exceeding the given unique circumstances; it was a matter, therefore, of the total victory of that subjective discovery of the world in its infinite variety (a diversity which had developed out of the medieval interpretation of the world, combined as it was with transcendental presuppositions) that now itself became a *Weltanschauung* formulating a source of art based upon its own principles.

This can certainly not be explained solely in terms of a new artistic technique which, as astonishing as it was, still signified

"Timotheos," by Jan van Eyck. *Reproduced by courtesy of the Trustees of the National Gallery, London.*

ONE HUNDRED THIRTY-NINE

only a continuation of a developmental line extending far back into the past and observable in many contemporary artists, although to a lesser extent; rather it was based on a new un-medieval artistic attitude pioneered by a highly gifted artist. The origin of this compositional limitation is to be sought in this attitude, not as though this restriction can be interpreted as a lack of imagination—a position assumed by authors who have but scant acquaintanceship with artistic processes—for in reality it signifies a revolutionary act which was to open unto art a new and undreamed-of wealth, a new world in the fullest sense of the word. "The Portrait of a Man" (inscribed "Tymotheas Leal Souvenir 1432") in London or the "Cardinal of Santa Croce" (also known as the "Cardinal Albergat" portrait) in Vienna appear so far distant from medieval art and have the same effect on the naive viewer as modern pictures not because Jan van Eyck suddenly discovered an art based upon a modern conception of fidelity to nature or because he had seen reality differently than his predecessors; the difference lies instead in the fact that he limited himself to painting what could be represented as far as possible as a faithful and individual observation of nature within the means at his disposal and the framework of the problems of his art and times. One also encounters this same procedure wherever his pictorial invention does not rest solely upon the study of a model, as in his religious representations, but seeks rather to unite space and traditional pictorial concepts, objective fidelity and creative inventiveness.

In representations of this type, in contrast to Giottoesque paintings, Jan van Eyck strikingly renounced as much as possible every form of external action. In quiet solemnity, almost archaicly motionless, he paints the enthroned Madonna and her court, the holy men and women, the founder residing under their protection or even the married couple whom he unites in the form of a double portrait within the context of the pictorial relationship. If the art of the fourteenth century endeavored to overcome the rigid tectonic sequence-form of early Gothic art by means of a more vigorous mobility of figures, objectively founded on actions, and the resulting union of these figures into plastically and spatially effective groups, it appears that Jan van Eyck once again relinquished all of the accomplishments attained in favor of the old motionless and isolated poses. One can also conjecture here a certain acquiescence vis-à-vis what was attainable and solvable from the standpoint of the observation of nature; complicated motifs of motion and groups, if they were not to rest on old schemata, demanded a knowledge of the bodily organism; the study of the body based on abstract principles, a method of knowledge recognized in contemporary Italy as one of the most important goals of representational art, had to yield in Northern Europe in favor of an individual objective fidelity. Everything surrounding the figures in these paintings—their garments and implements, the architecture or vegetation and anything by way of material qualities, color or lighting that would transmit their sensual phenomenon to the viewer—had originated in the endeavor to create a portrait of reality which in Gothic art had been a complement to the concept of fidelity to nature and which now conferred upon the entire composition the appearance of a section of nature viewed as a unit and painted as a direct copy; the motivating concept was still conceived in terms of old Gothic addition and avoided as far as possible all aspects which, from the standpoint of an artistic truth so interpreted, were not representational.

However this would not have been possible if the artist had not had some notion of such a section of nature viewed as a unified whole which could serve a priori as an authoritative ideal unity. Herein lies a second source of the innovations which were decisive for the history of art in Northern Europe.

It is clear that neither the classical nor the new Italian system of spatial objective effects and representational means was appropriate for the portrait reproduction of a specified section of nature in its unique contingency or even for the representation of the appearance of such a unity. The artfully considered game, by means of which plastic bodies were united within a spatial construction to form a unified and convincing spatial effect, could of course be expanded into a legitimate [German original: *gesetzmässig*] and scrutinizable regularity as it had been in contemporary Italian art; this procedure was insufficient, however, when it was a matter of transmitting to the viewer the illusion of a free section of space isolated from the infinity of the continuous fluid spatial impressions engulfing man. At best this artistic game was applicable when it came to rendering auxiliary services, as was later the case; however as an independent goal it was opposed on principle to the interpretation of spatial representation developed in Northern Europe. The magic game that was to enable the artist to represent the impression of a free, compositionally unfettered section of unlimited space, filled with being and life, required a different system and other means.

First of all one must ask himself how it happened that the artist attempted to attain such a goal. Was it really a matter of something so completely new? or rather was it not that the artist adhered to things which were older but which formerly had a different significance, a conception founded upon the essence of Gothic painting and to a degree repressed only through the Italian influences in the fourteenth century?

Vis-à-vis the complicated structure of the Giottoesque paintings, the spatial composition in Jan van Eyck's pictures appears infinitely simplified: vertical and horizontal coulisses running parallel to the figures, enclosing them as though in a box, and then at times joined to a complementary view of a landscape that, without taking into consideration a limited and well thought-out interplay of forces, allows the tangible proximity of the vertical structure to overflow into the unbounded expanse of a horizontal plane in depth within which the landscape motifs are arranged as though they had been merely scattered about; or again attempts to combine the proximate view of the figural composition with such a depth perspective without the aid of any connecting links. In conjunction with the frontality and the simple sequence of the figures, to which we have earlier referred, all of this reminds one of the compositional system of the older Gothic art as it had developed in the sculpture and painting of Northern Europe before the forceful advent of Italian influence; nevertheless this system still remained dominant even after the influences from Italy had become an effective force in the great ecclesiastical art. For the basis of this system was that principle according to which the sequence of statues on the facades of the great Gothic cathedrals or the majestic figures of the early-Gothic stained-glass windows did not appear as objective material group formations but seemed to be united in infinite space by means of other aspects so that immaterial, unlimited space, with its concomitant concepts of infinity and expanse, as a higher form of spatial unity, became the foundation of the entire pictorial composition and so dominated it that everywhere, even in the reliefs and miniatures with a narrative content, the motifs of a concrete spatial scene are not represented as the real bearers of the spatial union but function only as connecting links!

The application and significance of this old Gothic compositional principle had, however, changed in the new Dutch painting. If Christianity, through its belief in a law of divine revelation governing all creation and all time, had taught man to unite infinity with the most important presuppositions of his *Weltanschauung*, at first as a transcendental concept of the ideal and then in Gothic art as real space in which supernatural forces dominate and metaphysical relationships exist, in the new Dutch painting even this fundamental progress in the relationship to the world was separated from its transcendental presuppositions and content; and, under the influence of the trend toward autonomy in artistic problems and of the self-assurance of observation, it was transformed into the point of departure for the natural and sensually perceptible union of objects within unlimited space.

The sense of validity and necessity of the infinity and

boundlessness of space became in other words a natural, aesthetic and fundamental factor presented to the viewer by means of distant horizons; this was a factor, however, which pertained to no less a degree to the smallest section extracted from the universe of the pictorial invention. The classical and Italian objective reconstruction and closed composition of space was replaced by union within space just as it is presented in its inexhaustible multiplicity and limitlessness to subjective experience and observation of reality. It is precisely here that the deeper meaning of the apparent simplification of spatial composition in the works of Jan van Eyck and their approximation of the old Gothic system is to be found.

In the representation of spatial relationships as well as of objects, the concept of subjectively recognized and experienced actuality which, in contrast to classical art, had developed out of the spiritual relationship of medieval man to the external world, became decisive for the continued development of the art in Northern Europe as opposed to the compositional abstraction of Italian art. This concept, however, was no longer incorporated into a transcendent world of ideas, nor was it there to serve this transcendent world or to be conditioned by it; under the influence of the spiritual and formal emancipation of art, this concept became decisive rather as a purely artistic problem and as a source of artistic perception, sensual apprehension and comprehension of the physical world which, because of this fact, man had begun to see with a new vision in its natural state; furthermore in this world man had also begun to discover phenomena, relationships, secrets and effects never before dreamed of, neither in classical antiquity nor in the Italian art of the fourteenth century.

This relationship will become fully clear if one considers how nearly not only the compositional structure and the relationship to the unlimited section of space but also the means of uniting figures in space harmonized with those points of view which we have come to recognize as characteristic innnovations of medieval as opposed to classical art.

As in Gothic art, so here too it was primarily immaterial aspects which united the almost immobile figures to one another within infinite space and at the same time with the viewer. These aspects were the following.

1. The participation in a spiritual community. The concatenation of figures into a closed composition by means of animated action and physical relationships corresponding to them, a technique preferred by Giottoesque art, once again fell into disfavor and was replaced on the one hand by a strong accentuation of only psychic approximation and on the other hand by an arrangement which, vis-à-vis all individual psychic or physical events, gave free rein to the compelling power of a commonly shared and higher spiritual significance, superior to these occurrences and effective not as action but as tranquil being. This new order was no longer merely the reflection of a transcendental ideal system as in the older Gothic art, whose monumental solemnity was based upon the endeavor to elevate mundane objects to a metaphysically timeless existence, nor did it consist solely of the bond uniting the elect of God to a transcendental kingdom of eternal values and encompassing the past, the present and the future; it rested rather upon spiritual depth and composure that removed Jan van Eyck's figures from mere commonplace existence and awakened a response in the pious devotions of the onlooker.

The foil for this new attitude was formed by the observation and admiration of an inexhaustible nature and the "tranquil" existence, growth and decay of natural objects, a process of maturation both independent of the human will and seemingly resplendent with the reflected splendor of eternity. From Gothic art with its conceptions of temporally and spatially unlimited forces of the divine governance in the history of the human race and in nature, a field of experience newly opened to the imagination, flowed the joy in spacious horizons and scenes which seem to stretch endlessly in depth and distance, which reveal to the viewer the beauty of nature and the multiplicity of life as far as the eye can see. Or again it depicts the joy in riches of observations which offer themselves to the artist, even where the material to be represented requires a limited circumscription, provided he will submerge himself in the view of the limitless world of wonder which contains reality even in the insignificant and monotonous aspects of one's milieu and which, when viewed with love, is capable of producing in a reflective mind by means of sense impressions a comprehension of a being and life superior to the individual will and action, even though this superior form of being might be viewed only in the most humble of its phenomena. Upon these two aspects rests the inspired mood that seems to hover about the figures on muted wings and transports the viewer into a kingdom where passions are silenced and everything is so transfigured as though to reflect the holy and tranquil atmosphere of the Lord's sabbath. The human soul in its needs and in its secrets and the complexity of nature and life, both considered as the point of departure of the relationship to the transitory world and as the mirror of its deeper meaning—these two important criteria of the new Christian art of the Middle Ages once again step forward as the unifying spiritual content of composition but are no longer, as they had been in Gothic art, the reflection of a supernatural subservience to established law [German original: *Gesetzmässigkeit*] within the soul of man or in nature, but on the contrary they function as a natural value-concept inherent in life and experience, in cogitation as well as in observation. By means of this value judgment, and in order to fulfill its religious stipulations, art was able above all to elevate man spiritually and to awaken within him religious sentiments.

2. The second means of spatial union in the new Dutch painting also stands in a similar relationship to the great legacy of Gothic art. Here the principal matter of concern is the illu-

mination which fills the space with an immaterial movement and lightly touches individual forms in a playful manner, in combat with twilight darkness and in competition with shadows seemingly flitting back and forth. Here too one must point out the role which light played in the preceding development of Christian art as a compositional means, at first in the early Middle Ages as an abstract ideal factor and then in Gothic art as real light which, in conjunction with the art of stained-glass windows, was used to increase the impression of a free supernatural sense of floating of the holy figures and thus increase their effect on the viewer, simultaneously uniting phenomena within space. Thus natural light became a part of the artistically seen and a represented section of the universe as well as a means of uniting the phenomenon in space. Moreover it remained thus even when it no longer was a matter of treating transcendental relationships once art had begun to concentrate upon natural combinations in a real section of space; and in this way a shift of emphasis was transformed into an independent problem of the art of painting. What the Middle Ages had discovered by way of bringing the marvelous closer to man in visionary perception, now became a source for viewing nature—still far distant from a complete dissolution of all phenomena into phenomena of illumination and their unified and logically consistent formation and execution, but doubtlessly the first step toward the realization of such a technique —the first step toward that Northern art which as no other had begun to construct pictorial unity on immaterial elements of the transitory optical phenomenon.

It certainly is not expedient to trace in detail how the tasks of color representation and patternization [German original: *Modellierung*] changed because of this shift of emphasis; no longer being reproduced in an abstract or isolated form, color, as a phenomenon influenced by lighting and physical milieu, was now conceived as an element of uniting objects in space. These are well known facts. However it is necessary to emphasize once

ONE HUNDRED FORTY-SEVEN

again that the presupposition of all these innovations and, because of this fact, in the final analysis the main source of the new pictorial invention was not, as in the new contemporary Italian art, a logically constructed and rationally examined unity, that is to say that, now as before, it was fundamentally not an abstract unity.

3. Rather on the whole the power of subjective perception which, permeating the picture down to its last recess, bestowed upon every object its own characteristic life. One scarcely inquires if the relationship will bear logical scrutinization; its effect is convincing solely because of the fact that all the objects in their own sensual value, in their form and materiality and in their relationship to one another, as either successive or juxtaposed figures, appear as forms of reality pictorially conceived as equal and faithfully reproduced. With this consideration I again arrive at the general point of departure of the artistic revolution encountered in the works of Jan van Eyck.

I have heard that Jan van Eyck shattered the old idealistic norms of pictorial composition because they no longer corresponded to the new spiritual position vis-à-vis art and nature and logically replaced them with studies of nature which did correspond to what the new peoples of the Middle Ages in conjunction with their entire spiritual development and *Weltanschauung* had achieved as a new concept of being true to nature [German original: *Naturwahrheit*]. This concept was also the basis from which he proceeded when it was a matter of combining individual naturalistic studies to form a pictorial unity. As Ernst Heidrich cleverly remarked,[84] it is correct that in the process of unifying these individual efforts a residue of the old conception of a final cause in artistic invention still prevails over perception and that the observations have not logically developed from their natural causality, as from the naturalistic positivism of the modern era, but, as one is accustomed to say today, they were strung together to a great extent "unnaturally" and joined to an abstract compositional construction. In so doing, the relationship was completely altered so that it was no longer a matter of what was actually attained but of new goals and views, of a new spiritual position to art and its relationship to nature and life. Out of the growing conviction of the independent significance of that view of nature and life based upon subjective observation, a view which in the Middle Ages had developed as a conditioned element of a transcendental explanation of the world, arose, in the form of an ingenious spiritual revolution concomitant to the loosening of this bond of conditionality, a new artistic credo, a new interpretation of what primarily constituted the form of art. Here lay its most important problems, namely by which means within its own sphere of influence could it elevate man to a higher realm of a spiritual consciousness of the world and what actually enjoined the most important content of artistic responsibility.

Because of this feeling of responsibility, the medieval art form was burst asunder in the form of a bold, personal action and one of the greatest geniuses of painting began to concentrate upon practical truth which was then transformed from an explanatory accessory into the highest goal of the struggle in art. The words "as I can" which Jan van Eyck was accustomed to inscribe on the frames of his paintings resound not like the expression of medieval modesty but rather like a modern justification; and even if everything which they propose by way of pioneering innovations might have been propounded somewhat in the manner of a naive foregone conclusion peculiar to the Middle Ages, there can be no doubt that an art, which found the purest and highest reflection of its own nature in a fidelity to portraiture detail, an almost photographic reproduction of objects—one need but compare the portraits of Judokus Vydt or of Canon van der Pael—signified not only material progress in the imitative reproduction of nature but also a conscious victory over the past (a victory of which one was just as conscious in the North as in the South although contemporary Italy had arrived at the same point by other means) and a triumph not of new means but of a totally new interpretation of the relationship between man, art and the physical world. And this interpretation gave expression to a general spiritual reorganization of art far exceeding the limits of the normal progress of pictorial creation bound to specific presuppositions. As formerly in prehistoric ages out of geological catastrophes new mountain ranges arose from whose heights today one can view gripping panoramas, so also were born in the spiritual crises filling the history of Europe in the Middle Ages new spiritual possibilities for experiencing the world. When the times were ripe, these were to serve as the point of departure for a gifted reformer in the field of art who, breaking old chains, would base his artistic creation upon the new concept of truth and artistic obligation contained in these possibilities of experience and would see in them the most important guide to artistic expression; thereby in principle he would surmount in art the transcendental idealism of the Middle Ages.

This is a phenomenon which will hardly be surprising if one considers that it stood at the threshold of an age in which a radicalism of spiritual demands, based upon subjectively recognized truth and conviction, had become the signature of an era. It not only rendered to every idea of reform in all spiritual concerns a tremendous range and resonance, but it also produced a new type of spiritually independent and leading men. It is, however, characteristic that this transformation in art was perfected relatively early and initially, not accidentally (in addition to Italy), in the Netherlands where two hundred years later a new phase in the spiritual development of the Northern peoples was also to find its purest expression in the field of pictorial creation.

NOTES

1. Translator: Cf. especially *Die kirchliche Baukunst des Abendlandes.* Stuttgart: J. G. Cotta, 1884–1901.

2. Translator: Cf. especially Karl Schnaase (1798–1875) *Geschichte der bildenden Künste.* 7 Vols. Düsseldorf: Buddeus, 1843–1864; 2nd edition 8 Vols. Stuttgart: Ebner und Seubert, 1866–1879.

3. Cf. Georg Dehio (q.v.), *Kunsthistorische Aufsätze.* München: Oldenbourg, 1914, p. 6.

4. Wilhelm Worringer (q.v.), *Formproblem der Gotik.* München: Piper, 1911. (Translator's note: English translation as *Form Problems of the Gothic.* Authorized American edition. New York: Stechert, 1920; authorized British edition with an Introduction by Sir Herbert Read. London: Tiranti, 1957.)

5. Even the most recently published comprehensive book by Achille Pellizzari (q.v.) about medieval art treatises (*I trattati attorno le arti figurative in Italia. I. Dall' antichità classica al sec. XIII.* Napoli: Perrella, 1915) suffers from this bias. Pellizzari's rather verbosely attempted proof that remnants of practical art literature of classical antiquity have been preserved in uninterrupted tradition in the alchemistic, natural scientific and technical treatises and in the recipe books is valuable. However the value of these writings for the art of the Middle Ages as well as for a critical examination of this art is excessively overestimated, for these writings offer little assistance in assessing the vivifying and unbroken development of conceptions of art and have become important only since the fourteenth century when, in connection with the progressive dissolution of the medieval transcendental conditionality of art, they were associated to an ever-increasing degree with theoretical rules of art and art evaluation.

6. In patristic and medieval literature one can find innumerable verifications of this basic change in the interpretation of art. Undoubtedly it is most beautifully expressed in the familiar verses which Suger, Abbot of Saint-Denis (q.v.), had engraved on the bronze doors of his monastery church. (Cf. Adolphe Napoléon Didron [q.v.], *Iconographie Chrétienne. Histoire de Dieu.* Paris: Imprimerie royale, 1843, p. vii). (Translator's note: The verses of Suger referred to above are the following:

> "Mens hebes ad verum per materialia surgit,
> Et, demersa prius, hac visa luce resurgit."

Freely translated they could be rendered thus: "The weak [or untutored] mind is able to rise toward the truth when aided by material objects, and the soul plunged in darkness is able to rise again by that light which art causes to shine before his eyes." Didron pointed out that Suger's verses express, although with greater beauty of phrasing and depth of thought, an idea analogous to two lines from Horace's *De Arte poetica:*

"Segnius irritant animos demissa per aurem
    Quam quae sunt oculis subjecta fidelibus. . . ."

"Those things [to be learned] excite the mind of man more slowly through his hearing [ears] than do those which are subjected to our faithful sight [eyes].)

7. Translator's note: For Dilthey's discussion of this particular problem compare his *Gesammelte Schriften.* I. Band, II. Buch, III. Abschnitt: "Metaphysisches Stadium der neueren europäischen Völker." 4., unveränderte Auflage. Stuttgart: Teubner; Göttingen: Vanderhoeck und Ruprecht, 1954, pp. 250–350; for a French translation of this work, cf. *Introduction à l'Etude des Sciences humaines. Essai sur le fondement qu'on pourrait donner à l'étude de la société et de l'histoire.* Translated by Louis Sauzin. Paris: Presses Universitaires de France, 1942.

8. These general presuppositions of the spiritual life of the Middle Ages have been most penetratingly, most felicitously and, for the art historian, most instructively formulated by Ernst Troeltsch (q.v.) in his study *Die Soziallehren der christlichen Kirchen und Gruppen.* Tübingen: Mohr, 1912. For what has just been stated and for the following few lines, compare especially pp. 181 ff.

9. *Ibid.,* pp. 182 ff.

10. It is certainly not pure chance that its inception can be traced back to the early Christian era where new spiritual needs resulted in a striving for the dematerialization of eccclesiastical buildings.

11. Cf. Dehio, *op. cit.,* p. 44.

12. Tertullian (q.v.) had already given voice to this sentiment in a most passionate manner in his treatise "De idolatria liber": "At ubi artifices statuarum et imaginum et omnis generis simulacrorum diabolus saeculo intulit, rude illud negotium humanae calamitatis, et nomen de idolis consecutum est, et profectum. Exinde jam caput facta est idolatriae ars omnis, quae idolum quomodo edit." "De idolatria liber," c. 3, *Patrologiae Cursus Completus* (seu bibliotheca universalis, integra, uniformis, commoda, oeconomica, omnium SS. Patrum, doctorum, scriptorumque ecclesiasticorum, sive Latinorum, sive Graecorum, qui ab aevo apostolico ad tempora Innocentii III [anno 1216] pro Latinis et Concilii Florentini [anno 1439] pro Graecis floruerunt. . . . Recusio chronologica). Rev. Jacques Paul Migne (1800–1875), ed. *Series Latina.* Paris: Garnier, 1844– 1903; Supplementum, 1958–1960, Vol. I, col. 740. (Hereafter the *Patrologiae Cursus Completus. Series Latina* will be referred to as Migne, *PL,* the *Series Graeca* [1857–1892] as Migne, *PG*). (Translator's note: "But when the devil introduced into the world artificers of statues and of images, and of every kind of likenesses, that former rude business of human disaster attained from idols both a name and a development. Thenceforward every art which in any way produces an idol instantly became a fount of idolatry." "On Idolatry," Chap. 3, *The Ante-Nicene Fathers. Translations of the Writings of the Fathers down to A.D. 325.* Edited by Rev. Alexander Roberts, D.D. and James Donaldson, LL.D. Vol. III. New York: Scribner's Sons, 1926, p. 62.) However if one were to object that artists too must live from their work, the same excuse might also

be offered for *fures balneanos et ipsos latrones* (rogues and vagabonds and even thieves). The positive aspect of the new program was expressed most succinctly by St. Augustine when he said: "Non in aligua mole corporea inspicanda est pulchritudo." "Epist. ad Consentium," c. 4, n. 20, Migne, *PL*, Vol. XXXIII, col. 462. (Translator's note: "Certainly it is in this beauty, rather than in the body [that we are made to the image of God]." "Letter to Consentius," *Saint Augustine. Letters [83–130]*, p. 316. Translated by Sister Wilfrid Parsons, S.N.D. This volume forms Vol. XVIII of the series *The Fathers of the Church. A New Translation*. Edited by Roy Joseph Deferrari, *et al*. New York: Fathers of the Church, Inc., 1953.)

    13. Wilhelm Vöge (q.v.), *Die Anfänge des monumentalen Stiles im Mittelalter*. Strassburg: Heitz, 1894, p. 50.

    14. Translator's note: I. Julius Lange (1838–1896), Danish art historian. His principal work appeared in Danish in three parts: 1) *Billedkunstens fremstilling af menneskeskikkelsen i dens aeldste periode indtil højdepunktet af den graeske kunst*. Avec un résumé en francais: "Etude sur la représentation de la figure humaine dans l'art primitif jusqu'à l'art grec du ve siècle av. J.-C." København: B. Lunos Kgl. hof-bogtrykkeri (F. Dreyer), 1892; 2) *Billedkunstens fremstilling af menneskeskikkelsen i den graeske kunsts første storhedstid*. Avec un résumé en francais: "Etude sur la représentation de la figure humaine dans la première grande periode de l'art grec." København: B. Lunos Kgl. hof-bogtrykkeri (F. Dreyer), 1898; 3) *Menneskefiguren i kunstens historie fra den graeske kunsts anden blomstringstid indtil vort aarhundrede*. København: Det nordiske forlag, E. Bojesen, 1899. A German translation of this work appeared in two parts: 1) *Darstellung des Menschen in der älteren griechischen Kunst*. Translated by Mathilde Mann. Edited and foreword by A. Furtwängler with the collaboration of C. Jörgensen. Strassburg: Heitz, 1899; 2) *Die menschliche Gestalt in der Geschichte der Kunst von der zweiten Blütezeit der griechischen Kunst bis zum XIX. Jahrhundert*. Translated by Mathilde Mann. Edited by P. Köbke. Strassburg: Heitz, 1903. To date none of Lange's works has appeared in English translation. II. Emanuel Löwy (1857–1938), Austrian archaeologist and professor of art history in Rome and Vienna. His principal works are: 1) *Untersuchungen zur griechischen Künstlergeschichte*. Wien: Gerold's Sohn, 1883; 2) *Inschriften griechischer Bildhauer*. Leipzig: Teubner, 1885; 3) *Griechische Inschrifttexte*. Wien und Prag: Tempsky, 1888; 4) *Lysipp und seine Stellung in der griechischen Plastik*. Hamburg: Sammlung gemeinverständlicher wissenschaftlicher Vorträge, 1891; 5) *Die Naturwiedergabe in der älteren griechischen Kunst*. Rom: Loescher, 1900; 6) *Die griechische Plastik*. 2 Bde. Leipzig: Klinkhardt und Biermann, 1911; 7) *Stein und Erz in der statuarischen Kunst*. Innsbruck: Wagner, 1915; 8) *Neuattische Kunst*. Leipzig: Seemann, 1922; 9) *Die Anfänge des Triumphbogens*. Wien: Schroll, 1928; 10) *Polygnot. Ein Buch von griechischer Malerei*. 2 Bde. Wien: Schroll, 1929; 11) *Ursprünge der bildenden Kunst*. Wien: Hölder-Pichler-Tempsky, 1930; 12) *Zur Chronologie der frühgriechischen Kunst. Die Artemistempel von Ephesos*. Wien: Hölder-Pichler-Tempsky, 1932. Of Löwy's many works only one has appeared in English, namely number 5 above: *The Rendering of Nature in Early Greek Art*. Translated by John Fothergill. London: Duckworth, 1907. In the context of Dvořák's statement compare the works number 1, 5, 10 and 11, especially 11.

15. Vöge, *op. cit.*, pp. 52 ff.

16. "The age of the spirit has now arrived," Amalrich von Bena (q.v.) wrote around 1200. (Cf. Heinrich von Eicken [q.v.], *Geschichte und System der mittelalterlichen Weltanschauung.* Stuttgart: Cotta, 1887, p. 605.)

17. *Ibid.*

18. Karl Borinski (q.v.), *Die Antike in Poetik und Kunsttheorie vom Ausgang des klassichen Altertums bis auf Goethe und Wilhelm von Humboldt.* Leipzig: Dieterich, 1914, pp. 67 ff.

19. Thus even in Dante: "non è se non splendor di quella idea, che parto-risce amando il nostro Sire," (*Paradiso*, XIII, 52–75).

> All that which dies and all that dieth not
>   Is naught but splendour of the Idea that knows
>   The Father's Love whereby It is begot;
>
> Because the living Luminance that flows
>   Forth of Its Luminant, yet parts not thence,
>   Nor from the Love that aye in-trines with Those,
>
> Doth, of Its grace, converge Its radiance,
>   Glassed as it were, in nine subsistences,
>   Itself still One, eterne in permanence;
>
> Which radiance thence to the last potencies
>   Descends, from act to act, becoming even
>   Such as to make mere brief contingencies—
>
> An epithet, as I conceive it, given
>   To things engendered, formed, as requisite,
>   From seed, or seedless, by the moving heaven.
>
> Now, more or less of light such things transmit
>   When stamped with the Idea, so variable
>   Are both the wax and that which stampeth it;
>
> Wherefore the tree brings forth good fruit or ill
>   After its kind, and mortals are born rich
>   In various gifts of intellectual skill.
>
> Were the wax always wrought to perfect pitch,
>   Might at full power the spheres unchanging stand,
>   The signet's light would shine complete in each. . . .

The Comedy of Dante Alighieri The Florentine. Cantica III. Paradise. Trans-lated by Dorothy L. Sayers and Barbara Reynolds. Baltimore: Penguin Books, Inc., 1962, Canon XIII, 52–75.) Cf. Hubert Janitschek (q.v.), *Dantes Kunstlehre und Giottos Kunst.* Leipzig: Brockhaus, 1892.

20. It is noteworthy that already in the writings of Gregory Nazianzen (q.v.) an attack on color-impressionism can be noted. (Cf. Βίβλος Β΄. Ἔπη Ἱστόρικα. Τομή. Α΄. Περὶ ἑαυτου [*Carmen de seipso*], v. 739 ff., Migne, *PG.*, Vol. XXXVII, col. 1220). (Translator's note: The verses referred to above are the following:

Ἦ καὶ γραφέων ἄριστος οὗτός σοι δοκεῖ,
Οὐχ ὅς γράφει κινούμεν' ἁπλοῖς χρώμασι,
Ζεῦξίς τις, ἢ Πολύκλειτος, ἢ τις Εὐφράνωρ,
'Αλλ' ὅς μὲν ἀνθηραῖς τε καὶ παντασκίοις
Βαφαῖς ἄμορφα σώματ' ἐξεργάζεται,
Ὧν Καλλίμαχος, κα'ι Κάλαϊς ἤστην, ὡς δοκῶ,
Μόγις γράφοντες εἰκόνας τῶν εἰκόνων;
Τοιοῦτός ἐστι πᾶς ἀνὴρ πολύτροπος.

English translation: "To you it seems that the best painter is not he who repro-
duces animate objects with simple colors, as do Zeuxis, Polycletus or Euphranor, but rather he who gives expression to amorphic bodies with gaudy colors,
completely devoid of shadow, among which painters, it seems to me, Callimachus and Calais are [to be included]—painters who can barely paint imitations
of imitations. Anyone of such a nature is [indeed]deceitful." In the Migne edition of Nazianzen's works the Greek original is followed by two Latin versions, one a more or less literal translation from the Greek, the other a poetic
rendering. For the sake of scholarship it is rather interesting to compare the
variants. The direct translation is:

An pictorum tibi praestantissimus ille videtur,
Non qui pingit simplicibus coloribus,
Ut Zeuxis quidam, aut Polycletus, aut Euphranor,
Sed qui floridis et nusquam umbrosis
Coloribus informia exprimit corpora,
Quales Callimachus et Calais fuere, ut mihi quidem videtur,
Qui vis imagines imaginum efficiebant?
Talis est omnis homo versutus.

The poetic version is:

An tibi videtur esse pictor inclytus,
Non qui colore viva pingit simplici,
Polycletus, aut Euphranor, aut Zeuxis novus;
Qui floridis vero, nec umbrosis quidem,
Informe corpus exprimit coloribus,
Callimachus alter et Calais, ut sentio,
Qui vix imagines debant imaginum?
Talis profecto quilibet vir callidus.)

The history of the Middle Ages affords sufficient proof of their belief in the
superiority of their own art over the artistic productions of classical Greece
and Rome. That the classical authors were regarded as an antithesis to true
knowledge is evidenced by the *Bataille des Arts* (*Battle of the Seven Liberal
Arts*, ca. 1236) of the thirteenth-century French author Henri d'Andeli (q.v.).
(Cf. Freiherr Rochus von Liliencron [q.v.], *Über den Inhalt der allgemeinen
Bildung im Zeitalter der Scholastik* [Festrede gehalten in der öffentlichen
Sitzung der königlichen bayerischen Akademie der Wissenschaften zu München
zur Feier ihres 117. Stiftungsfestes am 29. März, 1876]. München: Bayerische
Akademie der Wissenschaften, 1876 [*Concerning the Content of General Edu-
cation in the Age of Scholasticism*].)

21. In this sense repeated reference was made especially to the new style of sketching in medieval art.

22. Cf. the following statement of Rudolf Kautzsch (q.v.): "The process which had been enacted in Egypt repeats itself: a world of forms typically rigidified in every feature proclaims from every wall the religion's deeds of salvation." (*Die bildende Kunst und das Jenseits.* Jena und Leipzig: Diederichs, 1905, p. 41.)

23. "Pulchrum respicit vim cognoscitivam" (Thomas Aquinas, *Summa Theologica,* I, q. 5, a. 4, ad. 1). (Translator's note: "Beauty and goodness in a thing are identical fundamentally, for they are based upon the same thing, namely, the form; consequently goodness is praised as beauty. But they differ logically, for goodness properly relates to appetite [goodness being what all things desire], and therefore it has the aspect of an end [the appetite being a kind of movement toward a thing]. On the other hand, *beauty relates to a cognitive power,* for those things are said to be beautiful which please when seen. Hence beauty consists in due proportion, for the senses delight in things duly proportioned, as in what is like them—because the sense too is a sort of reason, as is every cognitive power. Now since knowledge is by assimilation and since likeness relates to form, beauty properly belongs to the nature of a formal cause." *Basic Writings of Saint Thomas Aquinas.* Edited by Anton C. Pegis. Vol. I. New York: Random House, 1945. Hereafter referred to as *Aquinas-Pegis.*

24. The origins of this procedure are likewise traceable to pre-Carolingian times where one can follow its development in art as well as in the literary discussions about the external appearance of the saints. Compare the following statement of Clement of Alexandria (q.v.): "The Spirit gives witness through Isaias that even the Lord became an unsightly spectacle: 'And we saw Him, and there was no beauty or comeliness in Him, but His form was despised, and abject among men' [Cf. *Isaias,* 53, 2]. Yet, who is better than the Lord? He displayed not beauty of the flesh, which is only outward appearance, but the true beauty of body and soul: for the soul, the beauty of good deeds; for the body, that of immortality." (*Paedagogus,* Bk. III, Chap. 1; Cf. J[oseph] Jungmann [q.v.], *Aesthetik.* [3rd enlarged and revised edition. 2 Vols. Freiburg im Breisgau: Herder'sche Verlagsbuchhandlung, 1886], pp. 43 ff.). (Translator's note: The English version just quoted can be found in Clement of Alexandria, *Christ as Educator.* Translated by Simon P. Wood, C.P., New York: Fathers of the Church, Inc., 1954, p. 201. This work forms Vol. XXIII of the series: The Fathers of the Church. A New Translation. The original Greek version and a Latin translation thereof will be found in Migne, *PG,* Vol. VIII, col. 557–560 as Clementis Alexandrini *Paedagogus,* Liber Tertius, Caput I:

Τὸν δὲ Κύριον αὐτὸν τὴν ὄψιν αἰσχὸν γεγόνεται, διὰ 'Ησαΐου τὸ Πνεῦμα μαρτυρεῖ· "Καὶ εἴδομεν αὐτὸν, καὶ οὐκ εἶχεν εἶδος, οὐδὲ κάλλος· ἀλλὰ τὸ εἶδος αὐτοῦ ἄτιμον, ἐκλεῖπον παρὰ τοὺς ἀνθρώπους." Καὶ τίς ἀμείνων Κυρίου; "Αλλ' οὐ τὸ κάλλος τῆς σαρκός, τὸ φαντασιαστικὸν, το δὲ ἀληθινὸν καὶ τῆς ψυχῆς καὶ τοῦ σώματος ἐνεδείξατο κάλλος· τῆς μὲν τὸ εὐεργετικὸν, τὸ δὲ ἀθάνατον τῆς σαρκός.

Latin translation: "Ipsum autem Dominum fuisse aspectu deformen, testatur Spiritus per Isaiam: 'Et vidimus ipsum, et non habebat speciem, nec pulchritudinem; sed species ejus vilis, et deficiens prae hominibus.' Quis autem Domino praestantior? Sed non carnis pulchritudinem, quae visione apprehenditur, sed veram animae et corporis ostendit pulchritudinem; animae quidem, beneficentiam; carnis vero, immortalitatem.") St. Thomas Aquinas takes the opposite position: "Oportet quod omnes nobilitatis omnium creaturarum inveniantur in Deo nobilissimo modo et sine aliqua inperfectione!" ("It is necessary that all noble qualities of all creatures be found in God in the most noble manner and without any imperfection!") (Cf. *Sancti Thomae Aquinatis Commentum in Quatuor Libros Sententiarum Magistri Petri Lombardi.* [Hereafter referred to as *Sent.*] Volumen Primum, Distinctio II, Quaestio I, Articulus II, Solutio in *Sancti Thomae Aquinatis Opera Omnia.* Vol. VI. Original editor, Petrus Fiaccadorus. New general editor, Vernon J. Bourke. New York: Musurgia Publishers, 1948, p. 22, col. 1. All further references to the Latin texts of the works of Thomas Aquinas will be from this edition of his *Opera Omnia.*) This difference of opinion is the result of the entire intervening medieval development.

25. Scholastic philosophy is rich in commentaries on this speculative procedure. Of the various treatises on this subject, the theories of St. Thomas Aquinas were formulated the most beautifully and ingeniously—cf. *Summa Theologica,* I, q. 77, a. 2 c.

26. In this connection cf. St. Thomas Aquinas, *Summa Theologica,* I, q. 77, a. 2 c: "Dicendum est ergo quod res, quae sunt infra hominem, quaedam particularia bona consequuntur et ideo quasdam paucas et determinatas operationes habent et virtutes. Homo autem potest consequi universalem et perfectam bonitatem, quia potest adipisci beatitudinem. Est autem in ultimo gradu secundum naturam eorum quibus competit beatitudo. Et ideo multis et diversis operationibus et virtutibus indiget anima humana. Angelis vero minor diversitas potentiarum competit. In Deo vero non est aliqua potentia vel actio praeter ejus essentiam." (Translator's note: "We conclude, therefore, that things which are below man acquire a certain limited goodness, and so have a few determinate operations and powers. But man can acquire universal and perfect goodness, because he can acquire beatitude. Yet he is in the lowest degree, according to his nature, of those to whom beatitude is possible; and therefore the human soul requires many and various operations and powers. But to angels a smaller variety of powers is sufficient. In God, however, there is no power or action beyond His own Essence." *Aquinas-Pegis.* Vol. I, p. 723.) Similar ideas are to be found in the writings of Hugh of St. Victor (q.v.), especially in his *Expositio in Hierarchiam coelesten S. Dionysii Areopagitae* c. 3. (Translator's note: cf. Migne, *PL,* Vol. CLXXV, col. 929–930.) This fundamental theory can be found in popular form in the "school texts" of Vincent de Beauvais. (Translator's note: a list of the works and various editions thereof of Vincent de Beauvais [Vincentius Bellovacensis] has been reprinted in the *British Museum's General Catalogue of Printed Books.* Photolithographic edition to 1955. London: The Trustees of the British Museum, 1964, Vol. CCXLIX, col. 249–252.) (Cf. Liliencron, *op. cit.,* pp. 12 ff.)

27. For a discussion of the relationship between these various types of representations and the general medieval assortment of artistic forms, cf. Wilehlm (sic) Vöge, "Eine deutsche Malerschule um die Wende des ersten Jahrtausends. Kritische Studien zur Geschichte der Malerei in Deutschland im 10.

und 11. Jahrhundert," *Westdeutsche Zeitschrift für Geschichte und Kunst* (Trier), IX: Ergänzungsheft no. 7 (1891), p. 377.

28. The familiar, often-quoted passages in this respect are the following: *Summa Theologica*, I, q. 39, a. 8; *Summa Theologica*, II, q. 145, a. 2 and 1. *Sent.*, d. 31, q. 2, a, 1 ("Pulchritudo habet claritatem" ["Beauty has clarity"]). Even a few passages from the "Opusculum de pulcro" might be cited, as for example: "Omnis forma per quam res habet esse, est participatio quaedam divinae claritatis." ("The form of everything, through which the thing has its being, participates in some manner in divine clarity.") For the interpretation of the medieval concepts of being and beauty, the commentary on Pseudo-Dionysius (q.v.) is of importance, although the question of whether the "Opusculum de pulcro" discovered by Uccelli can be attributed to St. Thomas or not is quite secondary. The content of the manuscript corresponds without a doubt *in toto* to the views of the great scholastic. (Cf. Pellizzari, *op. cit.*, pp. 303 ff.) The older literature concerning the aesthetic principles of St. Thomas Aquinas stems in great part from theologians and therefore offers the art historian little, precisely because it does not investigate these views historically but rather because it attempts primarily to demonstrate their desirability even for the present; this attempt is founded on an historical basis and motivated by the endeavor to realize a new form of art whose content is both religious and moral. Compare, for example, Joseph Jungmann's *Aesthetik* (*op. cit.*) which is an attempt, more broad than it is profound, to construct a manual and system of aesthetics based on Thomistic principles; or the work of the Abbé P. Vallet, *L'Idée du Beau dans la Philosophie de Saint Thomas d'Aquin*. Paris: Robert et Chernoviz, 1883 (2nd edition, revised and augmented 1887). New investigations—for example, those on Marcelino Menéndez y Pelayo (q.v.) (*Historia de las Ideas estéticas en Espana*. 5 vols. Madrid, 1883–1891; 2nd edition 1909, 1931; cf. especially Vol. I) or Maurice de Wulf (q.v.) (*Histoire de la Philosophie mediévale*. 4th edition. Paris [Louvain], 1912 (Cf. also the English and German translations of this work: *History of Medieval Philosophy*. Translated by Ernest C. Messenger. 2 vols. London: Longmans, 1926. Vol. I revised in 1952; *Geschichte der mittelalterlichen Philosophie*. Translated by Rud. Eisler. Tübingen: Mohr, 1913)—elucidated to a great degree the interconnections between the art theories of Thomas Aquinas and the development of scholasticism, but they fail completely to take into consideration the relationship with medieval art which alone can explain the full import of these theories. One will find a few references to the agreement between Thomas Aquinas and Giotto in Hubert Janitschek's monograph *Die Kunstlehre Dantes und Giottos Kunst* (*op. cit.*). Giotto's position, however, no longer rests completely on the bases of the development of art which found its philosophic expression in the aesthetics of Thomas Aquinas.

29. "Perfectum autem dicitur, cui nihil deest secundum modum suae perfectionis" (*Summa Theologica*, I, q. 5, a. 5c). (Translator's note: "Now a thing is said to be perfect if it lacks nothing according to the mode of its perfection." *Aquinas-Pegis*, Vol. I, p. 48) . . . "quae enim diminuta sunt, hoc ipso turpia sunt" (*Summa Theologica*, I, q. 39, a. 8c). (Translator's note: ". . . since those things which are impaired are by that very fact ugly . . ." *Ibid.*, p. 378).

30. "Ratio pulchri consistit in quadam consonantia diversorum." ("The

essence of the beautiful consists in a certain harmony of different elements."
["Opusculum de pulchro"]). (Translator's note: No English version of this
work is available, in fact even the attributing of the authorship to St. Thomas
is disputable. A reprinting of the treatise can be found, however, in the five
volume collection *S. Thomae Aquinatis Opuscula Omnia* [Genuina quidem
necnon spuria melioris notae debito ordine collecta cura et studio R. P. Petri
Mandonnet. Tomus Quintus: Opuscula Spuris]. Parisiis: Sumptibus P. Lethielleux, Bibliopolae Editoris, 1927, pp. 417–443. The above quotation can be found
on page 418). "Dicendum quod, sicut ad pulchritudinem corporis requiritur,
quod sit proportio debita membrorum . . . ita ad rationem universalis pulchritudinis exigitur proportio aliqualium ad invicem vel partium, vel principiorum,
vel quorumcumque. . . . ("One must say that just as for beauty of the body it
is necessary that there be a due proportion of its members, so for the essence
of beauty in general a proportion of things to one another is required, either
of parts or principles or whatever they may be. . . ." [*Ibid.*, pp. 425–426.])
"Deus dicitur pulcher (sicut) universorum consonantiae et claritatis causa."
("God is said to be beautiful and the cause of the harmony and clarity of all
things."). (Translator's note: Dvořák erroneously attributed this quotation to
the *Summa Theologica*, I, q. 39, a. 8. In reality it is taken from the *Summa
Theologica*, II–II, q. 145, a. 2. It is of interest to compare this statement with a
similar statement in the disputed "Opusculum de pulchro," *ibid.*, p. 425: "Dicit
ergo primo ibi quod supersubstantiale pulchrorum dicitur pulchritudo, sicut
causa consonantiae universorum, id est, proportionis et claritatis." ["He (Dionysius) says therefore in the first place there (*De Divinis Nominibus*) that the
super-essential aspect of those things which are beautiful is what we call
beauty because it is the cause of the harmony in all things, i.e., of proportion
and clarity."] This quotation is taken from the commentary of St. Thomas on
an excerpt from the *De Divinis Nominibus* of Dionysius, reprinted at the beginning of the "Opusculum de pulchro," *ibid.*, p. 417: "Supersubstantiale vero
pulchrum pulchritudo quidem dicitur, propter traditam ab ipso omnibus exist-
entibus juxta proprietatem uniuscujusque pulchritudinem, et sicut universorum
consonantiae, et claritatis causa, ac similitudinem luminis cum fulgora immittens
universis pulchrificas fontani radii ipsius traditiones, et sicut omnia ad seipsum
vocans." ["But the Super-Essential Beautiful is called 'Beauty' because of that
quality which It imparts to all things severally according to their nature, and
because It is the Cause of the harmony and splendour in all things, flashing
forth upon them all, like light, the beautifying communications of Its originating ray; and because It summons all things to 'fare' unto Itself. . . ." Dionysius
the Areopagite (q.v.), *On the Divine Names* and *The Mystical Theology*,
Translated by C. E. Rolt. New York: Macmillan, 1940, p. 95].) Cf. also *Summa
Theologica*, I, q. 44, a. 4 c; *Summa Theologica*, II–II, q. 145, a. 8; Dionysius,
De Divinis Nominibus, Cap. IV, Lect. V.

    31. "[Dicendum quod] pulchrum in ratione sui plura concludit; scilicet
splendorem formae substantialis vel actualis [Dvořák has: 'accidentalis'] supra
partes materiae proportionatas et terminatas [Dvořák has: 'ac determinatas]
. . ." ("Opusculum de pulchro," *ibid.*, p. 420). (Translator's note: "It must be
said that the notion of beauty includes several elements, namely splendor of the
substantial and actual [Dvořák has: 'accidental'] form, plus external parts pro-

portionate to and terminated by [Dvořák has: 'determined by'] the matter. . . .")

32. Cf. for example St. Thomas Aquinas, *Summa Theologica*, I, q. 16, a. 1 c: "Et inde est, quod res artificiales dicuntur verae per ordinem ad intellectum nostrum: dicitur enim domus vera, quae assequitur similitudinem formae quae est in mente artificis." (Translator's note: *Aquinas-Pegis*, Vol. I, p. 160: "And thus it is that artificial things are said to be true as being related to our intellect. For a house is said to be true that fulfills the likeness of the form in the architect's mind.") Further *Summa Theologica*, I, q. 14, a. 8: "Scientia autem artificis est causa artificiatorum, eo quod artifex operatur per suum intellectum. Unde oportet, quod forma intellectus sit principium operationis: sicut calor est principium calefactionis." (Translator's note: *Aquinas-Pegis*, Vol. I, p. 147: "Now the knowledge of the artificer is the cause of the things made by his art from the fact that the artificer works through his intellect. Hence the forms in the intellect must be the principle of action; as heat is the principle of heating.")

33. Felix Witting (q.v.), *Die Anfänge christlicher Architektur. Gedanken über Wesen und Entstehung der christlichen Basilika*. Strassburg: Heitz, 1902 (Vol. X of the series: "Zur Kunstgeschichte des Auslandes") and *Von Kunst und Christentum. Plastik und Selbstgefühl. Von antikem und christlichem Raumgefühl. Raumbildung und Perspektive. Historisch-ästhetische Abhandlungen*. Strassburg: Heitz, 1903.

34. Wilhelm Pinder (q.v.), *Einleitende Voruntersuchungen zu einer Rhythmik romanischer Innenräume in der Normandie*. Strassburg: Heitz, 1904 (Vol. XXIV of the series: "Zur Kunstgeschichte der Auslandes" and *Zur Rhythmik romanischer Innenräume in der Normandie. Weitere Untersuchungen*. Strassburg: Heitz, 1905 (Vol. XXXVI of the series: "Zur Kunstgeschichte des Auslandes").

35. Cf. Vöge, *op. cit.* (cf. footnote no. 13, p. 153), pp. 313 ff.

36. Cf. Worringer, *op. cit.* (cf. footnote no. 4, p. 151), pp. 48 ff. To be sure, one must disregard Worringer's generalizations in this respect.

37. Cf. Vöge, *loc. cit.*

38. Concerning the significance of sculpture in the Middle Ages and modern times, conditioned as it is by Christianity and thus basically differentiated from classical sculpture, compare Witting's interesting and detailed arguments (*Von Kunst und Christentum* [cf. footnote no. 32, *supra*] 1st essay: "Plastik und Selbstgefühl" ["The Plastic Arts and Self-Reliance"]). However I cannot share his final conclusions.

39. The origin of this method of representation can be traced back into pre-Christian times. In the Middle Ages it underwent numerous revisions and thereby attained in Gothic art a new significance.

40. Considered from this point of view, the strong Byzantine influences in occidental sculpture and painting from the eleventh century on appear as a unified movement that reached its apex in Italy and also to some extent in Germany only in the thirteenth century; furthermore this movement was considerably enriched by new points of contact in the interpretation of the formal problems. The monographic literature to this chapter of the Byzantine question is extensive; however a comprehensive presentation is, although greatly to be desired, still wanting.

41. The initial beginnings of this development are to be found in the Carolingian Renaissance.

42. Cf. Pinder, *Zur Rhythmik romanischer Innenräume in der Normandie*, *op. cit.*, 39 ff. (Cf. footnote no. 34, p. 160.)

43. "Ein Blatt aus der Geschichte des Kolorits," *Ausgewählte Schriften*. ("A Page from the History of Coloring," *Selected Works*). Vol. II. Ed. by P. Köbke. Translated from the Danish by Mathilde Mann. Strassburg: Heitz, 1903, pp. 130 ff.

44. A beautifully stated, definitive formulation of this whole process can be found in Thomas Aquinas: "God rejoices absolutely in all things because each one of them stands in actual agreement with His being" (cf. *Jungmann, op. cit.*, p. 92).

45. This will be discussed later at greater length, especially when treating the problems of the new statuary, monumental style. Without a doubt the renewal of statuary art, which in the age of artistic antimaterialism had lost every justification for existence, is to be traced back either directly or indirectly to classical stimuli. In no sense, however, can one speak of either attempts to imitate classical models or of a sense of competition with classical statuary. Is it really true, as has been asserted, that the man of the Middle Ages was entirely stupid and blind to the beauty of a classical reproduction of the human body? Is the only reason why the Middle Ages ignored this form of art actually that the artists of this period had no understanding of or appreciation for the sublime excellences of their classical prototypes, since they themselves were completely ignorant in the reproduction of the human form? That this was not the case is unequivocally proven by the fact that, although classical influences can be repeatedly observed in Northern European art, until the dawn of the Renaissance with but few exceptions there were neither attempts nor tendencies to enrich the solutions of artistic problems in this direction or to oppose classical statuary with something individualistically new or different. In spite of the surging Renaissance movement in the thirteenth century, all attempts in this vein, even in statuary art, remained timorous and were practically ineffectual—until suddenly in the fifteenth century a revolution, arising from causes which will be discussed within a different context, occurred. Between the "Venus" of Pisa and let us say Donatello's bronze figure of "David" lies a chasm which demands an explanation more penetrating than the mere assumption of a newly acquired understanding of classical art ushered in by naturalistic progress. Certainly the naturalistic accomplishments of Gothic art were the external prerequisites for this transformation, but in no sense were they the actual inner cause thereof.

46. Cf. Kurt Freyer, "Entwicklungslinien in der sächsischen Plastik des dreizehten Jahrhunderts," *Monatshefte für Kunstwissenschaft* (Leipzig, 1908–1922), Vol. IV (1911), pp. 261 ff. This article is a noteworthy attempt to reach an understanding of the artistic problems of Gothic sculpture within one particular region limited by time and place.

47. Thus Paulinus Nolanus, when besought by Sulpicius Severus for a portrait of himself and of his wife, refused the request with the words: "Qualem cupis ut mittamus imaginem tibi? Terreni hominis an coelestis? Scio quio tu illam incorruptibilem speciem concupiscis, quam in te rex coelestis adamavit."

(Epistola XXX, *PL*, Vol. LXI [1847], cols. 322–325; quotation located in col. 322). (Translator's note: "What type of portrait do you desire that we send you? That of the earthly or the celestial man? I know that you desire that incorruptible species which the King of Heaven loved in you.") That which had to appear to the classically educated bishop as incompatible with the essence of art and, therefore, as a sufficient reason for refusing the requested portrait was gradually transformed in the following generations into the point of departure in art for a wholly new representation of man. Similar views are repeatedly expressed by medieval writers: "Quid namque eorum, quae in facie lucent, si internae cuiuspiam sanctae animae pulchritudini comparetur non vile ac foedum recto appareat aestimatori?" (Bernard of Clairvaux, in *Sermonese in Cantica*, no. 27, *PL*, Vol. CLXXXIII [1854], cols. 912–921; quotation located in col. 913). (Translator's note: "For what of those qualities, which shine forth in the human countenance, will not appear vile and corrupted to one who judges rightly, if it be compared to the interior beauty of any holy soul?"). Or the words of St. Thomas Aquinas: "Perfectissima formarum id est anima humana, quae est finis omnium formarum naturalium." (*Quaestiones Disputatae*. "De spiritualibus Creaturis," q. 1, a. 2: "Utrum substantia spiritualis possit uniri corpori"). (Translator's note: "The most perfect of all forms is the human soul which is the end of all natural forms." Cf. St. Thomas Aquinas, "De spiritualibus Creaturis," *Opera omnia*. Edited by S. E. Fretté. Paris: Vivès, 1875, Vol. XIV, p. 12, col. 2.) According to St. Thomas, and in agreement with the art of his age, psychic and bodily beauty no longer signify an insurmountable contradiction in terms, for which reason, therefore, he sought a more narrowly constricted delimitation. While physical beauty was considered to be the lowest degree of beauty (pulchritudo ima, extrema) by St. Augustine, the classicist among the Fathers of the Church (cf. *De vera Religione*. Bk. 1, c. 40, n. 74, *PL*, Vol. XXXIV [1841], col. 155), St. Thomas attempted to do justice to the bodily factor of man as well as to his spiritual side; this view definitely corresponded to the new art of his own day: "Visio corporalis est principium amoris sensitivi. Et similiter contemplatio spiritualis pulchritudinis vel bonitatis est principium amoris spiritualis." (*Summa Theologica*, Prima Secundae, q. 27, a. 2). (Translator's note: "Corporal vision is the principle of physical love. And likewise the contemplation of spiritual beauty or goodness is the principle of spiritual love." For the Latin version cf. *Opera omnia*. Vol. II, p. 102, col. 1; for an English translation cf. *The Summa Theologica* in 3 Vols. Translated by the Fathers of the English Dominican Province. New York, *et al.*: Benziger Brothers, 1947, Vol. I, p. 707.)

48. The cadaverous heads, which are for the contemporary viewer perhaps the most horrifying examples of this type of art, were created only as late as the twelfth century at the very outset of the new Gothic art, and the direction from which they had originated dominated individual schools of art even in France and even at a time when the new style had been completely developed. Cf. Vöge, *op. cit.*, p. 44, illustration no. 15.

49. Borinski, *op. cit.*, p. 73.

50. Ernst Troeltsch, *Augustin, die christliche Antike und das Mittelalter.* München-Berlin: Oldenbourg, 1915, pp. 112 ff. Cf. also Alois Riegl. *Die spätrömische Kunstindustrie nach den Funden in Österreich.* 2 Vols. Wien: Österreichische Staatsdruckerei, 1901–1923, pp. 211 ff.

51. Cf. St. Thomas Aquinas, *Summa Theologica*, I, sec. q. 5, 27 and 39 and II, sec. q. 145, a. 2, as well as his commentary to the *De Divinis Nominibus* of Dionysius the Areopagite, c. 4, lect. 5. (Translator's note: *Summa Theologica* in Aquinas' *Opera omnia*. Vol. I: Pars Prima, q. 5 ["De bono in communi"], pp. 17–21; q. 27 ["De processione divinarum personarum"], pp. 117–120; q. 39 ["De personis ad essentiam relatis"], pp. 134–162; Vol. III: Secunda Secundae, q. 145 ["De honestum"], a. 2 ["Utrum honestum sit idem quod decorum"], pp. 484–485. For an English translation of the questions in "Pars Prima" cf. *Aquinas-Pegis*, Vol. I, pp. 42–50 ["On Good in General"], pp. 274–281 ["The Procession of the Divine Persons"], pp. 363–381 ["The Persons in Reference to the Essence"]: English version of the question in "Secunda Secundae" cf. *The Summa Theologica of St. Thomas Aquinas*. Translated by the Fathers of the English Dominican Province. New York, *et al.*: Benziger Brothers, 1912, QQ. CXLI–CLXX, pp. 42–49 ["Of Honesty"], especially pp. 44–46 ["Whether the Honest is the same as the Beautiful"]. For Aquinas' commentary on the work of Dionysius the Areopagite cf. "In Librum Beati Dionysii de Divinis Nominibus" in *Opera Omnia*. Vol. XV, pp. 259–405; c. 4, lect. 5 pp. 305–307 ["De pulchro divino et qualiter attribuitur Deo"]. There is no English translation available to date.)

52. This new conception of artistic truth is also expressed in the writings of St. Thomas Aquinas: "Ad hoc [. . .] ergo quod vere aliquid sit imago, requiritur quod ex alio procedat, simile ei in specie, vel saltem in signo speciei." *Summa Theologica*, I, q. 35, a. 1. (Translator's note: "I answer . . . therefore that for a true image it is required that one proceeds from another like to it in species, or at least in specific sign." Cf. *Aquinas-Pegis*, Vol. I, p. 339.) A similar thought is to be found in his commentary on the works of Pseudo-Dionysius: ". . . [nam] pulchrum addit supra bonum ordinem ad vim cognoscitivam illud esse huius modi" (c. 4, lect. 5). (Translator's note: Cf. *Sancti Thomae Aquinatis Opuscula Theologica* [quorum specialem mentionem facit De-Tocco]. Opusculum VII: "In Librum Beati Dionysii de Divinis Nominibus," Caput 4, lectio 5: "De pulchro divino et qualiter attribuitur Deo," from the *Opera Omnia*. New York: Musurgia Publishers, 1950, Vol. XV, p. 307, col. 2. Translation: ". . . that it be thus in some manner, as regards man's cognitive faculties, he ranked the order of the beautiful above the order of the good.") Duns Scotus goes even farther when he states: "Nunc autem in toto opere naturae et artis etiam hunc videmus, quod omnis forma, sive plurificatio, semper est de imperfecto et indeterminato ad perfectum et determinatum. . . ." ("De rer. princ.", q. 8, a. 4: 28, p. 53b, Leidener edition, 1639). (Translator's note: Cf. "Quaestiones Disputates de Rerum Principio." Quaestio 8, articulus 4:28 in *B. Ioannis Duns Scoti . . . Quaestiones Disputates de Rerum Principio. Tractatus de Primo Rerum Omnium Principio*. New edition by R. P. Marianus Fernandez Garcia, O.F.M., Ad Claras Aquas [Quarachi] prope Florentiam: Ex Typographica Collegii S. Bonaventurae, 1910, p. 170. Translation: "Thus, however, in the total manifestation of nature and art, we always perceive this order, [namely] that all external form and reproduction [thereof] are always imperfect or indeterminate with regard to that which is perfect and determinate.")

53. In the Middle Ages the following verses of Prudentius were often paraphrased: "Non est inanis aut anilis fabula—Historiam pictura refert, quae tradita

libris—veram vetusti temporis monstrat fidem . . ." (*Liber Peristephanon*. Hymnus IX, in Migne, *PL*, Vol. LX, col. 434–435). (Translator's note: "[A] fable is not inane or silly—[a] picture refers to [a] historical fact which is transmitted through books [and] illustrates the actual reality of ancient times. . . .") In the early Middle Ages the practical aim of these verses was naively stressed. Gregory the Great once wrote to Bishop Serenus: "Pictures in the House of God ought to be for simple men that which books are to the learned." (Cf. *Monumenta Germaniae Historica. Epistolarum Tomus* II. Liber IX, epistola 208. Berlin: Weidmann, 1899, p. 195.) (Translator's note: Dvořák's quotation would seem to be a paraphrase of the remarks of St. Gregory the Great which are as follows: "Idcirco enim pictura in ecclesiis adhibetur, ut hi qui litteras nesciunt saltem in parietibus videndo legant, quae legere in codicibus non valent." Translation: "Therefore, picture[s] are brought into churches so that those who are illiterate might nevertheless, by looking upon the walls, read about those things which they are not able to read in books.") The decrees of the Synod of Arras of the year 1025 reflect similar views (cf. Didron, *op. cit.*, p. 6). Since the twelfth century, references to the ideal worth of art have generally replaced the pedagogical basis in such considerations. Compare, for example, the following: St. Thomas Aquinas, *Summa Theologica*, I, q. 75, a, 5c; II, sec. q. 167, a. 2c and the treatise of St. Bonaventure "De reductione artium ad theologiam." (Translator's note: This treatise can be found in *S. Bonaventurae Opera Omnia*. Vol. V. Florentiam [Florence]: Ex Typographia Collegii S. Bonaventurae, 1891, pp. 319–325.)

54. Cf. the statement of St. Bernhard: "Ligna et lapides docebunt te—quod a magistris audire non possis." (Translator's note: "Lines and stones will teach you what you will not be able to hear from teachers.") Concerning medieval symbolism cf. Borinski, *op. cit.*; concerning the particular role of the *exemplum* in medieval art cf. Julius von Schlosser (q.v.), "Zur Geschichte der künstlerischen Überlieferung im späten Mittelalter," *JbSAK*, Vol. XXIII, p. 284 and his "Materialien zur Quellenkunde der Kunstgeschichte," Sitzungsberichte (meeting notes) of *AÖAW*, Vol. I:77 (1914), Section 3, p. 86.

55. Cf. Liliencron, *op. cit.*; concerning the relationships between the *Speculum* of Vincent of Beauvais and the contemporary art of his period cf. Emile Mâle (q.v.), *L'Art religieux du XIIIe siècle en France. Etude sur l'iconographie du moyen âge et sur ses sources d'inspiration*. Paris: Colin, 1902. (Translator's note: the original edition appeared in Paris: Leroux, 1898.) It must be emphasized, however, that here it was undoubtedly not a matter of direct borrowings.

56. According to Vincent of Beauvais, man ascends from the lower to the higher degrees of knowledge, and thus through the perception of created being to the knowledge of God; man ascends, therefore, from the consideration of an image to the comprehension of its primal idea. (Cf. Liliencron, *op. cit.*, p. 13).

57. Cf. Vöge, "Die Bahnbrecher des Naturstudiums um 1200," *ZbK*, Vol. XXV (1914), pp. 193 ff.

58. Cf. Arthur Weese (q.v.), *Die Bamberger Domskulpturen*, 2nd edition. Strassburg: Heitz, 1914, p. 160.

59. Cf. Adolph Goldschmidt (q.v.), "Das Naumberger Lettnerkreuz im Kaiser-Friedrich-Museum in Berlin," *JbkpK*, Vol. XXXVI (1914), pp. 137 ff.

60. John Ruskin, *Gotik und Renaissance*. Translated from the English by

Jakob Feis. This work forms Vol. II of the series "Wege zur Kunst." Strassburg: Heitz, 1898. (Translator's note: *Wege zur Kunst. Eine Gedankenlese aus den Werken des John Ruskin*. Aus dem Englischen übersetzt und zusammengestellt von Jakob Feis. 4 vols. Strassburg: Heitz (Heitz und Mündel), 1898.

    Vol. I: Extracts from various books;

    Vol. II (*Gotik und Renaissance*): Extracts from *The Stones of Venice;*

    Vol. III (*Vorlesungen über Kunst*): A translation of the greater part of *Lectures on Art;*

    Vol. IV (*Aratra Pentelici*): A translation of the greater part of that work. [cf. *The Works of John Ruskin*. Ed. by E. T. Cook and Alexander Wedderburn. New York: Longmans, Green, and Co., 1912, Vol. XXXVIII, p. 38]).

    61. Cf. Johann Heinrich Loewe (q.v.), "Der Kampf zwischen dem Realismus und Nominalismus im Mittelalter," *AkbGW*, Series VI, Vol. VIII, pp. 44 ff.

    62. Maurice de Wulf's note-worthy opinion—namely, that one cannot speak of a consistent Nominalism, in the full sense of the word, before the thirteenth century since all the older nominalistic theories are to be conceived only as preparatory stages and nominalistic tendencies within the general framework of Realism—is confirmed by what can be observed in art. Cf. de Wulf's article in the *Archiv für Geschichte der Philosophie* (Berlin), Vol. II, pp. 427 ff. and his *L'Histoire de la philosophie du moyen âge*. 4th French edition. Louvain: Institut supérieur de philosophie, 1912, p. 208.

    63. See footnote 44, p. 161.

    64. Cf. de Wulf, *op. cit.*, p. 323.

    65. Wilhelm Windelband, *Lehrbuch der Geschichte der Philosophie*. 4th edition. Tübingen: Mohr, 1907, p. 258.

    66. His famous maxim: "Sine experientia nihil potest sufficienter sciri" ("Without experience nothing can be sufficiently known") should be further supplemented with his statement: "[Argumentum concludit et facit nos concludere quaestionem, sed] non certificat neque removet dubitationem, ut quiescat animus in intuitu veritatis [nisi eam inveniat via experientiae]. . . ." (*Opus Majus*, Part VI, chapter 1). (Translator's note: cf. *Fratris Rogeri Bacon, Ordinis Minorum, Opus Majus* . . . Ed. by S. Jebb, M.D. London: Bowyer, 1733, p. 445. Translation: "[Reasoning draws a conclusion and makes one grant the conclusion, but] does not make the conclusion nor does it remove doubt so that the mind may rest on the intuition of truth [unless the mind discovers it by the path of experience]. . . ." *The Opus Majus of Roger Bacon*. A Translation by Robert Belle Burke. 2 Vols. New York: Russell and Russell, 1962, Vol. II, p. 583 [First published in 1928 concurrently by the University of Pennsylvania Press and the Oxford University Press (London)].)

    67. Cf. Max Maywald, *Die Lehre von der zweifachen Wahrheit. Ein Versuch der Trennung von Theologie und Philosophie im Mittelalter. Ein Beitrag zur Geschichte der scholastischen Philosophie*. Berlin-München: Ackermann, 1871.

    68. Ernst Heidrich (q.v.), *Die altdeutsche Malerei. 200 Nachbildungen mit geschichtlicher Einführung und Erläuterungen*. Jena: Diederichs, 1909.

    69. Translator's note: Dvořák was unable to execute this work before his death.

70. Wilhelm Dilthey, *Das Erlebnis und die Dichtung.* 3rd edition. Leipzig: Teubner, 1910, p. 4.

71. The annalistic arrangement of facts, foregoing any pragmatic connection, is indeed the given correlative to the legendary and supernatural explanation of facts and is analŏgous to the relationship between the raw block-form and the spiritual system of a figural and architectonic composition.

72. Joseph Bédier (q.v.), *Les Légendes épiques. Recherches sur la formation des Chansons de geste.* Vol. IV. Paris: Champion, 1908–1913; cf. also Samuel Singer (q.v.), *Mittelalter und Renaissance. Die Wiedergeburt des Epos.* Tübingen: Mohr, 1910.

73. Eduard Wechssler (q.v.), *Das kulturgeschichtliche Problem des Minnesanges. Studien zur Vorgeschichte der Renaissance.* 2 Vols. Halle: Niemeyer, 1909; cf. also Richard Heinzel, *Über den Stil der altgermanischen Poesie.* Strassburg: Trübner, 1875.

74. Franz Wickhoff, "Die Gestalt Amors in der Phantasie des italienischen Mittelalters," *JbkpK,* Vol. XI (1890), p. 41.

75. Karl Vossler (q.v.), *Die Göttliche Komödie. Entwicklungsgeschichte und Erklärung.* 2 Vols. Heidelberg: Winter, 1907–1910. Cf. Vol. II, part 1, p. 47: "The great Italian theologians belong to the Italian people more because of their birth than because of their studies, their effectiveness and their works." (Translator's note: The English translation of this work is entitled *Mediaeval Culture. An Introduction to Dante and His Times.* 2 vols. Translated by William Cranston Lawton. New York: Harcourt and Brace, 1929.)

76. The pertinent passages in Aquinas have been assembled by Pellizzari, *op. cit.,* pp. 308 ff.: cf. also Maurice de Wulf, *Etudes historiques sur l'esthétique de St. Thomas d'Aquin.* Louvain: Institut supérieur de philosophie, 1896. (Translator's note: The English version of this work is entitled *Mediaeval Philosophy. Illustrated from the System of Thomas Aquinas.* Cambridge, Mass.: Harvard University Press, 1922.)

77. Borinski, *op. cit.* Concerning the new position of the artist cf. Albert Dresdner (q.v.), *Die Kunstkritik. Ihre Geschichte und Theorie.* München: Bruckmann, 1915–, Vol. I, pp. 64 ff.

78. Cf. the work of Karl Maria Swoboda on the Florentine baptistry. (Translator's note: *Das Florentiner Baptisterium.* Berlin: Bard, 1918 [In the series "Wiener kunstgeschichtliche Forschungen"].) Moreover the comprehensive literature on the antique, southern Italian sculpture of the thirteenth century and on Niccolò Pisano should be taken into consideration here. Important material concerning the history of a new Italian interpretation of pictorial problems can be found in Joseph Wilpert's (q.v.) extensive publication of the Roman mosaics and paintings. (Translator's note: *Die römischen Mosaiken und Malerei der kirchlichen Bauten vom 4ten bis zum 13ten Jahrhundert.* 4 vols. Freiburg im Breisgau: Herder, 1916.) New observations of Friedrich Rintelen (q.v.) can also be found in his work on Giotto. (Translator's note: *Giotto und die Giotto-Apokryphen.* München-Leipzig: Müller, 1912), p. 68.

79. Rintelen, *ibid.,* passim.

80. The first attempt at a theoretical explanation of this distinction whose roots, as we have stated above, are to be sought in the philosophy of St. Thomas Aquinas can be found in the writings of St. Bonaventure (cf. Lib.

III, Sentent., distin. 23, dub. 4). (Translator's note: *S. Bonaventurae . . . Opera Omnia*. Iussu et auctoritate R. P. Bernardini a Portu Romatino. Vol. III: Commentaria in Quatuor Libros Sententiarum Magistri Petri Lombardi. Sententiarum Liber III, Distinctio XXIII, Dubium IV. Ad Claras Aquas [Quaracchi] prope Florentiam: Ex Typographia Collegii S. Bonaventurae, 1887, pp. 503–505.)

81. Cf. Friedrich Winkler (q.v.), *Der Meister von Flémalle und Rogier van der Weyden*. Strassburg: Heitz, 1913, p. 139. (Translator's note: This work forms Vol. CIII in the series "Zur Kunstgeschichte des Auslandes.")

82. [Jacob Burckhardt] (q.v.), *Weltgeschichtliche Betrachtungen*. Berlin-Stuttgart: Spemann, 1905, p. 105.

83. Apart from his so-called youthful products, which I do not consider to be Jan's works. Cf. my article: "Die Anfänge der holländischen Malerei" ("The Beginnings of Dutch Painting"), *JbkpK*, Vol. XXXIX (1918), pp. 51 ff.

84. Ernst Heidrich (q.v.), *Altniederländische Malerei*. Jena: Diedrichs, 1910, p. 15.

SELECTED BIBLIOGRAPHY

Part I: Works by Max Dvořák—Monographs

1. *Gesammelte Aufsätze zur Kunstgeschichte.* Edited by Julius Wilde and Karl M. Swoboda. München: R. Piper & Co. 1929. (Contents: 1. "Les Aliscans"; 2. "Die kunstgeschichtliche Bedeutung der Mosaiken in der Markuskirche zu Rom"; 3. "Byzantinischer Einfluss auf die Miniaturmalerie des Trecento"; 4. "Die Illuminatoren des Johann von Neumarkt"; 5. "Spanische Bilder einer österreichischen Ahnengalerie"; 6. "Zur Entwicklungsgeschichte der barocken Deckenmalerei in Wien"; 7. "Eine illustrierte Kriegschronik"; 8. "Denkmalkultus und Kunstentwicklung"; 9. "Francesco Borromini als Restaurator"; 10. "Alois Riegl"; 11. "Franz Wickhoff"; 12. "Buchbesprechungen; Adolfo Venturi, Storia dell' arte italiana. I–III"; 13. "Neuste Literatur zur Geschichte der karolingischen Kunst"; 14. "Friedrich Rintelen, Giotto und die Giotto-Apokryphen"; 15. "Zur Diskussion über Cimabue"; 16. "Marie Luise Gothein, Geschichte der Gartenkunst"; 17. "Bibliographie der Schriften Max Dvořáks.")

2. *Geschichte der italienischen Kunst im Zeitalter der Renaissance. Akademische Vorlesungen.* Vol. I (14th and 15th cent.), Vol. II (16th cent.) Edited posthumously by Karl Maria Swoboda and Julius Wilde. München: Pieper, 1927–1928.

3. *Idealismus und Naturalismus in der gotischen Skulptur und Malerei.* München: Oldenbourg, 1918.

4. *Kunstgeschichte als Geistesgeschichte. Studien zur abendländischen Kunstenwicklung.* Edited posthumously by Karl Maria Swoboda and Julius Wilde. München: Pieper, 1924. Reprinted 1928 (Contents: 1. "Vorwort des Herausgebers," pp. IX–XII; 2. "Katakombenmalerei. Die Anfänge der christlichen Kunst," pp. 1–40; 3. "Idealismus und Naturalismus in der gotischen Skulptur und Malerei," pp. 41–147; 4. "Schongauer und die niederländische Malerei," pp. 149–189; 5. "Dürers Apokalypse," pp. 191–202; 6. "Über die geschichtlichen Voraussetzungen des niederländischen Romanismus," pp. 203–215; 7. "Pieter Bruegel der Ältere," pp. 217–257; 8. "Über

Greco und den Manierismus," pp. 259–276 [English translation by John Coolidge: "El Greco and Mannerism," *Magazine of Art*. Vol. XLVI:1 [1953], pp. 14–23].)

5. *Der Palazzo di Venezia in Rom.* Written in conjunction with Philip Denegel and Herman Egger. Wien: Malota, 1909.

6. *Das Rätsel der Kunst der Brüder van Eyck.* With an appendix devoted to the origins of Dutch painting. München: Pieper, 1925.

Part II: Works by Max Dvořák—Essays

1. "Les Aliscans," *Beiträge zur Kunstgeschichte. Franz Wickhoff gewidmet.* Wien: Schroll, 1903, pp. 12–24; cf. also Dvořák's *Gesammelte Aufsätze zur Kunstgeschichte* (above), pp. 4–18.

2. "Alois Riegl," *MkkZ*, 3.F. Vol. IV (1905), pp. 255–276.

3. "Das alte Rautterhaus in Villach," *MkkZ* (1904), p. 336.

4. "Anfänge der holländischen Malerei," *JbkpK*, Vol. XXXIX (1918), pp. 51–79.

5. "Betrachtungen über die Entstehung der neuzeitlichen Kabinettmalerei," *JbSW*, Vol. XXXVI: 1 (1923). (Printed from Dvořák's literary remains with an appended essay by Ludwig Baldass: "Sittenbild und Stilleben im Rahmen des niederländischen Romanismus".)

6. "Byzantinischer Einfluss auf die Miniaturmalerei im Trecento," *MIÖG*, Vol. VI (1900), pp. 792, 821.

7. "Denkmalkultur und Kunstentwicklung," *KJb*, Vol. IV (1911), Beibl., pp. 1–32.

8. "Denkmalpflege," *Österreichs Bau-und Werkkunst.* 2 Vols. Wien: Krystall, 1925, Vol. II, pp. 32–37.

9. "Deutsche Kunst Topographie," *KA* (1907), pp. 59–65.

10. "Einführung" (Introduction), *Die Gemälde Peter Bruegels des Älteren.* Wien: Schroll, 1941.

11. "Einführung" (Introduction), *Pieter Bruegel der Ältere. 37 Farbenlichtdrucke nach seinen Hauptwerken in Wien und eine Einführung in seine Kunst.* Wien: Hölzel, 1926.

12. "Einrichtungen des Kunstschutzes in Österreich," *Kunstschau im Kriege.* Edited by P. Clemens. Leipzig: Seemann, 1921, Vol. II, pp. 1–10.

13. "Entstehung der christlichen religiösen Kunst," *JbWK*, N.F. Vol. I–II (1925), pp. 1–13.

14. "Erzherzog Franz Ferdinand," *MkkZ*, 3.F. Vol. XIII–XIV (1915), p. 157.

15. "Francesco Borromini als Restaurateur," *KJb*, Vol. I (1908), Beibl., p. 89.

16. "Franz Wickhoff, Professor der Kunstgeschichte," *BioJb*, Vol. XIV (1912), pp. 317–326.

17. "Idealismus und Naturalismus in der gotischen Skulptur und Malerei," *HZ*, Vol. CXIX (1919), pp. 1–62, 185–246; this work first appeared as a monograph (cf. above) and was later included in the volume *Kunstgeschichte als Geistesgeschichte* (cf. above).

18. "Die Illuminatoren des Johann von Neumarkt," *JbSAK*, Vol. XXII: Heft 2 (1901), pp. 35–126.

19. "Illuminierte Handschriften in Osterreich," *MöVB* 1906), pp. 69–76.

20. "Sgraffiti im Schlosse zu Leitomischl," *JbZK* (1907), Beibl., pp. 77–84.

21. "Sgraffiti im Schlosse zu Neutomischel," *KJb*, Vol. I (1908), Beibl., pp. 72 ff.

22. "Italienische Kunstwerke in Dalmatien," *KJb*, Vol. V (1911), p. 1.

23. "Königsburg und Restaurierung," *KJb*, Vol. II (1908), Beibl., pp. 1–7.

24. "Kunstbetrachtung," *Bel*, Vol. V: 27 (1924), pp. 85–91.

25. "Mittlelalterliche Wandmalerei in Muggia Vecchia," *JbZK* (1907), Beibl., pp. 15–27.

26. "Monumenta deperdita in Prag, Pilsen und Wien," *KJb*, Vol. IV (1911), p. 175.

27. "Museen und Denkmalpflege," *MkkZ*, 3.F. Vol. XII–XIV (1915), pp. 17–24.

28. "Der politische Bezirk Raudnitz. II. Teil. Raudnitzer Schloss." *Topographie der historischen und Kunst-Denkmale im Königsreich Böhmen von der Urzeit bis zum Anfange des XIX. Jahrhunderts.* Written in conjunction with Boh. Matcjka. Prag-Leipzig: Hiersemann, 1910.

29. "Das Rätsel der Kunst der Brüder van Eyck," *JbSAK*, Vol. XXIV: 5 (1904), pp. 161–317; reprinted as a separate monograph in 1925 (cf. above).

30. "Rembrandts 'Die Nachtwache,'" *Meisterwerke der Kunst in Holland* (Rijksmuseum, Amsterdam). Wien: Filser, 1920–1921.

31. "Restaurierung des Buvinatores am Dom zu Spalato," *KJb*, Vol. III (1910), Beibl., pp. 118–142; reprinted in *MkkZ*, 3.F. Vol. VII (1910), pp. 347 ff.

32. "Spanische Bilder einer österreichischen Ahnengalerie," *JbZK* (1907), Beibl., pp. 13–27; reprinted in *KJb*, Vol. I (1908), pp. 13–28.

33. "Statuengruppierung der heiligen Franz Xaverius, Ignatius und Luitgardis an der Karlsbrücke zu Prag," *MkkZ*, 3.F. Vol. VI (1909), pp. 152–160.

34. "Ein Stilleben des Bueckelaer, oder Betrachtungen über die Entstehung der neuzeitlichen Kabinettmalerei," *JbSW*, Vol. XXXVI (1925), pp. 1–14.

35. "Verbauung des Ausblickes an dem Emauser Kloster zu Prag," *MkkZ*, 3.F. Vol. IX (1910), p. 190.

36. "Von Manes zu Svabinsky," *Die graphischen Künste*. Wien: Gesellschaft für vervielfältigende Kunst, 1904, pp. 29–52.

37. "Zur Diskussion über Cimabue," *KA* (1913), Beibl., pp. 75–83.

38. "Zur Entwicklungsgeschichte der barocken Deckenmalerei in Wien," *Österreichische Kunstbücher*. Vol. I–II. Wien: Hölzel, 1920.

Part III: Works edited by Max Dvořák et al.

1. *Beschreibendes Verzeichnis der illuminierten Handschriften in Österreich* (Wien). Dvořák *et al.*

2. *Kunstgeschichtliche Anzeigen.* Beiblatt der *Mitteilungen des Instituts der österreichischen Geschichtsforschung* (Wien), 1910 ff. Dvořák *et al.*

3. *Kunstgeschichtliches Jahrbuch der kaiserlich-königlichen Kommission für Erforschung und Erhaltung der Kunst- und historischen Denkmale* (Wien), Vol. I ff., 1907 ff. Dvořák *et al.*

4. *Österreichische Kunsttopographie* (Wien); Czech edition 1907, German edition 1910. Dvořák *et al.*

5. Riegl, Alois. *Die Entstehung der Barockkunst in Rom.* Edited by Max Dvořák and Arthur Burda. 2nd edition. Wien: Schroll, 1923.

6. Wickhoff, Franz. *Gesammelte Schriften.* 2 vols. Edited by Max Dvořák. Berlin: Meyer und Jessen, 1912 (only Vols. 2 and 3 appeared).

For a list as complete as possible of Dvořák's works, including lecturers and book reviews by him, cf. Max Dvořák, *Gesammelte Aufsätze zur Kunstgeschichte*. München: Pieper, 1929, pp. 371–381.

Part IV: Works about Dvořák

1. Alker, E. "Max Dvořák," *Hld*, 25. Jhrg. Vol. II (1928), pp. 313–318.

2. Benesch, Otto. "Max Dvořák," *NÖB*, Vol. X (1957), pp. 189–189.

3. ———. "Max Dvořák," *RKwt*, Vol. XVLIV (1924), pp. 159–197.

4. Böckelmann, Walter. *Die Grundbegriffe der Kunstbetrachtung bei Wölfflin und Dvořák*. Dresden: von Baensch Stiftung, 1938 (Originally a Doctoral Dissertation).

5. Braun, Felix. "Max Dvořáks letzte Vorlesungen," *Lit*, Vol. XXX (1928), p. 701.

6. Dell'Acqua, Gian Alberto. *L'Arte italiana nella Critica di Max Dvořák*. Firenze: Sansoni, 1935.

7. ———. "Max Dvořák," *Dizionario Letterario Bompiani degli Autori di tutti i Tempi e di tutte le Letterature*. Vol. I (A–F). Milano: Bompiani, 1963, pp. 687–688.

8. Frey, Dagobert. "Max Dvořáks Stellung in der Kunstgeschichte," *JbWK*, Vol. I (1921–1922).

9. *Ein Gedenkblatt zur Trauerfeier für Max Dvořák*. Wien: Filser, 1922 (Contains: Dagobert Frey, "Max Dvořáks Stellung in der Kunstgeschichte" and Max Dvořák, "Über Greco und den Manierismus").

10. Köhler, W. "Max Dvořák," *MIÖG*, Vol. XXIX (1923), pp. 314–320.

11. Kohte, I. "Max Dvořák, Kunsthistoriker," *Dpf*, 23. Jhrg. (1921), p. 40.

12. "Max Dvořák," *NFP*, February 9 and 11, 1921.

13. Praehauser, L. "Max Dvořák und das Problem der Stilentwicklung in der bildenden Kunst," *DnW* (1927), pp. 609–616.

14. Santifaller, Leo. "Max Dvořák," *MIÖG*, no. 176 (1950).

15. Schlosser, Julius. "Max Dvořák," *AÖAW*, 71. Jhrg. (1922), pp. 253–259.

16. ———. "Die Wiener Schule der Kunstgeschichte," *MIÖG*, Supplementary Vol. XII (1934).

17. Schubert-Soldern, F. "Professor Doktor Max Dvořák," *MZKE*, 3. F. Vol. XVI (1924), p. 91.

18. Sedlmayr, Hans. "Kunstgeschichte als Geistegeschichte. Das Vermächtnis Max Dvořáks," *WuW*, Vol. IV (1949), pp. 264–277.

19. Swoboda, Karl Maria. "Max Dvořák," *NDB*, Vol. IV (1959), pp. 209–210.

20. Tietze, Hans. "Max Dvořák," *KuK*, Vol. LVI. (1921), p. 441.

21. ———. "Max Dvořák," *Kunstwissenschaft der Gegenwart in Selbstdarstellungen.* Leipzig: Meiner, 1924.

22. ———. "Max Dvořák, Kunsthistoriker," *DBJb*, Vol. III (1930), p. 74.

23. ———. "Max Dvořáks gesammelte Werke," *NFP*, Jan. 4, 1924.

24. Weingartner, J. "Max Dvořák und die kunsthistorische Wiener Schule," *Hld*, 21. Jhrg. Vol. I (1924), pp. 345–351.

25. Weiss, K. "Max Dvořák," *Gyd*, Vol. III (1924), p. 187.

BIOGRAPHICAL-BIBLIOGRAPHICAL DATA

AMALRIC OF BENA (died ca. 1207), scholastic philosopher, was born in Bena near Chartres and taught at Paris. In a series of pantheistic doctrines, which had many points of contact with those of Erigena, he maintained, *inter alia*, that God was the one essence underlying all created beings and that those who remain in the love of God cannot sin. He founded the sect known as the "Amalricians," who further developed his teachings. His principal theses were explicitly condemned by a synod at Paris in 1210 and again at the Lateran Council of 1215.

Principal sources concerning him:

1. Bäumker, Clemens, editor. "Contra Amaurianos. Ein anonymer wahrscheinlich dem Garnerius von Rochefort zugehöriger Traktat gegen die Amalrikaner aus dem Anfang des XIII. Jahrhunderts," *BGPM*, Vol. XXIV: 5–6 (1926).

2. Caesarius Heisterbacensis, monachi ordinis Cisterciensis. *Dialogus Miraculorum*. Edited by Joseph Strange. Köln: Heberle, 1851, pp. 304–307.

3. Capelle, Germaine Catherine. *Autour du Décret de 1210:III. Amaury de Bène. Etude sur son Panthéisme formel.* Preface by Etienne Gilson. Paris: Vrin, 1932 (Vol. XVI of the series issued by the "Bibliothèque Thomiste, Section historique" [Paris and Kain, Belgium]).

4. Oppaviensis, Martin. "Chronicon Pontificum et Imperatorum," edited by L. Weiland. *MGH*, Scriptores, Vol. XXII (1872), p. 438.

5. Überweg, Vol. II, pp. 250–251; bibliography pp. 707–708.

ANSELM, ST. (1033–1109), Archbishop of Canterbury, was born at Aosta in Piedmont of noble Lombard parents. Having left home because of his father's harshness, he finally settled at the renowned Abbey of Bec in Normandy where in 1060 he became a monk and in 1063 succeeded his master Lanfranc as prior. Chosen Abbot of Bec in 1078, he visited the abbey's possessions in England and won many friends there. Upon the death of Lanfranc as Archbishop of Canterbury, the King, William Rufus, resisting the general desire for Anselm as new archbishop, kept the seat vacant for four years until 1093 when he reluctantly consented to the consecration of Anselm and then only because he supposed himself to be on his deathbed. However Rufus recovered and repented his decision, for Anselm demanded that he be invested with the insignia of his office by the Pope and not by the King. Although the quarrel was smoothed over, Anselm went to Rome in 1097 where he remained until William's successor, Henry I, recalled him in 1100. The dispute over lay investiture was revived, however, and was not settled until 1107 when it was agreed that bishops should do homage to the king for their lands but must be invested with the symbols of their spiritual functions by the Church. Anselm died at Canterbury, April 21, 1109, and was canonized in 1494.

In the realm of thought, Anselm's achievement was threefold:

1. In the field of Christian dogma he elaborated a revolutionary interpretation of the doctrine of the Atonement, according to which the sacrifice of Christ was a ransom offered not to the Devil—as had previously been believed—but to God; the new theory quickly won general acceptance.

2. In considering the problem of the relation between reason and faith, Anselm, inspired by the teaching of St. Augustine, maintained that faith is the necessary presupposition of rational speculation; his celebrated phrases, "Faith seeking knowledge," *fides quaerens intellectum*, and "I believe in order that I may know," *credo ut intelligam*, became watchwords of the Augustinian school, and before the advent of St. Albertus Magnus and St. Thomas Aquinas the majority of his successors deferred to his opinion.

3. His supreme achievement, however, was the formulation of the ontological argument which professes to show that the very conception of God involves His existence, an argument which has been repeatedly restated, championed and attacked by eminent philosophers since his time.

Anselm's important writings include the *Monologion*, the *Proslogion, De veritate* and *Cur Deus homo*—the last contains his famous exposition of the theory of the Redemption.

Critical editions of Anselm's *Opera omnia*:

1. Gerberon, O.S.B., Dom Gabriel. Paris: Billaine, 1675; new edition 1721.
2. Migne, *PL*, Vols. CLVIII–CLIX. Paris: Migne, 1845.
3. Raynaud, S. J., Theophil. Lyons: Durand, 1630.

Biographies of St. Anselm:

1. *Eadmeri Historia novorum in Anglia et opusculo duo, de vita Sancti Anselmi et quibusdam Miraculi ejus.* Edited by John Selden. London: Stanesbeius, 1623; re-edited in *P.L.*, Vol. CLVIII and by Martin Rule. London: Longman, 1884.
2. Charma, Antoine. *Saint Anselme. Notice biographique, littéraire et philosophique.* Paris: Hachette, 1853.
3. Church, Richard William. *Saint Anselm.* London: Macmillan, 1937 (First published 1870).
4. Croset-Mouchet, Abbe J. *Saint Anselme. Histoire de sa Vie et de son Temps.* Paris: Lethielleux, 1859.
5. Hasse, Friedrich R. *Anselm von Canterbury.* 2 Vols. Leipzig: Engelmann, 1843–1852.
6. Hook, Walter. *Lives of the Archbishops of Canterbury.* London: Bently, 1860.
7. Ragey, le Père (Marianist). *Vie de Saint Anselme.* Lyon: Delhomme et Briquet, 1892.
8. Raymond-Baker, E. "The Youth of Anselm," *CW*, Vol. XXXVII (1883), pp. 334–347.
9. Remusat, Comte Charles-François-Marie de. *Saint Anselme de Cantobery. Tableau de la Vie monastique et de la Lutte du Pouvoir spirituel avec le Pouvoir temporel au onzième Siècle.* Paris: Didier, 1850.
10. Rule, Martin. *Life and Times of Saint Anselm, Archbishop of Canterbury, Primate of the Britains.* London: Kegan Paul, 1883.

Works about Anselm's theology:

1. Baeumker, Franz. *Die Lehre Anselms von Canterbury über den Willen und seine Wahlfreiheit.* Münster: Aschendorff, 1912 (Cf. *BGPM*, Vol. X).
2. Möhler, Johann A. *Gesammelte Schriften und Aufsätze.* Edited by Johann Döllinger. 2 Vols. in one. Regensburg: Manz, 1839–1840.

3. Ragey, le Père (Marianist). *Saint Anselme Professeur*. Paris: Roger et Chernoviz, 1890.

4. Überweg, Vol. III, especially pp. 192–203, 698–700.

5. Webb, Clement C. *Studies in the History of Natural Theology*. Oxford: The Clarendon Press, 1915.

BÉDIER, JOSEPH (i.e. CHARLES MARIE JOSEPH), professor of French language and literature, was born in Paris on January 28, 1864, and died there in 1938. From 1903 until his death he was Professor of Old French language and literature at the Collège de France.

Major Writings:

1. *Bibliographie des travaux de Gaston Paris*. Paris: Bouillon, 1904.

2. *La chanson de Roland*. Paris: Piazza (L'Edition d'art), 1927.

3. *Les chansons des croisades* (avec leurs mélodies publiées par Pierre Aubry). Paris: Champion, 1909.

4. *Chevalerie*. Tours: Mame, 1931.

5. *Etudes critiques*. Paris: Colin, 1903 (Articles on Aubigné, Pascal, Le Maistre, Diderot, Chénier, Chateaubriand).

6. *Les fabliaux. Etudes de littérature populaire et d'histoire littéraire du moyen âge*. Paris: Bouillon, 1893.

7. *Les légendes épiques*. Paris: Champion, 1908–1913. (In this work Bédier sought to connect the origin of the medieval epic poetry with the places visited by the vast number of pilgrimages throughout Europe and the Middle East).

8. *Le roman de Tristan et Iseult*. Paris: Piazza, 1900. (Translated into German by the German poet Rudolf Binding as *Der Roman von Tristan und Isolde*. Leipzig: Insel, 1911; the story was also reworked as a drama with music accompaniment, cf. *Tristan et Iseult* [Pièce en trois actes, un prologue et huit tableaux, musique de scène de Paul Ladmirault]. Paris: Imprimerie de l'Illustration, 1929.)

BELOW, GEORG ANTON HUGO VON (1858–1927), German historian, was born in Königsberg, January 19, 1858, into a family that had distinguished itself in both the military and the civil service; he died in Badenweiler, October 20, 1927. Destined for a career either in the state or the church, he decided instead to study history, was graduated from the University of Bonn in 1883 and took over the publication of the records of the diet of Jülich-Berg (*Die Landtagsakten*

von Jülich-Berg. 1400–1600. Düsseldorf: Voss und Co., 1895–1907).
In 1889 he accepted a professorship at the university in Königsberg
where he lectured until 1891. He then taught successively at Münster (1891), Marburg (1897), Tübingen (1901) and Freiburg in Br.
(1905), from which university he retired *emeritus* in 1924.

Below's comprehensive writings are devoted mainly to con-
stitutional and economic history, yet he remained enough of a universal historian to refrain from giving any undue preference to
political over cultural history in the learned controversies waged in his
day. In conformance with his natural critical inclinations, most of his
work was occasioned by a personal antithetical opposition to the
views sponsored by one of his colleagues in the field or sprang from
his desire to set off in sharp relief some basic problem, formulated as
it were in almost judicial-legalistic terms. Although he was attracted
to the origins of institutions and their motivations, the main concern
of his research was his endeavor to delineate in terms of the legalistic
concepts of his day the basic character of the state, beginning with
its inception up to his own period, and to free the idea "state" from
suffocating concepts of overly personal rights, either in the sense of
a patrimonial state or one based on the principle of a confederation
of politically equal and independent but commercially interdepend-
ent territorial units (*Genossenschaftstheorie*). His chief work, *Der
deutsche Staat des Mittelalters.* Vol. I. (Leipzig: Quelle und Meyer,
1915), however, remained only a torso and barely proceeded beyond
the critical fundamentals of the total projected work.

His method of presentation was one of historical objectivity and
demanded equal validity for all areas of research and well-documented
superstructure for analysis. He categorically rejected the assumption
of compulsive laws of causality in history as well as the concept of
basic developmental patterns and stressed on the contrary the significance of the individual and individual events in the progress of historical growth. Having found justification in the accepted demarcation between the cultural and the natural sciences, he challenged
with equal vigor the intrusions of materialistic, positivistic or naturalistic interpretations of history. Affected by a romantic idealism
whose values he firmly adhered to, Below primarily derived these
values from his Protestant religiosity and secondarily from a vivid
national consciousness, entirely German in orientation in spite of his
dominant Prussian background. Consequently in his historiographic
works, he emphasized the significance of the Romantic Period on

the development of German historiography in the nineteenth century.

Politically Below was active as the leader of a free conservative group from 1907 until his death and founded (*et al.*) the periodical *Deutschlands Erneuerung* (München, 1917 ff.) and the periodical series *Herdflamme. Sammlung der gesellschaftswissenschaftlichen Grundwerke aller Zeiten und Völker* (Jena, 1922–1934). He also served as one of the editors of the *Vierteljahrsschrift für Sozial-und Wirtschaftsgeschichte* (Stuttgart, 1903 ff.) and the historical reference series *Handbuch der mittelalterlichen und neueren Geschichte* (München-Berlin: Brackmann).

Basic writings:

1. *Deutsche Geschichtsschreibung von den Befreiungskriegen bis zu unseren Tagen.* Leipzig: Quelle und Meyer, 1916.

2. *Die Entstehung der deutschen Stadtgemeinde.* Düsseldorf: Voss, 1889.

3. *Die mittelalterliche Stadtwirtschaft und die gegenwärtige Kriegswirtschaft.* Tübingen: Mohr, 1917.

4. *Territorium und Stadt.* München-Leipzig. Oldenbourg, 1900.

5. *Über historische Periodisierung mit besonderem Blick auf die Grenze zwischen Mittelalter und Neuzeit.* Berlin: Deutsche Verlagsgesellschaft für Politik und Geschichte, 1925.

6. *Die Ursachen der Reformation.* München-Berlin: Oldenbourg, 1917.

7. *Die Ursachen der Rezeption des römischen Rechts in Deutschland.* München-Berlin: Oldenbourg, 1905.

8. *Der Ursprung der deutschen Stadtverfassung.* Düsseldorf: Voss, 1892.

9. *Vom Mittelalter zur Neuzeit.* Leipzig: Quelle und Meyer, 1924. An autobiographical sketch of Below can be found in *Geschichtswissenschaft in Selbstdarstellungen.* Edited by Sigfrid Steinberg. Vol. I. Leipzig: Meiner, 1925.

Some selected essays devoted to von Below:

1. Baier, G. "Georg von Below," ZGORh, Vol. LXXXII, N.F. Vol. XLIII (1930), pp. 598–609.

2. Below, Minnie. *Georg von Below. Ein Lebensbild für seine Freunde.* Stuttgart: Kohlhammer, 1930.

3. Dopsch, A. "Georg von Below," *AÖAW*, Vol. LXXVIII (1928), pp. 259–263.

4. *Gedächtnisschrift für Georg von Below.* Edited by his students and friends. Berlin: Deutsche Verlagsgesellschaft für Politik und Geschichte, 1928.

5. "Georg von Below," *ADB*, Vol. XLVI.

6. Herre, P. "Georg von Below," *Altpreussische Biographie* (Königsberg), Vol. I (1941).

7. Klaiber, Ludwig. *Georg von Below. Verzeichnis seiner Schriften.* Stuttgart: Kohlhammer, 1929.

8. Lamprecht, Karl. *Die historische Methode des Herrn von Below. Eine Kritik.* Berlin: Gaertner; Freiburg in Br.: Heyfelder, 1899.

9. Schmidt, Alfred. *Ahnentafel des Geschichtsschreibers Georg von Below.* Leipzig: Zentralstelle für deutsche Personen- und Familiengeschichte, 1938 (In the series: "Ahnentafel berühmter Deutscher," 4.F., Heft 14).

BORINSKI, KARL (1862–1922), German literary historian, was born in Kattowitz (Upper Silesia), June 11, 1862, and died in Munich, January 12, 1922. He studied under Michael Bernays and Konrad Hoffman at the University of Munich where he became a *Privatdozent* (unsalaried university lecturer) in 1894. In 1906 he was promoted to the rank of assistant professor (*ausserordentlicher Professor*), and was named a member of the Bavarian Academy in 1917.

His chief accomplishments were in the area of poetry and the investigation of the literary survival of classical literature in the individual national literatures of Europe. His extensive background in universal and comparative literature, coupled with his generally broad humanistic education, enabled him to discuss the influence of classical literature on contemporary culture. In an age and a politico-socio-economic milieu which emphasized external far more than internal values, Borinski appears to be one of the last significant representatives of the best that the scholarly tradition of the nineteenth century produced. It remained one of the sorrows of his academic career that his penetrating criticism and original ideas had so limited an effect during his lifetime.

His basic writings:

1. *Die Antike in Poetik und Kunsttheorie.* 2 Vols. Leipzig: Dieterichsche Verlagshandlung, 1914–1924.

2. *Balthasar Gracian und die Hofliteratur in Deutschland.* Halle: Niemeyer, 1894.

3. *Deutsche Poetik*. Leipzig: Göschen, 1895 ("Sammlung Gö-schen," Vol. XL).

4. *Geschichte der deutschen Literatur*. 2 Vols. Stuttgart: Union, 1921.

5. *Lessing*. 2 Vols. Berlin: Hofmann, 1900.

6. *Die Poetik der Renaissance und die Anfänge der literarischen Kritik in Deutschland*. Berlin: Weidmann, 1886.

7. *Die Rätsel Michelangelos und Dantes*. München: Müller, 1908.

8. *Die Weltwiedergeburtsidee in den neuen Zeiten*. München: Franzscher, 1919 (In the series: "Sitzungsberichte der bayerschen Akademie der Wissenschaften zu München").

Literature concerning Borinski:

1. Arens, F. "Eines Münchner Gelehrten literarisches Ver-mächtnis, *GH*, 6. Jhrg. (1929–1930).

2. Behrend, Fritz. *Geschichte der deutschen Philologie in Bil-dern*. Marburg: Elwert, 1927, p. 63 (portrait).

3. Borcherdt, H. H. "Karl Borinski," *München-Augsburger Abend-Zeitung* (München-Augsburg: newspaper), January 13, 1922.

4. "[Karl] Borinski," *BioJbA*, Jahrg, 54, Vol. CCXIX:A (1928), pp. 15–23.

5. Hofmiller, Joseph. "Karl Borinski," *Münchner Neueste Nach-richten* (München: newspaper), January 12, 1922.

6. Kosch, Wilhelm. "[Karl] Borinski," *Literatur Lexikon. Bio-graphisches und bibliographisches Handbuch*. 2nd edition. Vol. I. Bern: Francke, 1949, pp. 201–202.

7. Muncker, Franz, "Karl Borinski," *JbBAW* (1922–1923), pp. 22–26.

8. Newald, Richard. "Karl Borinski," *DBJb*, Vol. IV (1929), pp. 16–21 (Werkverzeichnis, Literaturangaben und Totenliste); cf. also *NDB*, Vol. II (1955), p. 463.

9. Stemplinger, Eduard. "Karl Borinski," *Tägliche Rundschau* (Leipzig?: newspaper), January 19, 1922.

BURCKHARDT, JACOB, German art and cultural historian, was born on May 25, 1818, in Basel and died there on August 8, 1897. In most of his writings Burckhardt is generally rather skeptical toward philosophy and believes that it was philosophy that had destroyed the will to power, myth, religion and poetry among the Greeks. In opposition to philosophy as a means of reflection, he would substitute artistic perception. It was from the point of view of the artist that he admired the architectonics of the various systematic approaches to knowledge and attributed to ethics the liberating effect generally associated with philosophic speculation. Guided in his personal view by Schopenhauer's pessimistic skepticism, he particularly battled against the dogmatic superiority assumed by all philosophic systems; however he never completely renounced his European cultural heritage; indeed, he himself substantially contributed to the understanding and appreciation of this culture in its modern origins.

Of his numerous studies see especially the following:

1. *Beiträge zur Kunstgeschichte von Italien. Das Altarbild. Das Porträt in der Malerei. Die Sammler.* Basel: Lendorff, 1898.

2. *Briefe an einen Architekten, 1870–1889.* München: Müller & Rentsch, 1913.

3. *Der Cicerone. Eine Anleitung zum Genuß der Kunstwerke Italiens.* 2nd edition. Leipzig: Seemann, 1869: English translation: *The Cicerone or Art Guide to Painting in Italy. For the Use of Travellers.* Ed. by Dr. A. von Zahn. Translated by Mrs. A. H. Clough. London: Murray, 1873 (New edition: New York: Scribner's Sons, 1908).

4. *Die Cultur der Renaissance in Italien.* Basel: Schweighauser, 1860; English translation: *The Civilization of the Period of the Renaissance in Italy.* Translated by S. G. C. Middlemore. London: Kegan Paul, 1878 (And innumerable later editions and translations).

5. *Griechische Kulturgeschichte.* Ed. by Jakob Oers. Berlin-Stuttgart: Spemann, 1898–1902.

6. *Größe, Glück und Unglück in der Weltgeschichte.* Leipzig: Insel, 1932.

7. *Jacob Burckhardt. Gesamtausgabe.* Stuttgart: Deutsche Verlagsanstalt, 1929–.

8. *Rubens.* Wien-Leipzig: Bernina, 1937.

9. *Weltgeschichtliche Betrachtungen.* Berlin-Stuttgart: Spemann, 1905.

10. *Die Zeit Constantins des Großen.* Basel: Schweighauser, 1953.

Works concerning Burckhardt:

1. Andler, Charles. "Nietzsche und Jakob Burckhardt," *Elsässische Bibliothek* (Basel), Vol. XII.

2. Grisebach, Eberhard. *Jacob Burckhardt als Denker*. Bern-Leipzig: Haupt, 1943.

3. Joel, Karl. *Jacob Burckhardt als Geschichtsphilosoph*. Basel: Helbing & Lichtenhahn, 1918.

4. Kaphahn, Fritz, ed. *Jacob Burckhardt. Briefe zur Erkenntnis seiner geistigen Gestalt* (Mit einem Lebensabriss und 12 Abbildungen). Leipzig: Kröner, 1936.

5. Löwith, Karl. *Jacob Burckhardt. Der Mensch inmitten der Geschichte*. Luzern: Vita Nova, 1936.

6. Martin, Alfred von. *Nietzsche und Jacob Burckhardt. Zwei geistige Welten im Dialog*. München: Erasmus, 1941.

7. Martin, Kurt. *Jacob Burckhardt und die Karlsruher Galerie*. Karlsruhe, 1941.

8. Neumann, Carl. *Jacob Burckhardt*. München: Bruckmann, 1927.

9. Rehm, Walter. *Jacob Burckhardt*. Frauenfeld: Huber, 1930.

10. Roth, Paul. *Aktenstücke zur Laufbahn Jacob Burckhardts*. Basel, 1936.

11. Stadelmann, H. "Jacob Burckhardt und die Décadence," *Vom Schicksal des deutschen Geistes*. Berlin, 1934.

12. Winners, Richard. *Weltanschauung und Geschichtsauffassung Jacob Burckhardts. Ein Beitrag zur Geistesgeschichte*. Leipzig: Teubner, 1929.

BURIDANUS, JOANNIS, French nominalist and cleric, was born around the beginning of the fourteenth century in Béthune (Artois). As a disciple of Ockham, he served as the Rector of the University of Paris in 1327 and again in 1348. He died shortly after 1358. His significance in philosophy lies in the areas of logic, ethics and physics. In ethics he was particularly drawn toward the problem of the freedom of the will and reduced the problem to a psychological phenomenon in which indeterminism was freed from arbitrariness and determinism from the inescapable necessity of an all-dominating "nature" which would thus axiomatically exclude any considerations of moral responsibility. In physics he anticipated the law of inertia and its concepts of physical directive forces with his theory of "impetus." Having accepted as possible the proof for the existence of God by means of the argument of cause and effect, he became an opponent of his former mentor and his theological skepticism—in 1340 he even signed the document promulgated by the Faculty of Arts at Paris that prohibited the teaching of Ockham's doctrines.

Some of his major writings:

1. *In metaphysicen Aristotelis.* . . . Paris: Bade, 1518.
2. *Questiones et decisiones physicales.* . . . Paris: Bade, 1516.
3. *Questiones Joannis Buridani super X libros Aristotelis ad Nicomachum.* Paris: Hopyl, 1489.
4. *Questiones Joannis Buridani super X libros ethicorum Aritotelis.* . . . Paris: Le Preux, 1513.
5. *Quaestiones Johannis Buridani super VIII libros politicorum Aristotelis.* . . . Paris: Petit, 1513.
6. *Textus summularum Magistri Johannis Buridani.* Ed. by Johannes Dorp. Paris: Carchagni, 1487.
7. *Dialectices sitioribus questionum.* Paris: Senant, n.d.

Works concerning Buridanus:

1. Duhem, Pierre Maurice Marie. *Etudes sur Léonard de Vinci, ceux qu'il a lus et ceux qui l'ont lu.* 3 Vols. Paris: Hermann, 1906–1909, Vol. II, pp. 379–384, 420–423, 431–441; Vol. III, pp. 1–112, 113–259, 279–286, 350–360.
2. Michalski, C. "Les courants philosophiques à Oxford et à Paris pendant le XIVe siècle," *Bulletin international de L'Académie Polonaise des Sciences et des Lettres* (Cracow), Vol. LXXXII (1922).
3. Prantl, Carl von. *Geschichte der Logik im Abendlande.* Leipzig: Hirzel, 1855–1870, Vol. IV, pp. 14–38.
4. "Le temps et le mouvement selon les scolastiques," *Revue de Philosophie* (Paris), Vol. XIV (1914).
5. Verweyen, Johannes Maria. *Das Problem der Willensfreiheit in der Scholastik.* Heidelberg: Winter, 1909.

CLEMENT OF ALEXANDRIA, ST. (ca. 150–ca. 215), theologian, was an Athenian by birth who, after studying Christianity and philosophy in several places, became a pupil of Pathaenus, the head of the Catechetical School at Alexandria whom he succeeded in 190. In 202 he was forced to flee because of persecution. He was succeeded in turn by his pupil Origen. His chief works are the *Protrepticus* (*An Exhortation to the Greeks*), the *Paedagogus* (*Christian life and manners*) and the *Stromateis* (*Miscellaneous Studies*).

It was the age of Gnosticism, and Clement concurred with the Gnostics in holding "gnosis," religious knowledge or illumination, to be the chief element in Christian perfection. But for him the only true "gnosis" was that which presupposed the faith of the Church, was Apostolic in its foundation and possessed Divine revelation. Although thoroughly loyal to this faith, Clement explained and supplemented it with the ideas of Greek philosophy which he also regarded as a Divine gift to mankind. Christ, the Logos, the second Person of the Divine Trinity, was both the source of all human reason and the interpreter of God to mankind. He became man in order to posit a supreme revelation and to enable man through Him to partake of immortality. In the realization of this immortality the sacraments of Baptism and the Eucharist are instrumental. Clement saw ignorance and error as a more fundamental evil than sin, and although he held that not all men would attain the highest level of blessedness, he took an optimistic view of the ultimate destiny of even the most erring. His *Quis Dives Salvetur?* is a beautiful exposition of Mark X, 17–31 and ends with the narrative of the young man who was baptized, lost and re-won by St. John the Apostle. His name occurs in the earlier martyrologies; his feast day is assigned to December 4, but Clement VIII excised it on the grounds of the doubtful orthodoxy of some of Clement's writings.

The *Opera omnia* of Clement of Alexandria:
 1. Migne, *PG*, Vols. XVIII–IX.
 2. Stählin, Otto, editor. Critical edition in *GCS*, Vols. I–III (Text, 1905–1909); Vol. IV (Index, 1934–1936).

Literature concerning Clement:
 1. Altaner, pp. 159–164.
 2. Bardenhewer, Vol. II, pp. 15–62.
 3. Bardy, Abbé G. *Clément d'Alexandrie*. Paris: Gabalda, 1926 (Collection "Les Saints").
 4. Békés, G. "Clemente Alessandrino," *EC*, Vol. III (1950), cols. 1842–1857.
 5. Bigg, Charles. "Clement of Alexandria," *The Christian Platonists of Alexandria*. Edited by F. E. Brightman. Oxford: Claren-

don, 1913, pp. 72–150. (This is an enlarged edition of the original of 1886).

6. Borre, A. de la. "Clément d'Alexandrie," *DTC*, Vol. III (1908), cols. 137–199.

7. Faye, Eugène de. *Clément d'Alexandrie. Etude sur les Rapports du Christianisme et de la Philosophie grecque au IIe Siècle.* Paris: Leroux, 1898.

8. Freppel, Charles Emil. *Clément d'Alexandrie.* Paris: Bray, 1865.

9. Lazzati, Giuseppe. *Introduzione allo Studio di Clemente Alessandrino.* Milano: Società Editrice "Vita e Pensiero," 1939.

10. Merk, Carl. *Clemens Alexandrinus in seiner Abhängigkeit von der griechischen Philosophie.* Leipzig: Böhme, 1879.

11. Molland, E. "Clement of Alexandria on the Origins of Greek Philosophy," *SO*, Vols. XV–XVI (1936).

12. Mondésert, S. J., Claude. *Clément d'Alexandrie. Introduction à l'Etude de sa Pensée religieuse à partir de l'Ecriture.* Paris: Montaigne, 1944.

13. Patrick, John. *Clement of Alexandria.* London-Edinburgh: Blackwood, 1914 (The Croall Lectures for 1899–1900).

14. Tollington, Richard B. *Clement of Alexandria. A Study in Christian Liberalism.* 2 Vols. London: Williams and Norgate, 1914.

DEHIO, GEORG GOTTFRIED (1850–1923), German art historian, was born in Reval, November 22, 1850, and died in Tübingen, March 19, 1932. His family had emigrated from Holland to Schleswig and then to Reval early in the eighteenth century, where in the course of 200 years they served as doctors, goldsmiths, paper manufacturers and professors under both Russian and German governments. Georg studied in Göttingen and devoted himself almost exclusively to history and historiography. After graduating from Göttingen in 1872, he accepted a position in Munich (1877) as a *Privatdozent* (an unsalaried lecturer) and lectured primarily on art history. In 1883 he was called to the university in Königsberg as a university lecturer in art history (*ausserordentlicher Professor*) and received a full professorship (*Ordinariat*) the following year (1884).

While still in Munich he and a very close friend and associate, Gustav von Bezold, had begun a most extensive undertaking—the two volume study *Die kirchliche Baukunst des Abendlandes* (Stuttgart: Cotta, 1884–1901), a work which even today is considered basic for any research in that area. The studies, devoted solely to the architecture of the Middle Ages, were founded on such thorough investigations, with accompanying detailed drawings, that they became a primary source of research even outside Germany.

In 1892 he was called to the University of Strassburg where he remained until the university was taken over by the French government after the Treaty of Versailles in 1918. He then went to Tübingen where he spent the remainder of his productive life. Although his principal concern still remained art history, his attention had been directed toward the area of preservation of art monuments; this interest spawned the five volume publication *Handbuch der deutschen Kunstdenkmäler* (Berlin: Wasmuth, 1906–1914). In addition German art history is indebted to Dehio for the first unified comprehensive history of art (*Geschichte der deutschen Kunst.* 3 Vols. Berlin-Leipzig: Vereinigung wissenschaftlicher Verleger, 1919–1925) in which he endeavored to establish the precise interactions of general historical events and development on the concomitant expression of art in any given period. According to Dehio's interpretation, there were periods in German history (especially the Middle Ages, the ages of the Reformation and the Baroque) in which the spiritual life of the entire nation not only participated actively in the expressions of the plastic arts but also promoted them with every means available. Later, however, the psychic character of the German people had so changed that the plastic arts were unable to concretize their new inner condition.

For his extraordinary services to the causes of art scholarship and the humanities, Dehio received many awards and honorary doctorates, among them a Doctorate of Theology (Jena), Doctorate of Medicine, *honoris causa* (Frankfurt am Main), Doctorate of Engineering, *honoris causa*, the Peace Order Pour le Mérite and the Maximilian Order for Science and Art; he was also an active member of the Academies of Sciences of Berlin, Munich and Göttingen.

Some of his additional publications:
1. *Der Bamberger Dom.* München: Pieper, 1924.
2. *Die Denkmäler der deutschen Bildhauerkunst.* Edited by Georg Dehio and Gustav von Bezold. Re-edition of the *Handbuch der deutschen Kunstdenkmäler.* Berlin: Wasmuth, 1950 ff.
3. *Die Genesis der christlichen Basilika.* München: Franz, 1883.

4. *Influence de l'Art français sur l'Art allemand au XIII Siècle.* Translated by M. Bertaux. Paris: Leroux, 1900.

5. *Kunstgeschichtliche in Bildern.* Leipzig: Seemann, 1898–1901.

6. *Kunstgeschichte Aufsätze.* München: Oldenbourg, 1914.

7. *Ein Proportionsgesetz der antiken Baukunst und sein Nachleben im Mittelalter und in der Renaissance.* Strassburg: Trübner, 1895.

8. *Spätgotischer Kirchenbau in Oderdeutschland.* Leipzig: Seemann, 1922.

9. *Das Strassburger Münster.* München: Pieper, 1924.

10. *Untersuchungen über das gleichseitige Dreieck als Norm gotischer Bauproportionen.* Stuttgart: Cotta, 1894.

Literature concerning Dehio:

1. Clemen, P. "Zum Gedächtnis an Georg Dehio," *Dpf* (1932), pp. 76–78.

2. Engelhardt, Roderich von. *Die deutsche Universität Dorpat.* Reval: Reinhardt, 1933.

3. Gall, Ernst. "Georg Dehio," *ZKg*, Vol. I (1932), pp. 2–4; cf. also *NDB*, Vol. III (1957), pp. 563–564.

4. "[Georg] Dehio," *BioJbA*, Vol. XLVI (1926), pp. 28–29.

5. Lange, M. A bronze bust of Dehio executed by Lange is located in the Elsass-Lothringer Institut in Frankfurt am Main; a portrait of same can be found in *Die grossen Deutschen im Bild.* Edited by A. Hentzen and Niels Don Holst. Berlin: Staatliche Museen und die National-Galerie im ehemaligen Kronprinzen-Palais, 1936, p. 63.

6. Pinder, Wilhelm. "Georg Dehio zu seinem 70. Geburtstag," *KuK*, no. 7 (1920), pp. 121–129; reprinted in *JbBAW* (1931–1932), pp. 61–64.

7. Vitzthum, G. Gf. "Georg Dehio," *Nachrichten der Gesellschaft der Wissenschaften zu Göttingen* (Geschäftliche Mitteilungen). Göttingen, 1931–1932, pp. 1–5.

———

DE WULF, MAURICE (1867–1947), Belgian philosopher and theologian, was born near Ypres, Belgium, April 6, 1867, and died in Poperinghe, Belgium, December 23, 1947. Having studied at Alost, Louvain, Berlin, and Paris, he was awarded three doctorates. In 1893 he was named to the Chair of Thomistic Philosophy at the University of Louvain and in 1894, in conjunction with Désiré (later) Cardinal

Mercier, he founded the periodical *Revue Néo-Scholastique*, which he personally directed from 1907 until his death in 1947. He also founded the series of scholarly texts *Les Philosophes belges*. From 1914 to 1918 he taught at Poitiers; from 1920 to 1927 he held the Chair of Medieval Philosophy at Harvard. During his active career he also lectured at Cornell, Toronto, Princeton and Chicago.

Of his vast publications the following are particularly to be noted:

1. *Etudes historiques sur l'Esthétique de St.-Thomas d'Aquin*. Louvain: Institut supérieur de Philosophie, 1896.

2. *Guerre et Philosophie*. Paris: Bloud et Gay, 1915.

3. *Histoire de la Philosophie médiévale*. Louvain: Institut supérieur de Philosophie, 1900; 5th revised edition, *ibid.*, 1924–1925; 6th completely revised edition, *ibid.*, 1934. English translation by P. Coffey. 3rd edition. London-New York: Longmans and Green, 1909; also translated by Ernest C. Messenger. London-New York: Longmans and Green, 1925–1926; 3rd English edition based on the 6th French edition, *ibid.*, 1935–1936. German translation by Rudolf Eisler. Tübingen: Mohr, 1913.

4. *Initiation à la Philosophie thomiste*. Louvain: Institut supérieur de Philosophie, 1932.

5. *Mediaeval Philosophy. Illustrated from the System of Thomas Aquinas*. Cambridge, Mass.: Harvard University Press, 1922.

6. *Philosophy and Civilization in the Middle Ages*. Princeton: Princeton University Press, 1922.

DIDRON, ADOLPHE-NAPOLÉON (1806–1867), French archaeologist and professor of art, was born in Hautvillers (Marne) in 1806 and died in Paris in 1867. He was elected a member of the French Committee for the Preservation of Historical Monuments in 1835, and in 1838 he was appointed professor of Christian iconography at the Bibliothèque Royal in Paris. He founded the periodical *Annales Archéologiques* (1844) and remained its editor-in-chief until 1858. Through his efforts, sufficient capital was raised with which to reinaugurate on a national scale the study and restoration of archaeological monuments dating back to the French Middle Ages.

Of his various publications the following are most pertinent to our present study:

1. *Iconographie chrétienne. Histoire de Dieu.* Paris: Imprimerie royale, 1843.

2. *Iconographie de l'Opéra.* Paris: Didron, 1864.

3. *Manuel des Oeuvres de Bronze et d'Orfèvrerie du Moyen Âge.* Paris: Didron, 1859.

4. *Manuel d'Iconographie chrétienne, grecque et latine (Denys, Moine de Fourna-Agrapha).* Paris: Didron, 1845; German version: *Das Handbuch der Malerei vom Berge Athos.* Trier: Lintz, 1855 (Original text translated by Godeh-Schäfer with notes by A. Didron as well as his own).

DILTHEY, WILHELM (1833–1911), German philosopher of history and culture, was born on November 19, 1883, at Biebrich and died October 1, 1911, at Seis, near Bolzano. He was successively professor in Basle (1866), in Kiel (1868), in Breslau (1871) and Berlin (1882). As a member of the Prussian Academy of Sciences he was entrusted with its edition of the philosophical work of Immanuel Kant (1902 ff.).

As a supporter of positive Idealism, he regarded the external world as a representation arising out of pure experience and postulated that will as well as thought was a component factor of knowing and self-consciousness. His empirical tendency also appears in his historical approach to philosophy, a discipline of which he is virtually the creator in its modern form. In his *Einleitung in die Geistes-wissenschaften.* Vol. I (1883), he stressed the fundamental differences between the humanistic sciences employed in the study of culture, art and religion and those of the natural sciences. That the methods and aims of a basically empirically orientated psychology could not but fail to reach the depth and truly spiritual life of the human person, the central idea of his critical essay, *Ideen über eine beschreibende und zergliedernde Psychologie* (1894), was to form the nucleus of his remaining philosophical-historical studies; moreover such psychology based its conclusions on the mere accidentals of human life and completely ignored (by reason of its very orientation) the substance of man, his soul.

His remaining works were then, in essence, an attempt to realize the ideal method of a philosophy of history, namely a descriptive and analytic psychology of the human psyche considered from its historical aspects. Doubting the possibility of constructing a valid philosophy of history based upon the traditional views and concepts of philosophy itself—for Dilthey the spiritual life of man was far too complex to be comprehended in mere arithmetic-like formulae—he turned his attention more and more toward religious studies, the results of which (particularly in the area of hermeneutics) have proven most relevant in elucidating contemporary problems in biblical exegesis.

The bibliographic information concerning works by and about Dilthey is legion; the following list is, therefore, only selected.

Part I: Works by Dilthey

1. *Der Aufbau der geschichtlichen Welt in den Geisteswissenschaften.* I. Teil. Berlin: Reimer, 1910. (Note: G. Reimer was the official publisher for the "Königliche Preussische Akademie der Wissenschaften.")

2. "Die Entstehung der Hermeneutik" in *Philosophische Abhandlungen. Christoph Sigwart zu seinem 70. Geburtstag, 28. III. 1900.* Essays by Dilthey, *et al.* Tübingen: Mohr, 1900, pp. 185–202.

3. *Einleitung in die Geisteswissenschaften. Versuch einer Grundlegung für das Studium der Gesellschaft und der Geschichte.* Vol. I. Leipzig: Duncker und Humbolt, 1883.

4. *Das Erlebnis und die Dichtung: Lessing, Goethe, Novalis, Hölderlin.* Leipzig: Teubner, 1905 (12th edition 1950).

5. *Die Funktion der Anthropologie in der Kultur des 16. und 17. Jahrhunderts.* Berlin: Reimer, 1904.

6. *Gesammelte Schriften.* 9 Vols. Leipzig-Berlin: Teubner, 1914–1934; reissued 1959–1960.

7. *Die grosse Phantasiedichtung und andere Studien zur vergleichenden Literaturgeschichte.* Edited by Herman Nohl. Göttingen: Vanderhoeck und Ruprecht, 1954.

8. *Grundriss der allgemeinen Geschichte der Philosophie.* Edited by Hans-Georg Gadamer. Frankfurt/Main: Klostermann, 1949.

9. "Ideen über eine beschreibende und zergliedernde Psychologie" in *Sitzungsberichte der Königlichen Preussischen Akademie der Wissenschaften* (Berlin), Jhrg, 1894, pp. 1309–1407.

10. *Die Jugendgeschichte Hegels.* Berlin: Reimer, 1905.

11. *Das Leben Schleiermachers.* Berlin: Reimers, 1870; enlarged edition Berlin-Leipzig: de Gruyter, 1922.

12. *Philosophie des Lebens. Eine Auswahl aus seinen Schriften: 1867–1910.* Edited by Herman Nohl. Frankfurt/Main: Klostermann, 1946.

13. *Studien zur Geschichte des deutschen Geistes.* Leipzig: Teubner, 1927.

14. *Studien zur Grundlegung der Geisteswissenschaften.* Berlin: Reimer, 1905.

15. *Von deutscher Dichtung und Musik.* Leipzig-Berlin: Teubner, 1933.

Dilthey's Works in English:

1. *Meaning in History. His* [Dilthey's] *Thoughts on History and Society.* Translated with an Introduction by H. P. Rickman. London: Allen, 1961; reprinted as *Pattern and Meaning in History.* New York: Harper, 1962 ("Harper-Torchbook" series).

2. *Philosophy of Existence. Introduction to Weltanschauungslehre.* Translated by William Kluback and Martin Weinbaum. London: Vision Press, 1960.

Part II: Works about Dilthey

1. Bischoff, Dietrich. *Wilhelm Diltheys geschichtliche Lebensphilosophie.* With an appendix: "Eine Kantdarstellung Wilhelm Diltheys." Leipzig: Teubner, 1935.

2. Bollnow, Otto Friedrich. *Dilthey. Eine Einführung in seine Philosophie.* Stuttgart: Kohlhammer, 1955 (2nd edition).

3. Bork, Arnold. *Diltheys Auffassung des griechischen Geistes.* Berlin: Junker und Dünnhaupt, 1944.

4. Cüppers, Klem. *Die erkenntnistheoretischen Grundgedanken Wilhelm Diltheys.* Leipzig: Teubner, 1933.

5. Degener, Alfons. *Dilthey und das Problem der Metaphysik.* Bonn: Röhrscheid, 1933.

6. Dietrich, Rudolf. *Die Ethik Wilhelm Diltheys.* Düsseldorf: Schwann, 1937.

7. Englhauser, Johann. *Metaphysische Tendenzen in der Psychologie Diltheys.* Würzburg: Becker, 1938.

8. Erdmann, Benno. *Gedächtnisrede auf Wilhelm Dilthey.* Berlin: Reimer, 1912.

9. Erxleben, Wolfgang. *Erlebnis, Verstehen und geschichtliche Wahrheit. Untersuchungen über die geschichtliche Stellung von*

Wilhelm Diltheys Grundlegung der Geisteswissenschaften. Berlin: Junker und Dünnhaupt, 1937.

10. Glock, Karl Theodor. *Wilhelm Diltheys Grundlegung einer wissenschaftlichen Lebensphilosophie.* Berlin: Junker und Dünnhaupt, 1939.

11. Groeben, Margaret von den. *Konstruktive Psychologie und Erlebnis. Studien zur Logik der Diltheyschen Kritik an die erklärende Psychologie.* Stuttgart: Kohlhammer, 1934.

12. Günther, Hans R. "Wilhelm Dilthey" in *Persönlichkeit und Geschichte. Aufsätze und Vorträge.* Augsburg: Beyschlag, 1947.

13. Hennig, Johannes. *Lebensbegriff und Lebenskategorie. Studien zur Geschichte und Theorie der geisteswissenschaftlichen Begriffsbildung mit besonderer Berücksichtigung Wilhelm Diltheys.* Dresden: Risse, 1934.

14. Herder, Franz. *Der Begriff der Lebendigkeit in Diltheys Menschenbild.* Berlin: Junker und Dünnhaupt, 1940.

15. Heynen, Walter. "Diltheys Psychologie des dichterischen Schaffens" in *Abhandlungen zur Philosophie und ihrer Geschichte* (Halle), Vol. X:48 (1916).

16. Höfer, Josef. *Vom Leben zur Wahrheit. Eine katholische Besinnung an die Lebensanschauung Wilhelm Diltheys.* Freiburg: Herder, 1936.

17. Hodges, Herbert Arthur. *The Philosophy of Wilhelm Dilthey.* London: Routledge and Kegan Paul, 1952 (Contains a detailed Dilthey-Bibliography).

18.———. *Wilhelm Dilthey. An Introduction.* London: Kegan Paul, Trench, Trubnes, 1944 (Contains a detailed Dilthey-Bibliography).

19. Krakauer, Hugo. *Diltheys Stellung zur theoretischen Philosophie Kants.* Breslau: Koebnersche Buchhandlung, 1913.

20. Liebe, Annelise. *Die Ästhetik Wilhelm Diltheys.* Bleicherode: Nieft, 1938.

21. Liebert, Arthur. *Wilhelm Dilthey. Eine Würdigung seines Werkes. Zum 100. Geburtstag des Philosophen.* Berlin: Mittler, 1933.

22. Meurers, Josef. *Wilhelm Diltheys Gedankenwelt und die Naturwissenschaften.* Berlin: Junker und Dünnhaupt. 1936.

23. Misch, Clara (née Dilthey). *Der junge Dilthey. Ein Lebensbild in Briefen und Tagebüchern.* Berlin: Teubner, 1933.

24. Misch, Georg. *Vom Lebens- und Gedankenkreis Wilhelm Diltheys.* Frankfurt/Main: Schulte-Bulmke, 1947.

25. Spranger, Eduard. *Wilhelm Dilthey*. Leipzig: Weigandt, 1912.

26. Stein, Arthur. *Der Begriff des Geistes bei Dilthey*. Berlin: Drechsel, 1913; enlarged edition Tübingen: Mohr, 1926.

27. Stenzel, Julius. "Dilthey und die deutsche Philosophie der Gegenwart," *PV*, Vol. XXXIII (1934); also appeared as a monograph in Berlin: Pan-Verlagsgesellschaft, 1934.

28. Überweg, Vol. IV, pp. 551–555, bibliography, p. 720.

29. Unger, Rudolf. "Weltanschauung und Dichtung. Zur Gestaltung des Problems bei Wilhelm Dilthey" in *Schweizer Schriften für allgemeines Wissen*. Zürich, 1917.

Dionysius, the Pseudo-Areopagite (ca. 500), a mystical theologian, is the name given to the author of a *corpus* of theological writings attributed, until the sixteenth century, to Dionysius, the Bishop of Athens. Since the author quotes from Proclus (411–485) and is first cited by Severus, Patriarch of Constantinople (ca. 513), he is believed to have written about the year 500, probably in Syria.

His extant writings are: 1. the *Celestial Hierarchy* that explains how the nine orders of angels mediate God to man; 2. the *Ecclesiastical Hierarchy* which deals with the Sacraments and the three ways of spiritual life—purgation, illumination and union—exemplificative of the three ways in which human nature is deified; 3. the *Divine Names* which examines the being and attributes of God; 4. the *Mystical Theology* that describes the ascent of the soul to union with God. The Pseudo-Dionysian writings aim at achieving a synthesis between Christian dogma and neo-Platonism. Their thematic idea, which has made them the charter of Christian mysticism, is the intimate union between God and the soul, and the progressive deification of the man. This is to be obtained by a process of "unknowing," in which the soul leaves behind the perceptions of the senses as well as the reasoning of the intellect. The soul will then enter an obscurity in which it will be increasingly illuminated by the "Ray of Divine Darkness" and brought ultimately to the knowledge of the ineffable Being that transcends affirmation and negation alike.

The supposed apostolic authority of these writings, added to their intrinsic value, caused them to exercise a profound influence on medieval theology both in the West and East. They were commented on by such Doctors of the Church as Hugh of St.-Victor,

Albertus Magnus, St. Thomas Aquinas and St. Bonaventure as well as the late medieval mystics such as Tauler and Eckhart. Only the research efforts of modern scholars (especially Joseph Stiglmayr and Hugo Koch) have definitely established their late fifth-century origin and the relationship of the author with moderate Monophysitism (the belief that Christ had but one nature, or a composite nature of the human and the divine, a tenet still held by the Coptic Church).

The *Opera omnia* of Dionysius:

1. Migne, *PG*, Vols. III–IV. (This edition includes the original Greek and a Latin translation with commentaries; it is a complete re-printing of an earlier two-volume edition by B. Corderius, S.J., Antwerp, 1634; Erigena's translation into Latin of Dioysius' works is to be found in Migne, *PL*, Vol. CXXII, cols. 1023–1194.)

2. Parker, Rev. John, editor. English translation of the selected works of Dionysius. 2 Vols. London-Oxford: Parker, 1897–1899.

3. Rolt, C. E., translator-editor. *The Divine Names* and *Mystical Theology*. London: Society for Promoting Christian Knowledge; New York: Macmillan, 1920. (In the series: "Translations of Christian Literature. Series I, Greek Texts." Introduction, pp. 1–47, bibliography pp. 47–49.)

4. For a complete listing of the works, translations thereof and articles about Dionysius cf. *British Museum General Catalogue of Printed Books*, Vol. LIII, cols. 88–96.

Works concerning Dionysius:

1. Altaner, pp. 453–457.

2. Bardenhewer, Vol. IV, pp. 282–299.

3. Beck, O.S.B., E. and C. Fabro. "Dionigi l'Areopagita," *EC*, Vol. IV (1950), cols. 1662–1668.

4. Honigmann, E. "Pierre l'Ibérien et les Ecrits du Pseudo-Denys l'Aréopagite," *ARB*, Vol. XLVII (1932).

5. Koch, Hugo. "Pseudo-Dionysius Areopagitica in seinen Beziehungen zum Neoplatonismus und Mysterienwesen," *FcLDg*, Vol. I: 2–3 (1900).

6. Roques, Abbé René. *L'Univers dionysien. Structure hiérarchique du Monde selon le Pseudo-Denys*. Paris: Aubier, 1955.

7. Stiglmayr, S.J., Joseph. "Dionysius Areopagitica," *LTK*, Vol. III (1931), cols. 334–336.

8. ———. "Der Neuplatoniker Proclus als Vorlage des soge-

nannten Dionysius Areopagita in seiner Lehre vom Übel," *HJB*, Vol. XVI (1895), pp. 253–273, 721–748.

9. Théry, G. "Études dionysiennes," *EPM*, Vols. XVI and XIX (1932 and 1937).

10. Überweg, Vol. II, pp. 119, 126–128, bibliography pp. 667–668.

11. van den Daele, S.J., A. *Indices Pseudo-Dionysiani*. Louvain: Université de Louvain, 1941 (In the series: "Recueil des Travaux d'Histoire et de Philologie," Series 3).

DRESDNER, ALBERT, 1866–?

1. *Ibsen als Norweger und Europäer*. Jena: Diederichs, 1907.

2. *Die Kunstkritik, ihre Geschichte und Theorie*. München: Bruckmann, 1915.

3. *Kultur- und Sittengeschichte der italienischen Geistlichkeit im X. und XI. Jahrhundert*. Breslau: Koebner, 1890.

4. *Regesten zur Geschichte der Juden im fränkischen und deutschen Reiche bis zum Jahre 1273*. Ed. by Julius Aronius with the assistance of Albert Dresdner and Ludwig Lewinski. Berlin: Simion Nachf., 1902.

EICKEN, HEINRICH VON, German historian of the nineteenth century. I was unable to find definitively any biographical information concerning Eicken. Of his works the two following seem to be the only ones to ever gain general acknowledgement:

1. *Der Kampf der Westgothen und Römer unter Alarich*. Leipzig: Duncker und Humblot, 1876; 4th edition Stuttgart-Berlin: Cotta, 1923.

2. *Geschichte und System der mittelalterlichen Weltanschauung*. Stuttgart: Cotta, 1887; reprinted Stuttgart: Cotta, 1923 and Aalen: Scientia Verlag, 1964.

This last work, running to some 850 pages, seems to have been his *magnum opus*. The central theme of the work is the attempt to show that the ascetic ideal of the medieval Church and its struggle for world dominion, apparently incompatible, are in reality harmonious. Thus in large measure the book is a history of the ideas which determined the relations between Church and State in the Middle Ages. Its scope reaches back into the Roman, Greek and Jewish worlds of thought and extends into the Reformation. The treatment is philosophical rather than historical (in this connection cf. also Ernst Troeltsch, *Die Soziallehren der christlichen Kirchen und Gruppen*. Tübingen: Mohr, 1912, pp. 178–426), presupposes a thorough knowledge of the history of the Middle Ages and fails obviously on principle to formulate a systematic treatment of even the intellectual history of the period. For an extensive and detailed discussion of the book cf. Rev. Wilhelm Bernhardi, *HZ*, Vol. LXII (1889), pp. 101–108.

GOLDSCHMIDT, ADOLPH, 1863–?

1. *Der Albanipsalter in Hildesheim und seine Beziehung zur symbolischen Kirchensculptur des XII. Jahrhunderts*. Berlin: Siemens, 1895.

2. *Die byzantinischen Elfenbeinskulpturen des X. bis zum XIII. Jahrhunderts*. Berlin: Cassirer, 1930–.

3. *Die deutsche Buchmalerei*. Firenze: Pantheon, Casa Editrice; München: Wolff, 1928. English translation: *German Illumination*. Firenze: Pantheon; New York: Harcourt & Brace, 1928.

4. *Das Evangeliar im Rathaus zu Goslar*. Berlin: Bard, 1910 (Herausgegeben im Auftrag des Deutschen Vereins für Kunstwissenschaft).

5. *Die Kirchenthür des Heiligen Ambrosius in Mailand. Ein Denkmal frühchristlicher Skulptur*. Strassburg: Heitz, 1902.

6. "Das Nachleben der antiken Formen im Mittelalter" in *Vorträge der Bibliothek des Warburg Instituts*. Ed. by Fritz Saxl. Leipzig, 1923 (Vorträge, 1921–1922).

GREGORY OF NAZIANZUS, ST. (329–389), "the Theologian" and one of the Cappadocian Fathers, was the son of the Bishop of Nazianzus in Cappadocia. He studied at the University of Athens, where he was a contemporary of St. Basil. Soon afterwards he adopted the monastic life which he found very congenial to his contemplative and retiring spirit. Under pressure and against his will, he was ordained a priest (ca. 362) and ca. 372 was consecrated to the See of Sasima, a small village in Cappadocia, a See which he never visited, however. Until his father's death (374) he remained at Nazianzus to help him as suffragan bishop; he then retired for some years to Seleucia in Isauria. In 379 he was summoned to Constantinople where his eloquent preaching in the Church of the Anastasis not only was a great influence in restoring the Nicene Faith, but also was instrumental in its final establishment at the Council of Constantinople in 381. During the Council he was appointed Bishop of Constantinople, but he resigned the See before the end of the year and retired first to Nazianzus and later to his own estate, where he died.

His more important writings include his *Five Theological Orations* that date from his Constantinopolitan period and contain an elaborate treatment of the doctrine of the Holy Spirit; the *Philocalia*, a selection from the writings of Origen which he compiled in conjunction with St. Basil; several important letters against Apollinarianism; and a large collection of poems.

His Feast Day is celebrated in the East on January 25 and 30 and in the West on May 9. The best sources concerning his life are his autobiographical poem "De vita sua" (reprinted in *PG*, Vol. XXXVII [1862], cols. 1029–1166) and the biography of Gregory by a seventh-century presbyter named Gregory (also reprinted in *PG*, Vol. XXXV [1885], cols. 243–304).

Gregory's *Opera omnia* (Greek original with Latin translation):
1. Clémencet, O.S.B., Claude, and A. B. Caillau, editors. Latin translation by J. Billius. Paris: Desaint and Parent-Desbarres, Vol. I, 1778; Vol. II, 1840.
2. Migne, *PG*, Vols. XXXV (1885), XXXVI (1885), XXXVII (1862), XXXVIII (1862) (This is a reprinting of the Clémencet-Caillau edition).

Some critical editions of Gregory's *Orations:*
1. Engelbrecht, A., editor. "Novem Oratione," translated into Latin by Rufinus (Orations nos. 2, 6, 16, 17, 26, 27, 38, 39, 40), *CSEL*, Vol. XLVI (1910).
2. Browne, C. G. and J. E. Swallow, editors (With introduction and translation into English). *Select Orations and Letters* in *NPNCF*, Series II, Vol. VII (1894), pp. 185–498.
3. Mason, Arthur James, translator and editor. *Five Theological Orations*. Cambridge: Cambridge University Press, 1899 (In the series "Cambridge Patristic Texts").

Works concerning Gregory:
1. Altaner, pp. 256–260.

2. Bardenhewer, Vol. III, pp. 162–188.

3. Benôit, Abbé Alphonse. *Saint Grégoire de Nazianze—sa Vie, ses Oeuvres et son Epoche.* Marseille: Olive, 1876.

4. Catandella, Q. "Gregorio Nazianzeno," *EC,* Vol. VI (1951), cols. 1088–1096.

5. Clémencet, Abbé Claude. "Grégoire de Nazianze," *PG,* Vol. XXXV (1885), cols. 147–242.

6. Dräseke, J. "Neuplatonisches in des Gregorios von Nazianz Trinitätslehre," *BZ,* Vol. XV (1906), pp. 141–160.

7. Loofs, Friedrich. "Gregorius von Nazianz," *RpTK,* Vol. VII (1899), pp. 138–146.

8. Pellegrino, Mich. *La Poesia di San Gregorio Nazianzeno.* Milano: Società Editrice, "Vita et Pensiero," 1932.

9. Plagnieux, Jean. *Saint Grégoire de Nazianze Théologien.* Paris: Editions franciscaines, 1952 (In the series: "Etudes de Sciences religieuses").

10. Ullmann, Carl. *Gregorius von Nazianz der Theologe.* Darmstadt: Leske, 1825; 2nd edition Gotha: Perthes, 1866 (Vol. V of Ullmann's *Werke in fünf Bänden*); English translation by G. V. Cox. London, 1851.

HEIDRICH, ERNST, German art historian, was born in Nakel on July 5, 1880, and died near Dixmuiden on November 4, 1914. He was a student of the noted scholar Wölfflin and taught at Basel (1911) and Strassburg (1914).

His major works:

1. *Altdeutsche Malerei.* Jena: Diederichs, 1908.

2. *Altdeutsche Meister.* Jena: Diederichs, 1916.

3. *Altniederländische Malerei.* Jena: Diederichs, 1910.

4. *Beiträge zur Geschichte und Methode der Kunstgeschichte.* Basel: Schwabe, 1917.

5. *Dürers schriftlicher Nachlaß. Familienchronik. Gedenkbuch. Tagebuch der niederländischen Reise. Briefe. Reime. Auswahl aus den theoretischen Schriften.* Introduction by Heinrich Wölfflin. Ed. by Ernst Heidrich. Complete new edition. Berlin: Bard, 1910 (Original edition, 1908).

6. *Dürer und die Reformation.* Leipzig: Klinkhardt & Biermann, 1909.

7. *Geschichte des Dürerschen Marienbildes.* Leipzig: Hiersemann, 1906.

8. *Vlaemische Malerei.* Jena: Diederichs, 1913.

Concerning Heidrich cf.

1. Rintelen, Friedrich. "Nachruf auf Ernst Heidrich" in *Reden und Aufsätze.* Ed by Edith Rintelen. Basel: Schwabe, 1927.

HEINZEL, RICHARD, professor of the older German language and literature, was born in Capo d'Istria on November 3, 1838, and committed suicide in Vienna on April 2, 1905. He taught in Graz (1868) and Vienna (1873). In 1905 a monument was erected in his honor at the University of Vienna.

Some of his major writings:

1. *Abhandlungen zum altdeutschen Drama.* Wien: Gerold's Sohn, 1896.

2. *Beschreibung des geistlichen Schauspiels im deutschen Mittelalter.* Hamburg-Leipzig: Voss, 1898.

3. *Kleine Schriften.* Ed. by M. H. Jellinek and C. von Kraus. Heidelberg: Winter, 1907 (Contains a bibliography of his works).

4. *Über die französischen Gralsromane.* Wien: Tempsky, 1892.

5. *Über die Nibelungensage.* Wien: Gerold's Sohn, 1885.

6. *Über die ostgotische Heldensage.* Wien: Tempsky, 1889.

7. *Über den Stil der altgermanischen Poesie.* Straßburg: Trübner, 1875.

8. *Über Wolframs von Eschenbach Parzival.* Wien: Tempsky, 1893.

Concerning Heinzel cf.:

1. Schönbach, A. E. "Richard Heinzel," *Biographisches Jahrbuch und deutscher Nekrolog* (Berlin), Vol. X (1907).

2. Singer, Samuel. "Richard Heinzel," *Aufsätze und Vorträge.* Tübingen: Mohr, 1912.

HENRI D'ANDELI (Thirteenth-century trouvère) is best known for his didactic poem *Bataille des sept Arts* (written after 1235). In form the poem is of the verse-disput or "débat" genre, a literary type derived from late Latin verse. D'Andeli's work is said to have been inspired by the *Psychomachia* of the fourth-century Latin poet Prudentius; his was a lengthy metrical dispute between various virtues and their opposing vices.

A poet of more than average potential, D'Andeli's verses transcend the limits of the genre and display an individuality and enlightenment not often found in writers of singularly moralistic verse. The theme of the poem is based on the quarrel concerning the relative merits of the "ancients" versus the "moderns," a quarrel that forms the very core of later seventeenth-century philosophy and literature. Developing his theme as a defense of the classics (the point of view of the University of Orleans against that of the University of Paris), D'Andeli marshals a host of representative figures who defend the concept of pure literature ("grammaire") against the converts to the newer form of literary dialectical argumentation ("logique"). The champions of classical standards are defeated and consequently the poem, closing on a despairing note, bemoans that the times are completely given over to emptiness. Only with the dawn of a new, more sophisticated generation will true culture be restored to its rightful hegemony. Although somewhat too sanguine, if not actually pessimistic, D'Andeli did prophesy correctly, for within two generations the longed-for rebirth of culture in the classical vein was born again in the person of Petrarch.

Through his emphasis on the value and beauty of the standards and modes of the classics, D'Andeli definitely can be considered a herald of the dawning Renaissance and his poem, although not necessarily an exceptional work of art, does serve as a first-rank cultural document of thirteenth-century France.

HILDEBERT OF LAVARDIN (ca. 1056–1133/1134), Bishop of Le Mans, Archbishop of Tours and medieval poet, was born at the castle of Lavardin near Montoir on the Loire in 1056 and died December 8, 1133 (or 1134). He is first heard of in 1085 when he was made *scholasticus* at the cathedral school in Le Mans. Appointed archdeacon in 1091, he became Bishop of Le Mans five years later. When William II of England captured Le Mans in 1099, Hildebert was suspected of plotting against him with the French and was called to England. He returned to his See a year later.

A stern but just man, Hildebert banished from his dioceses any one convicted of heresy. He took part in many of the synods and councils of the twelfth century and presided over the Synod of Nantes (1127) whose decrees (preventing incestuous marriages, conferring of Holy Orders upon sons of ecclesiastics and obtaining of ecclesiastical benefices by inheritance) were ratified by Pope Honorius II in May, 1128. For a time Hildebert supported the antipope Anacletus II, elected after the death of Honorius II, but through the efforts of St. Bernard, who praised Hildebert as one of the great pillars of the Church, he was convinced of his error and became a supporter of Innocent II. Besides being one of the greatest hymnologists of the Middle Ages, he was also the author of numerous works in prose. His writings, both the genuine and the spurious, have been edited by Migne (Cf. *PL*, Vol. CLXXI, cols. 1–1459)— this is, however, an uncritical edition. The prose works proven genuine are:

1. Most of the epistles (*PL*, CLXXI, cols. 141–312).
2. The life of Queen Radegundis (*Ibid.*, cols. 967–988).
3. The life of St. Hugh of Cluny (*PL*, Vol. CLIX, cols. 857–894).
4. "De querimonia et conflictu carnis et spiritus" (an ascetical treatise) Vol. CLXXI, cols. 989–1004).

Of the poetical works the following are genuine:
1. "Versus de mysterio missae" (*P.L.*, Vol. CLXXI, cols. 1177–1196).
2. "De operibus sex diverum" (*Ibid.*, cols. 1213–1218).
3. "Inscriptionum christianarum libellus" (*Ibid.*, cols. 1281–1288).
4. "Vita Beatae Mariae Aegyptiacae" (*Ibid.*, cols. 1321–1340).
5. "Historia de Mahomete" (*Ibid.*, cols. 1345–1366).

Works about Hildebert of Lavardin:
1. Dieudonné, Adolphe. *Hildebert de Lavardin, Evêque du Mans, Archevêque de Tours. Sa Vie et ses Lettres.* Paris: Picard, 1898.
2. Barth, Franz Xaverius. *Hildebert von Lavardin und das kirchliche Stellenbesetzungsrecht.* Stuttgart: F. Enke, 1906 (In the series: "Kirchenrechtliche Abhandlungen," Hefte 34–36).
3. Deservilliers, Comte P. de. *Un Evêque du douzième Siècle. Hildebert et son Temps.* Paris: Bourguet et Calais, 1876.

4. Hauréau, Jean-Barthélemy. *Mélanges poétiques d'Hildebert de Lavardin.* Paris: Pedone-Lauriel, 1882.

5. Hébert-Duperrón, Abbé Victor. *De venerabilis Hildeberti, vita et scriptis.* Bayeux: Delarue, 1860.

HUGH OF ST. VICTOR (ca. 1096–1141), medieval theologian and mystic, is believed to have been born at Hartingham in Saxony and belonged to the family of the Counts of Blankenburg. Educated by the canons regular of St. Augustine at Hammersleben near Halberstadt, he took their habit and went to the monastery of St. Victor at Paris in 1115, which had become famous for its learning under William of Champeaux. In 1133 he was charged with the direction of studies and was made prior of the abbey.

As a philosopher and theologian, he was deeply influenced by the Platonic tradition transmitted through St. Augustine (he was called "Alter Augustinus") and Dionysius the Areopagite about whose *Celestial Hierarchy* he wrote a commentary. His principal theological work is the *De Sacramentis Christianae Fidei* in which he develops a symbolist conception of the universe, according to which every creature is the sensible expression of a Divine thought. The mystic way leads from natural thought (cogitation) through the intuitive meditation by which the soul tries to discover the Divine thoughts hidden under the veil of both creatures and the Scriptures (*meditatio*) to purity of life and thence to loving contemplation (*contemplatio*). Accordingly reason plays an important part in his system; faith is above reason and thus can tolerate rational investigation. He thus rescued the dialectic method from the discredit brought on it by Abelard and prepared the way for the great Schoolmen of the thirteenth century.

The *Opera omnia* of Hugh of Saint Victor:

1. *Hugonis de Sancto Victoire Opera Propuedeutica. Practica geometriae, De grammatica, Epitome Dindimi in philosophiam.* Edited by Roger Baron. Notre Dame, Ind.: University of Notre Dame Press, 1966 (Vol. 20 in Publications in Medieval Studies Series).

2. Migne, *PL*, Vols. CLXXV–CLXXVII.

Some individual editions:

1. "De Grammatica," translated into French by J. Leclercq, O.S.B. in *AHdlMA*, Vol. XVIII (1943), pp. 263–322.

2. "Epitome in Philosophiam" and "De Contemplatione et eius Speciebus," published by J.B. Arthélemy Hauréau in *Hughes de St.-Victor. Nouvel Examen de l'Edition de ses Oeuvres*. Paris: Pagnerre, 1859, pp. 161–175 and 177–210 respectively.

3. "De Sacramentis," translated into English by R.J. Deferrari in *Spec*, Vol. LVIII (1951).

4. "Soliloquium de Arrha Animae" and "De Vanitate Mundi" edited by K. Müller in *KTVU*, Vol. CXXIII (1913); English translation of the former by Frank Sherwood Taylor. *The Soul's Betrothal Gift*. London: Dacre, 1945.

5. "De Tribus Maximus Circumstantiis Gestorum," translated into English by W.M. Green in *Spec*, Vol. XVIII (1943), pp. 484–493.

Literature concerning Hugh of St. Victor:

1. Châtillon, J. "De Guillaume de Champeaux à Thomas Gallus. Chronique d'Histoire littéraire et doctrinale de l'Ecole de Saint-Victor," Section II, "Hughes de Saint-Victor," *RMA1*, Vol. VIII (1952), pp. 147–162.

2. Croydon, F.E. "Notes on the Life of Hugh of St. Victor," *JTS*, Vol. XL (1939), pp. 232–253.

3. Hauréau, J. Barthélemy. *Les Oeuvres de Hughes de Saint-Victor*. Paris: Hachette, 1886.

4. Mignon, Chanoine Armand. *Les Origines de la Scolastique et Hughes de Saint-Victor*. 2 Vols. Paris: Lethielleux, 1895.

5. Ostler, H. "Die Psychologie des Hugo von St. Viktor," *BGPM*, Vol. VI: Heft 1 (1906).

6. Piolanti, A. "Ugo di San Vittore,"*EC*, Vol. XII (1954), cols. 711–713 (Contains a current bibliography).

7. Überweg, Vol. II, pp. 261–267, bibliography p. 709.

8. Vernet, F. "Hughes de Saint-Victor," *DTC*, Vol. VII (Part 1, 1922), cols. 240–308 (Contains a bibliography).

9. Weisweiler, Heinrich. *Die Wirksamkeit der Sakramente nach Hugo von St. Viktor*. Freiburg im Br.: Herder, 1932.

JANITSCHEK, HUBERT (1846–1893), German art historian, was born in Troppau (Silesia), October 30, 1846, and died in Leipzig, June 21, 1893. He was educated at Gratz (Austria) from 1868 to 1873, pursued his study of the history of art in Italy (1873–1877) and then served as custodian of the Austrian Museum of Art and Industry in

Vienna for two years. He taught successively at Prague (1880), Strassburg (1881) and Leipzig (1891). His primary field of interest was the Italian Renaissance and its effects on the development of art in Germany.

Among his major writings:

1. *Die Gesellschaft der Renaissance in Italien und die Kunst. Vier Vorträge.* Stuttgart: Spemann, 1879.

2. *Die Geschichte der deutschen Malerei.* Vol. III of *Geschichte der deutschen Kunst.* 5 Vols. Berlin: Grote, 1887–1890. Contents:

Vol. I. *Die deutsche Baukunst* (R. Dohme)

Vol. II. *Die deutsche Plastik* (W. Bode)

Vol. III. *Geschichte der deutschen Malerei* (Janitschek)

Vol. IV. *Der deutsche Kupferstich und Holzschnitt* (E. v. Lützow)

Vol. V. *Das deutsche Kunstgewebe* (J. v. Falke)

3. *Die Kunstlehre Dantes und Giottos Kunst.* Leipzig. Brockhaus, 1892.

4. *Kunst und Künstler des Mittelalters und der Neuzeit. Biographien und Charakteristiken.* The entire series was edited by R. Dohme. Leipzig: Seemann, 1875–1880. Janitschek contributed:

a. *Andrea del Sarto* (Vol. XVI)

b. *Tintoretto* (Vol. XXVI)

c. *Paolo Veronese* (Vol. XXVII)

d. *Die Malerschule von Bologna* (Vols. LXV–LXVI)

e. *Giovanni Bellini* (Vols. LXVII–LXVIII)

5. "Zwei Studien zur Geschichte der karolingischen Malerei" in *Strassburger Festgruss an Anton Springer zum 4. Mai 1885.* Stuttgart: Spemann, 1885, pp. 1–30. (Also contains: A. Michaelis, "Michelangelos Leda und ihr antikes Vorbild," pp. 31–43.)

JUNGMANN, JOSEF (1830–1885), German priest-teacher and philosopher of sorts, was born in Münster, Westphalia, November 12, 1830, and died at Innsbruck, November 25, 1885. In 1850 he entered the German College in Rome and was ordained in 1855. He then entered the Jesuit Order and in 1858, even before completing his novitiate, he was chosen to fill the Chair of Elocution in the re-established Theological Faculty at the University of Innsbruck where he taught and counseled until his death.

Some of his many writings:

1. *Aesthetik.* 2 Vols. Freiburg im Br.: Herder, 1886.

2. *Die Andacht zum heiligen Herzen Jesu und die Bedenken gegen dieselbe.* Freiburg im Br.: Herder, 1885.

3. *Gefahren belletristischer Lektüre.* Innsbruck: Wagner, 1872.

4. *Das Gemüt und das Gefühlsvermögen der neueren Psychologie.* Innsbruck: Wagner, 1869; 2nd edition, *ibid.,* 1885.

5. *Die Schönheit und die schöne Kunst. Nach den Anschauugen der sokratischen und der christlichen Philosophie in ihrem Wesen dargestellt.* Innsbruck: Wagner, 1871.

6. *Theorie der geistlichen Beredsamkeit.* 2 Vols. 3rd edition. Innsbruck: Wagner, 1886.

Concerning his influence on his students and those with whom he worked cf.:

1. Croce, Walter "Joseph Jungmann," *ZKTh,* Vol. LXXX (1958), pp. 193–199.

2. "Joseph Jungmann," *BCJ,* Vol. IV, Col. 884.

3. Koch, L. "Joseph Jungmann," *JL,* Col. 944.

KAUTZSCH, RUDOLF (1868–1945), German art historian and son of the Protestant theologian and Hebraicist Emil Kautzsch, was born in Leipzig, December 5, 1868, and died in Berlin-Frohnau, April 26, 1945. He taught art history in Darmstadt (1903), Breslau (1911) and Frankfurt am Main (1915–1930). His major field of endeavor was medieval German architecture, evaluated within the total framework of German national and religious life. He was also particularly active in the movement to preserve the cathedrals in the Rheinland.

Some of his more important works:

1. *Die bildende Kunst und das Jenseits.* Jena: Diederichs, 1905.

2. *Die deutsche Illustration.* Vol. XLIV of *Aus Natur und Geisteswelt.* Leipzig: Teubner, 1904.

3. *Der Dom zu Worms.* Berlin: Deutscher Verein für Kunstwissenschaft, 1938.

4. *Die Entstehung der Frakturschrift.* Mainz: Gutenberg-Gesellschaft, 1922.

5. *Kapitellstudien. Beiträge zu einer Geschichte des spätantiken*

Kapitells im Osten vom 4. bis ins 7. Jahrhundert. Berlin: de Gruyter, 1936.

6. *Die Kunstdenkmäler in Wimpfen am Neckar.* Wimpfen: Denkmal Archiv zu Wimpfen, 1907.

7. *Der Mainzer Dom und seine Denkmäler.* 2 Vols. Frankfurt am Main-Berlin: Frankfurter Verlags-Anstalt, 1925.

8. *Romanische Kirchen im Elsass.* Freiburg im Br.: Urban, 1927.

9. *Der romanische Kirchenbau im Elsass.* Freiburg im Br.: Urban, 1944 (2nd edition 1948).

10. *Wandlungen in der Schrift und in der Kunst. Rede.* Mainz: Gutenberg-Gesellschaft, 1929.

LANGE, JULIUS (1838–1896), Danish art historian, was born in Vordingborg (Seeland), June 19, 1838, and died in Copenhagen, September 20, 1896. In 1870 he was appointed *Privatdozent* (unsalaried university lecturer) at the Danish Academy of Sciences and was awarded the same position at the University of Copenhagen the following year. In 1865 he was promoted to the rank of full professor, a rank and position which he maintained until his death.

The principal aim of his scholarly research was the representation of the human form as an object of artistic interest throughout the entire history of Western art; thereby he attempted to relate and evaluate the insights gained within the total framework of human history in general. In the course of his study he discovered what has become recognized as the "Law of Frontality" (i.e. a principle of sculpture [and by analogy] of painting and architecture) according to which the figure, painting or building is executed as viewed from full frontal position—in the strictest style the schematic composition of the front view is complete without lateral movement, the figure or building being divided into two symmetrical halves or arranged into one or more planes running parallel to the central plane with all lines converging at one central, albeit imaginary, point (cf. Herbert Read. *The Art of Sculpture.* New York: Pantheon Books, 1956, pp. 55, 61, 66, 75). Lange elaborates his theses in his monumental, three part study:

1. *Billedkunstens fremstilling af menneskeskikkelsen i dens aeldste periode indtil højdepunktet af den graeske kunst.* Avec un résumé en français: "Etude sur la représentation de la figure humaine dans l'art primitif jusqu'à l'art grec du ve siècle av. J.-C." Kjøbenhavn: Lunos Kgl. hof-bogtrykkeri (F. Dreyer), 1892.

2. *Billedkunstens fremstilling af menneskeskikkelsen i den graeske junsts første storhedstid.* Avec un résumé en français: "Etude sur la représentation de la figure humaine dans la première grande periode de l'art grec." Kjøbenhavn: Lunos Kgl. hof-bogtrykkeri (F. Dreyer), 1898.

3. *Menneskefiguren i kunstens historie fra den graeske kunsts anden blomstringstid indtil vort aarhundrede.* Kjøbenhavn: Bojesen, 1899.

A German translation of this work appeared in two parts:

1. *Darstellung des Menschen in der älteren griechischen Kunst.* Translated by Mathilde Mann. Edited and foreword by A. Furtwängler with the collaboration of C. Jörgensen. Strassburg: Heitz, 1899.

2. *Die menschliche Gestalt in der Geschichte der Kunst von der zweiten Blütezeit der griechischen Kunst bis zum XIX. Jahrhundert.* Translated by Mathilde Mann. Edited by P. Köbke. Strassburg: Heitz, 1903.

Some of his other important works:

1. *Breve (Correspondence).* Edited by P. Köbke. Kjøbenhavn: Gyldendal, 1903.

2. *Guder og Mennesker hos Homer (Gods and Men in Homer).* Kjøbenhavn: Gyldendal, 1881.

3. *Om Kunstvaerdi (On Art Values).* Kjøbenhavn: Gad, 1876.

4. *Udvalgte Skrifte (Selected Works).* Edited by P. Kölbe and Georg Brandes. 3 Vols. Kjøbenhavn: Gyldendal, 1900–1903.

Although none of his works has been translated into English, most of them have appeared in German. Besides his *magnum opus* mentioned above, four other important works should be noted:

1. *Briefe (Breve).* Translated by Ida Jacob-Anders. Strassburg: Heitz, 1903.

2. *Studien über Leonardo da Vinci.* Translated by Ida Jacob-Anders. Strassburg: Heitz, 1911.

3. *Studien über Michelangelo.* Translated by Ida Jacob-Anders. Strassburg: Heitz, 1903.

4. *Vom Kunstwert.* Translated by Ferdinand Nagler. Zürich: Amalthea, 1925.

Concerning Lange, cf.:

1. Brandes, Georg. *Julius Lange. Breve fra hans Ungdom.* Kjøbenhavn: [Gyldendal (?)] 1898; translated into German by Alfred Forster. Leipzig-Berlin: Brasdorf, 1899.

———

Liliencron, Rochus, Freiherr von (1820–1912), German musicologist and philologist, was born in Plön, December 8, 1820, and died in Koblenz, March 5, 1912. He taught in Bonn (1848), Kiel (1850) and Jena (1854) and in 1848 diplomatically represented Schleswig-Holstein at the Prussian court in Berlin. In 1854 he was appointed director of the Court Choir and chief librarian in Meiningen, a position which he maintained until 1869 when as managing editor of the *Allgemeine Deutsche Biographie* he moved to Munich. For a few years he also served as Monastery Provost in Schleswig.

Among his philological works, all of which demonstrate his thorough knowledge of the history, culture and music of medieval Germany, the most significant are: 1) *Über die Nibelungenhandschrift "C". Sendschreiben an Herrn Hofrat Professor Göttling.* Weimar: Böhlau, 1856—a work which proved that the "C" manuscript of the *Nibelungenlied* was its earliest manuscript form; 2) *Historische Volkslieder der Deutschen vom 13. bis zum 16. Jahrhundert.* 4 Vols., plus one volume of melodies. Leipzig: Vogel, 1865–1869—a valuable critical edition of the texts and music of Germany from the late Middle Ages until the time of Martin Luther; 3) *Deutsches Leben im Volkslied um 1530.* Berlin-Stuttgart: Spemann, 1885 (Vol. XIII of Kürschner's "Deutsche National-Literatur")—an unexcelled collection of songs that serve as a living monument of the culture of Reformation Germany. Of his music-historical studies the most noted are: 1) *Die liturgischmusikalische Geschichte des evangelischen Gottesdienstes von 1523 bis 1700.* Schleswig: Geigas, 1893; and 2) the four-volume *Lieder und Sprüche aus der letzten Zeit des Minnesanges.* Written in conjunction with W. Stade and arranged for a four-voiced male chorus. Weimar: Böhlau, 1854.

In 1900 he assumed the directorship of the series "Denkmäler deutscher Tomkunst," a project subsidized by the Prussian government. From 1875–1907 he directed the publication of the first fifty-three volumes of the *Allgemeine Deutsche Biographie*, a project that was completed by Alfred Dove in 1912. Liliencron also wrote a history of the series which he published in the *Göttingsche Gelehrte Anzeiligen*, Vol. CLX (1898). Among his many talents was also that of a *Novellendichter* as witnessed by his many charming if not great short stories (cf. *Zwei Novellen* ["Wie man in Amwald Musik macht" and "Die siebente Todsünde"]. Leipzig: Duncker und Humblot, 1903). A section of an incipient autobiography was published as *Frohe Jugendtage. Lebenserinnerungen.* Leipzig: Duncker und Humblot, 1902.

For information concerning Liliencron cf.:

1. Bettelheim, Anton. *Leben und Wirken des Freiherrn Rochus von Liliencron.* Berlin: Reimer, 1917.

2. Schröder, Edward. "Rochus von Liliencron," *BioJb*, Vol. XVII (1915).

LOEWE, JOHANN HEINRICH, 1808–1892

1. "John Bramhall, Bischof von Derry und sein Verhältniss zu Thomas Hobbes" in *Abhandlungen der Königlich-Böhmischen Gesellschaft der Wissenschaften* (Prag), VII. Folge, Vol. I (1886).

2. *Johann Emanuel Veith. Eine Biographie.* Wien: Braumüller, 1879.

3. *Lehrbuch der Logik.* Wien: Braumüller, 1881.

4. *Die Philosophie Fichtes nach dem Gesamtergebnisse ihrer Entwicklung und in ihrem Verhältnisse zu Kant und Spinoza.* Stuttgart: Nitzsche, 1862.

5. *Die speculative Idee der Freiheit, ihre Widersacher, ihre practische Verwertung.* Ed. by the Königlich-Böhmische Gesellschaft der Wissenschaften. Prag: Rivnác, 1890.

6. "Über ein angebliches ethisches Hinderniss der Abstammung der Menschheit von einem Menschenpaar" in *Abhandlungen der Königlich-Böhmischen Gesellschaft der Wissenschaften* (Prag), VI. Folge, Vol. I (1868).

LÖWY, EMANUEL (1857–1938), Austrian archaeologist and historian, was born in Vienna, September 1, 1857, and died there in 1938. As a young man Löwy travelled extensively, particularly in Greece and Asia Minor, and taught in both Rome (1899–1915) and Vienna (1918–1930). His major interest centered primarily in archaic and Hellenistic statuary, an area of art about which he wrote with both conviction and verve. His study *Die Naturwiedergabe in der älteren griechischen Kunst* (1900), tracing the representation of nature in archaic art forms, gave rise to an international controversy that as yet has not been fully resolved. The work was based on a positivistic preconception of a parabolic evolution in Greek art evincing a progressive conquest of naturalism and culminating in the works of Lysippus (about whom he wrote a monograph in 1891).

His basic writings:

1. *Die Anfänge des Triumphbogens*. Wien. Schroll, 1928.
2. *Griechische Inschrifttexte*. Wien und Prag: Tempsky, 1888.
3. *Die griechische Plastik*. 2 Vols. Leipzig: Klinkhardt und Biermann, 1911.
4. *Inschriften griechischer Bildhauer*. Leipzig: Teubner, 1885.
5. *Lysipp und seine Stellung in der griechischen Plastik*. Hamburg: Sammlung gemeinverständlicher wissenschaftlicher Vorträge, 1891.
6. *Die Naturwiedergabe in der älteren griechischen Kunst*. Rom: Loescher und Co., 1900.
7. *Neuattische Kunst*. Leipzig: Seemann, 1922.
8. *Polygnot. Ein Buch von griechischer Malerei*. 2 Vols. Wien: Schroll, 1929.
9. *Stein und Erz in der statuarischen Kunst*. Innsbruck: Wagner, 1915.
10. *Untersuchungen zur griechischen Künstlergeschichte*. Wien: Gerold's Sohn, 1883.
11. *Ursprünge der bildenden Kunst*. Wien: Hölder-Pichler-Tempsky, 1930.
12. *Zur Chronologie der frühgriechischen Kunst. Die Artemistempel von Ephesos*. Wien: Holder-Pichler-Tempsky, 1932.

Of Löwy's many works only one has appeared in English, namely number 6 above: *The Rendering of Nature in Early Greek Art*. Translated by John Fothergill. London: Duckworth and Co., 1907. In the context of Dvořák's statement, compare the works numbered 5, 8, 10 and 11, especially 11. Concerning Löwy, cf.:

1. Praschniker, C. "Emanuel Löwy," *AÖAW*, Vol. LXXXVIII (1938).

MÂLE, EMILE, French art historian, was born in Commentry (Allier) on June 2, 1862, and died at the Château Chalis (Département Oise) on October 10, 1954. In 1912 he was appointed professor of art his-

tory in Paris and in 1925 he was appointed the director of the Ecole
français d'archéologie in Rome. His discussions of the history of
French art history are accredited with having given new impulse to
iconographic research.

Some of his major studies include:

1. *L'art allemand et l'art français du moyen âge.* Paris: Colin,
1917 (5th edition 1940). (His whole interpretation was colored by
World War I and as a result he fell victim to a somewhat justified
censure and self-contradiction).

2. *L'art et les artistes du moyen âge.* Paris: Colin, 1927 (4th edition 1947).

3. *L'art religieux.* 4 vols. Paris: Colin, 1902–1932.

    a. *L'art religieux du XIIIe siècle en France* (1902).
(Translated into English from the third French edi-
tion by Dora Nussey as *Religious Art in France in the
XIII Century. A Study in Mediaeval Iconography and
its Sources of Inspiration.* London: Deut and Sons;
New York: Dutton, 1913).

    b. *L'art religieux de la fin du moyen âge en France.
Etude sur l'iconographie du moyen âge et sur les
sources d'inspiration* (1908).

    c. *L'art religieux du XIIe siècle en France. Etude sur les
origines de l'iconographie du moyen âge* (1922).

    d. *L'art religieux après le Concile de Trente. Etude sur
l'iconographie de la fin du XVIe siècle, du XVIIe siècle
du XVIIIe siècle en Italie, France, Espagne et Flan-
dres* (1932).

4. *La cathédrale de Reims.* Paris: Bloud & Gay, 1915.

5. *L'histoire de l'art.* Paris: Larousse, 1915.

MENENDEZ Y PELAYO, MARCELINO (1856–1912), Spanish literary critic
and aesthetician, was born in Santander, Spain, November 3, 1856,
and died there May 19, 1912. He studied for the most part at Barce-
lona and at the age of 22 was appointed to the Chair of Literature at
Madrid. At 25 he was chosen a member of the Spanish Academy.
Having mastered most of the major languages of Europe, he dominated scholarship in Spain at the turn of the century. In 1898 he gave
up his teaching career to become the director of the Biblioteca Na-

cional in Madrid. From 1910 until his death two years later he was also director of the Spanish Academia de la Historia. He twice served as a deputy in the Cortes, first in 1884 and again in 1891. His extensive and influential critical works are illuminated by his hyper-personalized combination of universal Christian principles vivified by his exuberant nationalism. From his prodigious output, I would cite three works that have pertinent reference to this present study, namely:

1. *Ciencia española*. Madrid: Pérez Dubrull, 1887–1888. (A study of the culture during and after the Inquisition.)

2. *Heterodoxes Españoles*. Madrid: Libreria católica de San José, 1880–1881. (A study of the politics, literature and history of Spain since the fourth-century Priscillian heresy [A type of Manichean dualism, advocating a modalistic doctrine of the Trinity and emphasizing the complete evil of all matter and bodily functions].)

3. *Historia de las Ideas esteticas*. Madrid: Pérez Dubrull, 1890–1903. (A history of European aesthetic philosophy and its influence on the arts).

He also wrote numerous volumes of poetry, studies on the origins of the Spanish novel, histories of medieval, mystical Latin-American poetry and edited several collections of Spanish classical drama (Calderón, Lope de Vega) as well as many anthologies of Spanish and Latin American prose and poetry.

Literature concerning Menendez y Pelayo:

1. Artigas Ferrando, Miguel. *La Vida y la Obra de Marcelino Menendez y Pelayo*. Zaragossa: Heraldo de Aragón, 1939 (Contains an excellent bibliography).

2. Bonilla y San Martín, Adolfo. *Marcelino Menendez y Pelayo*. Madrid: Fortanet, 1914.

3. Cayuela, Arturo Maria. *Marcelino Menendez y Pelayo. Orientador de la Cultura española*. Madrid: Nacional, 1939.

4. Eguía Ruiz, Constancio. *Literaturas y Literates. Estudios contemporáneos*. Madrid: Sáenz de Jubera, 1914, Vol. I, pp. 205–221.

5. García y García de Castro, Rafael. *Marcelino Menendez y Pelayo. El Sabio y el Creyente*. Madrid: FAX, 1940.

6. Laín Entralgo, Pedro. *Marcelino Menendez y Pelayo. Historia de sus Problemas intelectuales*. Madrid: Instituto de Estudios políticos, 1944.

7. Navarra, Enzo. "Marcelino Menendez y Pelayo," *EC*, Vol. VIII (1952), p. 682.

8. Torre, Guillermo de la. *Marcelino Menendez y Pelayo y las dos Españas*. Buenos Aires: Patronato hispano-argentino de Cultura, 1943.

MORELLI, GIOVANNI (1816–1891), Italian scholar and art critic, was born at Verona, February 25, 1816, and died at Milan, February 28, 1891. He studied medicine in Germany for a number of years, lived in Paris as an itinerant scholar for a time and then retired to his native Italy. He developed a new type of painting comparison (known today as the Morelli method) based on the assumption that the execution of smaller, individual details, e.g., ears or eyes, most faithfully represent the constant element of the personal style of any artist. He studied the collections of various galleries throughout Europe and uncovered many new and interesting facts concerning the true identity of disputed masterpieces. His basic writings were published under the pseudonym Iwan Lermolieff, an anagram based on the Italian form of his name.

Originally appeared in German:
1. *Kunstkritische Studien über italienische Malerei*. Vol. I: *Die Galerien Borghese und Doria Panfili in Rom*. Leipzig: Brockhaus, 1890; Vol. II: *Die Galerien zu München und Dresden*. Leipzig: Brockhaus, 1891; Vol. III: *Die Galerie zu Berlin*. Leipzig: Brockhaus, 1893. (This volume also contains a biographical study on Morelli by Gustav Frizzoni.)

His works appeared in English translation almost as soon as they appeared on the German market, cf.:
1. *Italian Masters in German Galleries. A Critical Essay on the Italian Pictures in the Galleries of Munich, Dresden and Berlin*. Translated by Mrs. Louise M. Richter. London: Bell and Sons, 1893.
2. *Italian Painters. Critical Studies of the Works*. Translated by Constance Jocelyn Ffoulkes. Introduction by the Right Hon. Sir A. H. Layard. London: Murray, 1892–1893.
For a minor biographical study of Morelli cf. Carl Brun, *ADB*, Vol. LII (1906).

"NAZARENES" is a designation for a group of young German artists who at the beginning of the nineteenth century not only opposed the accepted standards of the art academies which held to traditional classical art forms but also in a deepening of moral consciousness and religious sentiment perceived the necessary prerequisite for the vivification of a serious artistic spirit. In consequence of this basic orientation, they demanded a stringent self-discipline in the whole conduct of life of the members of their "school." Initially they derived their inspiration primarily from the religious artists of sixteenth-century Germany and then increasingly more from the early works of the Italian masters of the High Renaissance (Perugino, Raphael and Michelangelo).

On June 10, 1809, Friedrich Overbeck and five disciples from the Viennese Academy founded the society known as the "*Lukas-bruderschaft*," a brotherhood of artists established on the principles of a religious community. The society was transferred to Rome in 1810 where it moved into the vacant monastery of Sant'Isidoro. By 1811 the number of members had risen to twelve, at which time they were given the name "Nazarenes." At first the name was a term of ridicule, applied because of the supposed proselytizing efforts of the Catholic members who, under the guise of furthering art, were actually interested only in gaining converts to Catholicism. In point of fact several Protestant members did embrace the Catholic religion. Later, however, the name lost its sense of opprobrium and actually became a title of honor after the group had established its fame through the fresco decorations of the Casa Bartholdy and the paintings offered at the German art exhibition in Rome in 1819.

Until the majority of the group returned to Germany in 1830, their primary field of engagement was fresco painting; the most noted product of their combined effort was the Casino Massinio. After returning to Germany, the individual members began to pursue newer modes of personal expression; consequently by 1840 Nazarene art as a movement waned although the principles of the group continued to influence the German artists resident in Italy until late in the second half of the nineteenth century.

Literature concerning the group and its founder F. Overbeck:
    1. Brodnitz, Käthe. "Nazarener und Romantiker. Eine Studie zu

Friedrich Overbeck," *KS*, Heft 2 (1914).

2. Eberlein, Kurt Karl. "Kunst und Kunstgeschichte der Nazarener" in *Overbeck und sein Kreis* by Karl Georg Heise. München: Wolff, 1928.

3. Harnack, Otto. *Deutsches Kunstleben im Rom in Zeitalter der Klassik*. Weimar: Felber, 1896.

4. Kaufmann, Paul. *Auf den Pfaden nazarenischer und romantischer Kunst. Was meine Bilder erzählen*. Berlin: Stilke, 1922.

5. Noack, Friedrich. *Das deutsche Rom*. Dittmann, 1912.

6. ———. *Deutsches Leben in Rom*. Stuttgart: Cotta Nachf., 1907.

7. ———. *Das Deutschtum in Rom seit dem Anfang des Mittelalters*. 2 Vols. Stuttgart: Deutsche Verlagsanstalt, 1927.

PELLIZZARI, ACHILLE (1882–1948), Italian literary critic and professor of Italian literature, was born in Maglie (Lecce) in 1882 and died in Genova in 1948. From 1915 until his death he taught at the universities of Messina, Catania and Genova. Besides teaching and editing the periodical *Rassegna della letteratura italiana* (Genova), he produced a prodigious number of books; the list of books and articles written or edited by him is well over one hundred.

The following titles can only hint at the range of his literary pursuits:

1. *Biblioteca rara. Testi e Documenti di Letteratura, d'Arte e di Storia*. Napoli: Perrella, 1915.

2. *Dal Duecento all' Ottocento*. Napoli: Perrella, 1914.

3. *Il Dittamondo e la Divina Commedia*. Pisa: Mariotti, 1905.

4. *Orme di Dante in Val di Magra*. Sarzana: Costa, 1906.

5. *Il Quadrivio nel Rinascimento*. Napoli: Perrella, 1924.

6. *Studi manzoniani*. Napoli: Perrella, 1914.

7. *I Trattati attorno le Arti figurative in Italia e nella Penisola Iberica dall'Antichità classica al Rinascimento e al Secolo XVIII. Vo. I: Dall'Antichità classica al Secolo XIII*. Napoli: Perrella, 1915.

8. *Vita e Opere di Guittone d'Arezzo*. Pisa: Nistri, 1904.

Concerning Pellizzari cf. the articles about him in the *Annuario Università Messiana* (1911–1912), pp. 142 ff. and in the following volumes.

PETER LOMBARD (ca. 1100–1160), medieval philosopher, was born near Novara in Lombardy and died in Paris in 1160. After studying at Bologna and Reims, he went to Paris (1139) where he taught at the Cathedral School. In 1159, shortly before his death, he was appointed Bishop of Paris. His commentaries on the Pauline Epistles and on the Psalms were written before 1143 and his chief work, the *Sententiarum libri quator*, between 1148 and 1150.

This last work, to which he owes his fame, is arranged in four books: 1) the Trinity, 2) the Creation and Sin, 3) the Incarnation and the Virtues and 4) the Sacraments and the Four Last Things. It contains a wealth of quotations from the Latin Fathers but after Lombard's death was violently attacked on the grounds of its Abelardian Christological Nihilianism, i.e., the doctrine that Christ according to His human nature is nothing. However this view was offered only as an opinion. It was attacked again at the Fourth Lateran Council (1215) but was pronounced orthodox. After this latter rehabilitation, it became the standard textbook of Catholic theology during the Middle Ages. The book, which owed its success to its lucid arrangement, its comprehensiveness and its lack of subjective bias, was commented on by nearly all theologians of repute and was even versified. Although it was finally superseded by the *Summa Theologica* of St. Thomas Aquinas, in the seventeenth century, commentaries were still being produced, among the last being that of the Jesuit J.M. de Ripalda (1635).

The *Opera omnia* of Peter Lombard:
1. Migne, *PL*, Vols. CXCI–CXCII.

Literature concerning Peter Lombard:
1. Baltzer, O. "Die Sentenzen des Petrus Lombardus," *SGTK*, Vol. III:3 (1902).
2. Espenberger, J. N. "Die Philosophie des Petrus Lombardus und ihre Stellung im zwölften Jahrhundert," *BGPM*, Vol. III:5 (1901).
3. Ghellinck, S.J., J. de. *Le Mouvement théologique du XIIe Siècle*. Paris: Gabalda, 1914, pp. 73–244; reprinted in *ML*, "Section historique," Vol. X (1948), pp. 113–373.
4. ———. "Peter Lombard," *CE*, Vol. XI (1911), pp. 768–769.

5. ———. "Pierre Lombard," *DTC,* Vol. XII (Part 2, 1935), cols. 1941–2019 (Contains an excellent Lombard-bibliography).

6. Protois, Abbé Felix. *Pierre Lombard, Evêque de Paris . . . Son Epoque sa Vie, ses Ecrits, son Influence.* Paris: Palmé, 1880.

7. Schupp, Johann. *Die Gnadenlehre des Petrus Lombardus.* Freiburg im Br.: Herder, 1932.

8. Seeberg, S. "Petrus Lombardus," *RpTK,* Vol. XI (1902), pp. 630–642.

9. Überweg, Vol. II, pp. 274–276, bibliography pp. 710–711.

PINDER, WILHELM (1878–1949), German art historian, was born in Kassel, June 25, 1878, and died in Berlin, May 13, 1949. He taught art history in Darmstadt (1910), Breslau (1917), Strassburg (1918), Leipzig (1920) and München (1927). Gifted with an extraordinary sense of form and perspective, he devoted his life to the study and interpretation of German art within the total framework of European civilization with particular emphasis on the methods, aims and achievements of medieval and baroque architecture and sculpture.

The list of his published material is indeed vast; the following works serve only to indicate the scope of his interests:

1. *Der Bamberger Dom und seine Bildwerke.* 3rd edition. Berlin: Deutscher Kunstverlag, 1935.

2. *Deutsche Barockplastik.* Königstein im Taunus-Leipzig: Langewiesche, 1933.

3. *Deutsche Burgen und feste Schlösser.* Königstein im Taunus-Leipzig: Langewiesche, 1938.

4. *Deutsche Dome des Mittelalters.* Düsseldorf-Leipzig: Langewiesche, 1910.

5. *Die deutsche Plastik vom ausgehenden Mittelalter bis zum Ende der Renaissance.* Potsdam: Athenaion, 1924–1929.

6. *Gesammelte Aufsätze aus den Jahren 1907–1935.* Edited by Leo Bruhns. Leipzig: Seemann, 1938.

7. *Goethe und die bildende Kunst.* München. Verlag der Bayerischen Akademie der Wissenschaften, 1933.

8. *Der Kölner Dom.* Königstein im Taunus-Leipzig: Langewiesche, 1934.

9. *Das Problem der Generation in der Kunstgeschichte Europas.* Berlin: Frankfurter Verlagsanstalt, 1926.

10. *Zur Rhythmik romanischer Innenräume in der Normandie.* Strassburg: Heitz, 1904–1905 (Hefte 24 and 36 of the series "Zur Kunstgeschichte des Auslandes").

Literature concerning Pinder:

1. Boehlich, W. "Wilhelm Pinder," *HAR*, 3 Jhrg. (1948–1949), p. 524.

2. *Festschrift für Wilhelm Pinder zum 60. Geburtstag.* Leipzig: Seemann, 1938.

3. Jantzen, H. "Wilhelm Pinder," *ZKg*, Vol. I: 1–2 (1947), pp. 73–76.

4. Meyer, Bruno. *Wer die Sterne zu Freunden nahm. . . . Dank, Bekenntnis und Besinnung. Briefe an Wilhelm Pinder.* Leipzig: Goten, 1944.

5. Weigert, H. "Wilhelm Pinder zum 60. Geburstag," *DZ*, Vol. VI: 25 (1938), p. 8.

6. "Wilhelm Pinder zum 70. Geburtstag," *Aufbau* (Berlin), 4. Jhrg. (1948), p. 524.

RIEGL, ALOIS (1858–1905), Austrian art historian and scholar, was born in Linz, January 14, 1858, and died in Vienna, June 17, 1905. Like Wickhoff, he was also actively engaged in the Austrian Museum for Art and Industry and likewise accepted a professorship in art history at the University of Vienna (1897).

In his lectures and published works, he attempted to overcome the excessively "schoolish," aesthetically oriented rigidity vis-à-vis contemporary criticism and evaluation of art per se as well as the historical development of art. Basing his own criticism upon a severely formalistic approach, he developed a new psychical-historical method of interpretation by means of which he rediscovered the grandeur of late Roman art in all of its orginality; this was a period in the history of art that until his time had been considered a period of complete decadence. He not only illuminated its significance in the development of medieval art, but he also attempted to clarify decisively certain basic questions concerning the origins of classical and oriental ornamentation. In the last years of his life, he actively concerned himself with the problem of the renovation of art monuments and the extension of state aid in the erection and preservation of new but similar monuments and museums.

Some of his major works include the following:

1. "Altorientalische Teppiche," *JbSAK*, Vol. XIII (1892).

2. *Die Entstehung der Barockkunst in Rom. Akademische Vorlesungen.* Edited from his literary remains by Arthur Burda and Max Dvořák. Wien: Schroll, 1908.

3. Filippo Baldinucci's *Vita di Giovanni Lorenzo Bernini.* Translated into German and edited by A. Riegl. Edited from Riegl's literary remains by Arthur Burda and Oskar Pollak. Wien: Schroll, 1912.

4. *Gesammelte Aufsätze.* Edited from his literary remains by Karl Maria Swoboda with an Introduction ("Die Quintessenz der Lehren Alois Riegls") by Hans Sedlmayr. Augsburg-Wien: Filser, 1929.

5. "Das holländische Gruppenporträt," *JbSAK*, Vol. XXIII: 3/4 (1902). (This essay also appeared as a monograph in Wien: Österreichische Staatsdruckerei, 1931.)

6. *Die spätrömische Kunstindustrie nach den Funden in Österreich.* 2 vols. Wien: Österreichische Staatsdruckerei, 1901–1923.

7. *Stilfragen. Grundlegungen zu einer Geschichte der Ornamentik.* Berlin: Siemens, 1893.

For information concerning Riegl cf. Max Dvořák, "Alois Riegl," *MkkZ*, 3. F. Vol. IV (1905), pp. 255–276. (This essay was reprinted in Dvořák's *Gesammelte Aufsätze zur Kunstgeschichte.* Edited by Karl Maria Swoboda and Julius Wilde. München: Pieper, 1929, pp. 279–298.)

RINTELEN, FRIEDRICH

1. *Giotto und die Giotto-Apokryphen.* München-Leipzig: Müller, 1912.

2. *Reden und Aufsätze.* Ed. by Edith Rintelen. Basel. Schwabe, 1927.

ROSCELLINUS (1050–1122?), also known as Roscelin, Rucelinus, or Rousellin, a monk of Compiègne, generally regarded as the founder of nominalism, was born in northern France about the middle of the eleventh century. He studied at Soissons and Reims, was attached to the cathedral of Chartres and became canon of Compiègne.

He taught a pronounced nominalism and postulated the argument that particular substances alone exist and that general concepts are mere names and words by means of which particular objects are divined. When he applied this reasoning to the doctrine of the Trinity and argued that the oneness of the divine nature was not real but that the three persons of the Godhead were three gods, he was condemned for heresy by a council convoked at Soissons (1092) and was obligated to retract his Tritheism. Apparently, however, he continued to teach his nominalistic dialectic, for he was again condemned in 1094 by a council at Reims and sought refuge in England. He was compelled to leave soon after for having attacked Anselm's doctrine of the incarnation. Later he taught at Tours, Locmenach or Lioches (where Abelard was his pupil) and Besançon; he is known to have lived as late as 1121. A letter addressed to Abelard, dealing chiefly with his Trinitarian doctrine, is the only extant document from Roscellinus' own hand.

Concerning Roscellinus, cf.:

1. Adlboch, B. "Roscelin und Sankt Anselm," *PJb*, Vol. XX (1907), pp. 442–456.
2. Barach, Karl Sigmund. "Zur Geschichte des Nominalismus vor Roscelin," *Kleine philosophische Schriften*. Neue Gesamtausgabe. Wien: Braumüller, 1878 (1st edition 1866).
3. De Wulf, Maurice. *History of Mediaeval Philosophy*. Translated by P. Coffey. 3rd edition. New York: Longmans, 1909, pp. 157–160.
4. Picavet, François. *Roscelin, Philosophe et Théologien*. Paris: Imprimerie nationale, 1896.
5. Reiners, Joseph. "Der Nominalismus in der Frühscholastik," *BGPM*, Vol. VIII:5 (1910). (Includes a translation of Roscellinus' letter to Abelard.)
6. Taylor, Henry Osborn. *The Mediaeval Mind. A History of the Development of Thought and Emotion in the Middle Ages*. London: Macmillans, 1911, Vol. I, p. 303; Vol. II, p. 339.

SCHLOSSER, JULIUS VON, Austrian art historian, was born in Vienna on September 23, 1866, and died there on December 1, 1938. From 1901 to 1922 he served as the director of the Kunsthistorisches Museum in Vienna and from 1922 until his death he was a professor of art history at the University of Vienna. His major interest lay in the area of the study of original sources and the history of the literature treating the development of art.

His major works include:
1. *Die Kunst des Mittelalters.* Berlin-Potsdam: Athenaion, 1923.
2. *Die Kunstliteratur. Ein Handbuch zur Quellenkunde der neueren Kunstgeschichte.* Wien: Schroll, 1924.
3. *Die Kunst- und Wunderkammern der Spätrenaissance. Ein Beitrag zur Geschichte des Sammelwesens.* Leipzig: Klinkhardt & Biermann, 1908.
4. *Leben und Meinungen des Florentiner Bildners Lorenzo Ghiberti.* Basel: Holbein, 1941.
5. *Lorenzo Ghibertis Denkwürdigkeiten.* 2 vols. Berlin: Bard, 1912.
6. *Die Wiener Schule der Kunstgeschichte.* Innsbruck: Wagner, 1934.

Concerning von Schlosser cf.:
1. "Festschrift für Julius Schlosser zum 60sten Geburtstag," *JbSW*, N.F. Vol. I (1927).
2. *Julius Schlosser. Festschrift zu seinem 60sten Geburtstag.* Ed. by Arpad Weixlgärtner and Leo Planiscig. Wien: Amalthea, 1927.
3. "Julius von Schlosser" in *Die Kunstwissenschaft der Gegenwart in Selbstdarstellungen.* Ed. by Johannes Jahn. Leipzig: Meiner, 1924.

SCHNAASE, KARL (1798–1875), German art historian, was born in Danzig, September 7, 1798, and died in Wiesbaden, May 20, 1875. In 1829 he was appointed procurator of the County Court in Düsseldorf and in 1848 he became a councillor to the Supreme Court in Berlin, a position which he maintained until he permanently moved to Wiesbaden in 1866.

His major work is the *Geschichte der bildenden Künste.* 7 vols. Düsseldorf: Buddeus, 1843–1864; 2nd edition 8 vols. Stuttgart: Ebner & Seubert, 1866–1879. This monumental work on the plastic arts is divided into three major parts covering 1) classical art, 2) medieval art, 3) art of the fifteenth century. Contents.

Part I: Classical Period

Vol. I. *Die Völker des Orients.* In conjunction with Karl von Lützow (1832–1897). 1866.

Vol. II. *Griechen und Römer.* In conjunction with Karl Friedrichs (1831–1871). 1866.

Part II: Medieval Period

Vol. III. *Altchristliche, byzantinische, muhammedanische, karolingische Kunst.* In conjunction with Johann Rudolf Rahn (1841–1912). 1869.

Vol. IV. *Die romanische Kunst.* In conjunction with Alwin Schultz (1839–1908) and Wilhelm Lübke (1826–1893). 1871.

Vol. V. *Entstehung und Ausbildung des gothischen Stils.* In conjunction with Alfred Woltmann (1841–1880). 1872.

Vol. VI. *Die Spätzeit des Mittelalters bis zur Blüthe der Eyck'schen Schule.* 1874.

Vol. VII. *Das Mittelalter Italiens und die Grenzgebiete der abendländischen Kunst.* In conjunction with Eduard Dobbert (1839–1899). 1876.

Part III

Vol. VIII. *Geschichte der bildenden Künste im 15. Jahrhundert.* In conjunction with Oscar Eisenmann (1842–1933). Edited by Wilhelm Lübke. 1879.

As a student of Hegel, Schnaase introduced the latter's system into the history of art and thus it is that his work is permeated with the willed desire to encompass and to evaluate as objectively and as free from prejudice as possible the art of all peoples and times; his work ranges the achievements and development of art before the totality of a cultural and *geistesgeschichtlichen* background. In opposition to a materialistic theory of art, he argued that artistic form cannot be derived from either imitation of natural objects, from the base material of the artifact itself or from any practical purpose which the finished product might serve. Rather it is a deeply rooted spiritual need in man himself that must and has determined the "what" and the "how" of artistic expression; thus man concretizes as *art* the drives and yearnings of his psyche.

Cf. also the following:

1. *Niederländische Briefe.* Stuttgart-Tübingen: Cotta, 1834. (These letters are the result of a trip through Holland and Belgium and are conceived as contributions to the history of art.)

2. *Über das Verhältnis der Kunst zum Christentum und besonders zur evangelischen Kirche.* Berlin: Schultz, 1852. (A lecture delivered before the Evangelical Union to promote ecclesiastical activities, March 1, 1852.)

Literature concerning Schnaase:

1. Donop, Karl S. "Karl Schnaase," *ADB*, Vol. XXXII (1891).
2. Heidrich, Ernst. *Beiträge zur Geschichte und Methode der Kunstgeschichte.* Basel: Schwabe, 1917.
3. Lübke, Wilhelm. "Karl Schnaase. Biographische Skizze," Vol. VIII of Schnaase's *Geschichte der bildenden Künste.* Stuttgart: Ebner & Seubert, 1879, pp. XV–LXXXIV.
4. MacMillian, L. K. *Die Kunst- und Geschichtsphilosophie Karl Schnaases.* Dissertation, University of Bonn, 1933.
5. Waetzoldt, Wilhelm. *Deutsche Kunsthistoriker.* Vol. II. Leipzig: Seemann, 1924.

SEECK, OTTO (1850–1921), German historian whose primary field of scholarship was the Roman Empire, was born in Riga, February 2, 1850, and died in Münster (Westphalia), June 29, 1921. He taught history at Greifswald (1881, associate professor until 1887, then promoted to full professor) and Münster (1907 until his death). He is reputed to have been one of the most thoroughly informed historians of the Roman Empire. With a strongly positivistic-Darwinistic bias, Seeck sought to explain the decadence and final collapse of the ancient world as caused by what he termed "the extermination of the best minds" of the Empire with the barbarian invasions serving more as a catalytic agent to a process of decay well advanced from within. His first important work was his edition of the *Notitia dignitatum* (a project recommended to him by Theodor Mommsen, his teacher and friend at the University of Berlin)—a critical edition which even today is considered to be of primary importance in the field. His major work, the six volume *Geschichte des Untergangs der antiken Welt*, although undisputably influenced by the Darwinistic theories of biological materialism, is nevertheless one of the dominant monuments in modern historiography; its vast wealth of biographical information and politico-sociological detail far outweighs in significance the pervading spirit of his interpretation of these specific facts, an interpretation which is at best debatable, if not actually questionable.

His basic writings:

1. "Die Briefe des Libanius," edited by Otto Seeck. *TUGaL*, N.F. Vol. XV:3/4 (1906).

2. "Die charakteristischen Unterschiede der Brüder van Eyck," *KGW*, N.F. Vol. III (1899).

3. *Die Entwicklung der antiken Geschichtsschreibung und andere populäre Schriften*. Berlin: Siemenroth uni Troschel, 1898.

4. *Die Geschichte des Untergangs der antiken Welt*. 6 Vols. Berlin: Siemenroth und Troschel, 1897–1920. Contents:

Vol. I: Part 1. *Die Anfänge Constantins des Grossen* (1897)
Part 2. *Verfall der antiken Welt* (Plus Appendix) (1898)
Vol. II: Part 3. *Die Verwaltung des Reiches* (1901)
Part 4. *Religion und Sittlichkeit* (Plus Appendix) (1901)
Vol. III: Part 4. (Conclusion) (Plus Appendix) (1909)
Vol. IV: Part 5. *Die Constantinische Dynastie* (Plus Appendix) (1911)
Vol. V: Part 6. *Vallentinian und seine Familie* (1913)
Part 7. *Die Auflösung des Reiches* (Plus Appendix) (1913)
Vol. VI: Part 7. (Conclusion) (Stuttgart: Metzler, 1920).

5. *Kaiser Augustus*. Bielefeld: Velhagen und Klasing, 1902. (In the series: "Monographien zur Weltgeschichte," No. 17.)

6. *Die Kalendertafel des Pontifices*. Berlin: Weidmann, 1885.

7. *Notitia dignitatum. Accedunt notitia urbis Constantinopolitanae et laterculi provinciarum*. Edited by Otto Seeck. Berlin-Leipzig: Weidmann, 1876.

8. *Die Quellen der Odyssee*. Berlin: Siemenroth, 1887.

9. *Regesten der Kaiser und Päpste für die Jahre 311–476 nach Christi*. 2 half Vols. Stuttgart: Metzler, 1918–1919.

10. *Russen und Balten*. 3 Vorträge. Bielefeld: Velhagen und Klasing, 1917.

11. [*Q. Aurelius*] *Symmachi quae superunt.* Edited by Otto Seeck. *MGH*, Vol. VI: 1. Teil (1883).

12. *Zeitphrasen.* Berlin: Siemenroth und Worms, 1892. (Seeck's discussion of a work entitled: *Rembrandt als Erzieher. Von einem Deutschen.*)

For information concerning Seeck, cf., Ludwig Radermacher, "[Otto] Seeck," *BJFkA*, Jhrg. 52 (1926).

SINGER, SAMUEL, German philologist, was born in Vienna on July 12, 1860, and died in Bern on December 5, 1948. He studied at the University of Vienna and received a doctorate in philosophy and law. With H. Maync he co-edited the collection "Sprache und Dichtung."

Some of his major writings include:

1. *Arabische und europäische Poesie im Mittelalter.* Berlin: Verlag der Akademie der Wissenschaften in Kommission bei G. Reimer, 1918.

2. *Germanisch-romanisches Mittelalter. Aufsätze und Vorträge.* Zürich-Leipzig: Niehans, 1935.

3. *Literaturgeschichte der deutschen Schweiz im Mittelalter.* Bern: Francke, 1916.

4. *Mittelalter und Renaissance. Die Wiedergeburt des Epos und die Entstehung des neueren Romans.* Tübingen: Mohr, 1910.

5. *Neue Parzival-Studien.* Zürich-Leipzig: Niehans, 1937.

6. *Die religiöse Lyrik des Mittelalters. Das Nachleben der Psalmen.* Bern: Franck, 1933.

7. *Wolfram und der Gral. Neue Parzival-Studien.* Bern: Lang, 1939.

8. *Wolframs Willehalm.* Bern: Francke, 1918.

Concerning Singer cf.:

1. *Festgabe Samuel Singer* (Überreicht zum 12. VII. 1930 von Freuden und Schülern). Ed. by Harry Maync. Tübingen: Mohr, 1930.

2. Schirokauer, A. and W. Paulsen. *Corona. Festschrift zum 8osten Geburtstage*, 1940.

3. WB, "Samuel Singer," *Neue Züricher Zeitung*, Fernausgabe Nr. 337, 1948.

Suger (ca. 1081–1151), Abbot of St.-Denis, near Paris, was born of humble parents in or near Paris. He entered the Abbey of St.-Denis ca. 1091, where he was a fellow-student of King Louis VI. In 1106 he became secretary to the Abbot and in 1107 was nominated Provost of Berneval in Normandy and in Toury in 1109. Louis VI sent him to the court of Pope Gelasius II (1118) at Maguelonne and later he spent some time at the court of Callixtus II. On returning from Italy (1122), he became Abbot of St.-Denis. The next year he went to Rome again to attend the Ninth Lateran Council.

In his first years as Abbot he was chiefly concerned with matters of state, but from 1127 to 1137 devoted himself to the thorough reform and reorganization of his monastery. During Louis VII's absence on the Second Crusade, which Suger personally opposed, he was one of the regents and discharged his duties with such success that Louis, on his return, rewarded him with the title "Father of the Country." His two panegyrics on Louis VI and Louis VII are primary historical sources for his age. His new church at St.-Denis, consecrated in 1144, about which he has left an account in his *Libellus de Consecratione Ecclesiae S. Dionysii* was the first building erected in the Gothic style. His methods of monastic government are set out in his *Liber de Rebus in Administratione sua gestis.*

Suger's works:
1. *Opera omia.* Edited by A Lecoy de La Marche. Paris: J. Renouard, 1867. (Part of the series published by the "Société de l'Histoire de France." Includes the twelfth-century life of Suger by Père Guillaume, O.S.B., pp. 377–411.)
2. English translation of Suger's *Sancti Dionysii Liber* by Erwin Panofsky in *Abbot Suger on the Abbey Church of St. Denis and its Art Treasures.* Princeton, N.J.: Princeton University Press, 1946.

Concerning Suger:
1. Aubert, Marcel. *Suger.* Paris: Editions de Fontenelle, 1950 (In the series "Figures monastiques").
2. Cartellieri, Otto. "Abt Suger von Saint Denis, 1081–1151," *HS,* Vol. XI (1898).
3. Gervaise, O.S.B., François Armand. *Histoire de Suger.* 3 Vols. Paris: Musier, 1721.

4. Huguenin, Alexandre. *Etude sur l'abbé Suger*. Paris: Thunot, 1855.

TERTULLIAN, QUINTUS SEPTIMUS FLORENS (ca. 160–ca. 220), African Church Father, was a native of Carthage. He received a solid pagan education and later became a lawyer and probably lived in Rome. Having been converted to Christianity in 195 or 196, he returned to Carthage where he became a catechist and, according to St. Jerome, a priest. His rigorist views led him to sympathize with Montanism, and ca. 207 he officially joined the sect. He later founded his own party, the Tertullianists, who survived until the fourth century.

Tertullian was the author of a long list of apologetic, theological, controversial and ascetic works in Latin as well as of a few writings in Greek. Of the Latin works most have been preserved but only in one manuscript, the ninth-century *Codex Agobardinus* (1622), whereas those in Greek have all been lost. His celebrated defense of Christianity, the *Apologeticus* (ca. 197), is addressed to the prefects of the Roman provinces and deals chiefly with the absurdity of the accusations brought against the Christians. He maintains that the Christians are good citizens who refuse to give Divine honors to the Emperor because of their monotheistic religion. His polemical treatise *De Praescriptione Haereticorum* (ca. 200) contains an exposition of the Catholic principles of tradition and authority by which he denies all heretics the right to interpret the Scriptures. His treatise *Against Marcion* (207 onwards) is a lucid exposition of the unity of God and the identity of Christ with the Jewish Messiah against Gnostic dualism. His *De Corona Militum* (211) and *De Idololatria* (ca. 211-212) are already saturated with Montanist spirit that would debar Christians of the Empire from most professions because of their connection with paganism.

The same rigorism appears in most of his later writings. What appears to be the first Christian writing on psychology is his *De Anima* (ca. 210) in which he stresses the unity of the soul and its life although, owing to his anti-Gnostic prepossessions, he assigns it to a certain corporality. He was the first Christian theologian to write in Latin, and in spite of his difficult style he can be said to have formulated the language of Western theology. The fact of Montanism did not prevent him from remaining dogmatically orthodox in most respects, and his contributions to the elucidations of the Trinitarian and Christological doctrines place him beside St. Augustine as the greatest Western theologian of the patristic period.

Tertullian's *Opera omnia:*
  a. Beatus Rhenanus, editor. Basle: J. Froben, 1521.
  b. In the series "Corpus Christianorum," edited by Janus Borleffs and E. Dekkers. 2 Vols. Turnholti: Brepols, 1954.
  c. Migne, *PL*, Vols. I–III. Paris: Migne, 1844.
  d. Oehler, K., editor. 3 Vols. Leipzig: Weigel, 1851–1854.
  e. Semler, editor. 6 Vols. Halle: Hendel, 1769–1776.

Some of his more important treatises:
  1. *Ad Nationen.* Edited by Janus Borleffs. Leiden: Brill, 1929; German translation by Max Haidenthaller. Paderborn: Schöningh, 1942. (Also contains a German translation of Tertullian's *De Anima.*)
  2. *Apologeticus.* Edited by John Mayor (Introduction and commentaries) and Alexander Souter (Translation). Cambridge: Cambridge University Press, 1917.
  3. *De Anima.* Edited by Jan Waszink (Introduction and commentaries). Amsterdam: Paris, 1933 (More elaborate edition 1947).
  4. *De Baptismo.* Edited by R. F. Refoulé (French translation and notes). Paris: Cerf, 1952; English edition by J. M. Lupton. Cambridge: Cambridge University Press, 1908. (Cf. also the "Ante-Nicene Christian Library" [Edinburgh, 1869–1870]. Edited by S. Thelwall, P. Holmes, *et al.*, Vols. VII, XI, XV and XVIII.)
  5. *De Testimonio Animae.* Edited by Willem Scholte Amsterdam: Vermeulen, 1934; G. Quispel. Leiden: Brill, 1952.

Works concerning Tertullian:
  1. Adam, Karl. "Der Kirchenbegriff Tertullians," *FcLDg*, Vol. VI: 4 (1907).
  2. Alès, Adhémar d'. *La Théologie de Tertullien.* Paris: Beauchesne, 1905.
  3. Altaner, pp. 122–134.
  4. Bardenhewer, Vol. II, pp. 377–442.
  5. Bardy, G. "Tertullien," *DTC*, Vol. XV (Part 1, 1946), cols. 130–171.
  6. Dekkers, E. *Tertullianus en de Geschiendnis der Liturgie.* Brugge (Belgium): De Kinkhorn, 1947.

7. Hoppe, Heinrich. *Beiträge zur Sprache und Kritik Tertullians.* Lund: Berlingska Boktryckeriet, 1932.

8. Monceaux, Paul. *Histoire littéraire de l'Afrique chrétienne.* 7 Vols. Paris: E. Leroux, 1901–1923 (Cf. especially Vol. I, *Tertullien et les Origines* [1901], pp. 177–461).

9. Pellegrino, M. "Tertulliano," *EC*, Vol. XI (1953), cols. 2025–2033. (Contains a bibliography of recent publications concerning Tertullian and his works.)

10. Quasten, Johannes. *Patrology.* Utrecht: Het Spectrum, 1953, Vol. II (*The Ante-Nicene Literature after Irenaeus*), pp. 246–340.

11. Waltzing, Jean Pierre. "Le Codex Fuldensis de Tertullien," *BFPLUL*, Vol. XXI (1914–1917).

12. Warfield, Benjamin B. *Studies in Tertullian and Augustine.* New York-London: Oxford University Press, 1930.

TROELTSCH, ERNST (1865–1923), German theologian and philosopher, was born in Augsburg in 1865 and died in Berlin, February 2, 1923. He taught theology at Göttingen (1891–1892), Bonn (1892–1894) and Heidelberg (1894–1915); from 1915 until his death in 1923 he was a professor of the History of Philosophy and Civilization at the University of Berlin. While at Berlin he became an ardent advocate of German annexation of French iron and coal territories in the Saarland (April, 1918) and received a portfolio in the Prussian Cabinet the following year.

One of Germany's foremost theologians, he was considered for a long time to be the outstanding leader among the clergy in the Pan-German movement which had gained an unprecedented ascendancy in Germany from about the turn of the century until after World War I. His theological convictions were influenced to no small degree by the views of his somewhat older contemporary Albrecht Ritschl (1822–1889); he emphasized the irreducibility of religion to any form of "experience" whatsoever inasmuch as it is grasped by faith and not reason and rests, therefore, on value judgments and not intellectual apprehension of series of a posteriori facts. Hence according to this view, theology must reject all philosophic idealism as irrelevant to Christian faith which is in essence committed to the "community" and not to individuals per se. The assessment of the "communal" role played by religion in society and in the cultural development of Western man is traceable in part to the theories of another contemporary, Wilhelm Dilthey (q.v). For

Troeltsch (via Dilthey) religion is founded solely on a priori reason and is derived immediately from the presence of the "absolute spirit" in the conscience of each individual. Ethics and the "moral life" are thus one continual battle or tension between the absolute norms and their realization in this world.

It should be noted in passing that in this "scheme of salvation" the concept "grace," the most basic principle of orthodox Christianity, is totally ignored; moreover this scheme echoes to a degree the theories propounded by another of Troeltsch's intellectual mentors, the neo-Kantian philosopher Wilhelm Windelband (1848–1915).

Some of his basic writings:

1. *Die Absolutheit des Christentums und die Religionsgeschichte.* Tübingen: Mohr, 1901.

2. *Augustin, die christliche Antike und das Mittelalter.* München-Berlin: Oldenbourg, 1915.

3. *Die Bedeutung des Protestantismus für die Entstehung der modernen Welt.* München-Berlin: Oldenbourg, 1906; English version: *Protestantism and Progress.* Translated by W. Montgomery. London: Williams and Norgate; New York: Putnam's Sons, 1912.

4. *Gesammelte Schriften.* 4 Vols. Tübingen: Mohr, 1912–1925.

5. *Der Historismus und seine Probleme.* Tübingen: Mohr, 1922 (Vol. XXIII of his *Gesammelte Schriften*); English version: *Christian Thought. Its History and Application.* London: University of London Press, 1923.

6. *Psychologie und Erkenntnistheorie in der Religionswissenschaft.* Tübingen: Mohr, 1905.

7. *Die Soziallehren der christlichen Kirchen und Gruppen.* Tübingen: Mohr, 1912 (Vol. I of his *Gesammelte Schriften*); English version: *The Social Teachings of the Christian Churches.* Translated by Olive Wyon. New York: Macmillan, 1931.

8. *Vernunft und Offenbarung bei Johann Gerhard und Melanchton.* Göttingen: Vandenhoeck und Ruprecht, 1891.

Literature concerning Troeltsch:

1. Bornhausen, Karl. "Ernst Troeltsch und das Problem der wissenschaftlichen Theologie," *ZTK* (1923), pp. 196–223.

2. Köhler, Walter. *Ernst Troeltsch.* Tübingen: Mohr, 1941.

3. Spaleck, Gerhardt. *Religionssoziologische Grundbegriffe bei Ernst Troeltsch.* Bleicherode: Nieft, 1937.

4. Spiess, Emil. *Die Religionstheorie von Ernst Troeltsch.* Paderborn: Schöningh, 1927.

5. Überweg, Vol. IV, pp. 600–605, with bibliography p. 722.

6. Vermeil, E. *La Pensée religieuse de Ernst Troeltsch.* Strassbourg: Université Faculté de Théologie protestante de Strassbourg, 1922 (Vol. II of the series "Etudes d'Histoire et de Philosophie religieuse").

VÖGE, WILHELM (1868–1952), German art historian, was born in Bremen, February 16, 1868, and died in Ballenstedt im Harz, December 30, 1952. From 1897 until 1908 he was actively engaged as a member of various museums in Berlin, at first as a technical advisor and then later as directorial assistant. From 1908 to 1916 he was a professor of art history at the University of Freiburg im Br.; he then moved to Ballenstedt im Harz where he remained until his death.

Vöge was particularly interested in promoting the knowledge of the art of medieval sculpture and was the first to assemble and catalogue the vast number of manuscripts in the monastery at Reichenau. He was also one of the first German scholars to study thoroughly the plastic arts of medieval France and endeavored to clarify the basic characteristics of that art which rendered it peculiarly "French" and then to trace the influence of this art on the development of similar art forms in Germany. Thus far only a minor part of his work has been published of which the most important follows.

1. *Die Anfänge des monumentalen Stiles im Mittelalter. Eine Untersuchung über die erste Blütezeit französischer Plastik.* Straßburg: Heitz, 1894.

2. "Die Bahnbrecher des Naturstudiums," *ZbK*, N.F. Vol. XXV (1914).

3. *Bildhauer des Mittelalters. Gesammelte Studien.* Foreword by Erwin Panofsky. Berlin: Mann, 1959 (Detailed Vöge-bibliography by Countess Carla Rothkirch, pp. 245–248).

4. *Die deutschen Bildwerke und die der anderen cisalpinen Länder.* 2nd edition. Berlin: Reimer, 1910.

5. "Eine deutsche Malerschule um die Wende des ersten Jahrhunderts. Kritische Studien zur Geschichte der Malerei in Deutschland im 10. und 11. Jahrhundert," *WZGK*, Vol. VII (Jhrg. 1891–1894).

6. *Die Elfenbeinbildwerke der königlichen Museen zu Berlin.* Berlin: Spermann & Reimer, 1900.

7. *Jörg Syrlin der Ältere und seine Bildwerke.* Berlin: Deutscher Verein für Kunstwissenschaft, 1950.

8. *Raffael und Donatello. Ein Beitrag zur Entwicklungsgeschichte der italienischen Kunst.* Straßburg: Heitz, 1896.

9. *Nicolas Hagnower, der Meister des Isenheimer Hochaltars und seine Frühwerke.* Freiburg im Br.: Urban, 1931.

VOSSLER, KARL, German philologist, was born in Hohenheim (near Stuttgart) on September 6, 1872, and died in Munich on May 19, 1949. He studied at Tübingen, Geneva, Strassburg, Rome and Heidelberg, from which last university he graduated in 1909 with a degree in Romance Philology. He then taught Romance Philology at the University of Würzburg. Besides his teaching career, Vossler was a government councillor in Munich (*Geheimrat*), co-edited the Heinemann Goethe-Ausgabe (Bibliographisches Institut) and edited the *Deutsche Vierteljahrsschrift für Literaturwissenschaft und Geistesgeschichte* (Stuttgart) for a number of years. In contrast to the literary historians of the philological historical school, Vossler considered each literary work as an artistic entity in itself and consequently judged each according to strictly formalistic and aesthetic principles.

Some of his major works include:

1. *Aus der romanischen Welt.* Leipzig: Koehler & Amelang, 1940.

2. *Das deutsche Madrigal. Geschichte seiner Entwicklung bis in die Mitte des XVIII. Jahrhunderts.* Weimar: Felber, 1898.

3. *Einführung in die spanische Dichtung des goldenen Zeitalters.* Hamburg: Behre, 1939.

4. *La Fontaine und sein Fabelwerk.* Heidelberg: Winter, 1919.

5. *Frankreichs Kultur im Spiegel seiner Sprachentwicklung. Geschichte der französischen Schriftsprache von den Anfängen bis zur klassischen Neuzeit.* Heidelberg: Winter, 1913.

6. *Geist und Kultur in der Sprache.* Heidelberg: Winter, 1925.

7. *Die Göttliche Komödie. Entwicklungsgeschichte und Erklärung.* 2 vols. Heidelberg: Winter, 1907–1910

  a. Vol. I: Part 1—*Religiöse und philosophische Entwicklungsgeschichte*

    Vol. I: Part 2—*Ethisch-politische Entwicklungsgeschichte*

b. Vol. II: Part 1—*Die literarische Entwicklungsgeschichte*
Vol. II: Part 2—*Erklärung des Gedichtes.*
8. *Italienische Literaturgeschichte.* Leipzig: Göschen, 1900.
9. *Leopardi.* München: Musarion, 1923.
10. *Lope de Vega und sein Zeitalter.* München: Beck, 1932.
11. *Poetische Theorien in der italienischen Frührenaissance.* Berlin: Felber, 1900.
12. *Positivismus und Idealismus in der Sprachwissenschaft.* Heidelberg: Winter, 1904.

Concerning Vossler cf.:
1. Beckmann, Ewald. "Gelehrter und Künstler," *Schwäbische Landeszeitung* (Stuttgart), Nr. 60, 1949.
2. Feist, Hans. "Begegnungen in Deutschland," *Neue Züricher Zeitung,* Fernausgabe Nr. 133, 1947.
3. Hohoff, Karl. "Karl Vossler," *Rheinischer Merkur* (Koblenz), Nr. 22, 1949.
4. Klemperer, Victor. "Vosslers Verhältnis zu Dante," *Deutsches Dante-Jahrbuch* (Leipzig), Vol. XXIX/XXX (1951).
5. Lerch, Eugen. "Ein europäischer Gelehrter," *Hamburger Allgemeine Zeitung* Nr. 6, 1949.
6. Merian-Genast, Ernst. "Karl Vossler," *Basler Nachrichten,* Nr. 220, 1949.

WECHSSLER, EDUARD, 1869–
1. "Eros und Minne" in *Vorträge der Bibliothek des Warburg Instituts.* Ed. by Fritz Saxl. Leipzig: Warburg Institut, 1923 (Vorträge, 1921–1922).
2. *Die Generation als Jugendreihe und ihr Kampf um die Denkform.* Leipzig: Quelle & Meyer, 1930.
3. *Hellas im Evangelium.* Berlin: Metzner, 1936.
4. *Jugendreihen des deutschen Menschen, 1773–1933.* Leipzig: Meiner, 1934.
5. *Molière als Philosoph.* 2nd rev. edition. Marburg a. L.: Ebel, 1915.
6. *Die Sage vom Heiligen Gral in ihrer Entwicklung bis auf Richard Wagners Parsifal.* Halle: Niemeyer, 1898.
7. *Über die Beziehungen von Weltanschauung und Kunstschaffen* (Im Hinblick auf Molière und Victor Hugo). Marburg a.

L.: Ebel, 1911 (Vortrag gehalten in der allgemeinen Sitzung der 51. Versammlung deutscher Philologen und Schulmännern in Posen am 5. Oktober 1911).

8. *Über die verschiedenen Redaktionen des Robert von Borron zugeschriebenen Graal-Lancelot-Cyclus.* Halle: Niemeyer, 1895.

WEESE, ARTHUR, German art historian, 1868–

1. *Die Bamberger Domsculpturen. Ein Beitrag zur Geschichte der deutschen Plastik des XIII. Jahrhunderts.* Strassburg: Heitz, 1897.

2. *Baldassare Peruzzis Anteil an dem malerischen Schmucke der Villa Farnesina* (Nebst einem Anhange: "Il taccuino di Baldassare Paruzzi" in der Communalbibliothek zu Siena). Leipzig: Hiersemann, 1894.

3. *Die Kunst im Buchgewerbe.* Bern: Verlag der Schweizerischen Gutenbergstube, Historisches Museum, 1913.

4. *München, eine Anregung zum Sehen.* Leipzig: Seemann, 1906 (3rd revised edition, Leipzig: Seemann, 1955).

5. *Der schöne Mensch in Mittelalter und Renaissance.* München-Leipzig: Hirth, 1900.

6. *Skulptur und Malerei in Frankreich im XV. und XVI. Jahrhundert.* Wildpark-Potsdam: Athenaion, 1927.

WICKHOFF, FRANZ (1853–1909), professor and scholar of art and art history, was born in Steyr (Upper Austria) on May 7, 1853, and died in Venice on April 6, 1909. In 1880 he was appointed curator of the Austrian Museum of Art and Industry in Vienna and then in 1885 he accepted a professorship in art history at the University of Vienna, a position which he held until his death.

He was primarily concerned with the content of art and strived for an intensified interpretation of art as the expression of any particular *age* as opposed to the individual personality of the artist himself. From 1905 until his death in 1909, Wickhoff served as one of the editors of the series *Beschreibendes Verzeichnis der illuminierten Handschiften in Österreich.* Vols. I–VII (Wien-Leipzig: Hiersemann, 1905–1917).

His *magnum opus* was the extensive study of the "Wiener Genesis" that appeared in *JbSAK*, Jhrg. XII–XIII, Vols. XV–XVI (1894–1895), Beilage (Supplement); this study was written in conjunction with Wilhelm Ritter von Hartel and was one which opened a wide area of late classical art to contemporary investigation and understanding. In this combined effort Hartel undertook the description of the manuscripts themselves and the Greek texts while Wickhoff contributed a discussion of the pictures and plates as well as a general introduction to the work. His introduction and commentaries appeared as a separate monograph in English as: *Roman Art. Some of its Principles and their Application to Early Christian Painting*. Translated and edited by Mrs. S. Arthur Strong. London: Heinemann; New York: Macmillan, 1900.

Another interesting study by Wickhoff is his "Die Bilder weiblicher Halbfiguren aus der Zeit und Umgebung Franz I. von Frankreich," *JbSAK*, Vol. XXII: 5 (1901), pp. 221–245. His collected works were published posthumously and were edited by Max Dvořák (cf. Franz Wickhoff, *Gesammelte Schriften*. 2 Vols. Berlin: Meyer und Jessen, 1912). Dvořák wrote a eulogy in honor of his former mentor which appeared in *BioJb*, Vol. XIV (1912) and was reprinted in Dvořák's *Gesammelte Aufsätze zur Kunstgeschichte*. Edited posthumously by Karl Maria Swoboda and Julius Wilde. München: Pieper, 1929, pp. 299–314.

WILPERT, JOSEF, German art historian, was born in Eiglau (Upper Silesia) on August 22, 1857, and died in Rome on February 13, 1944, as a professor at the Papal Institute for Christian Archaeology.

Some of his major works include:

1. *Erlebnisse und Ereignisse im Dienste der christlichen Archäologie. Rückblick auf eine fünfundvierzigjährige wissenschaftliche Tätigkeit in Rom*. Freiburg im. Br.: Herder, 1930.

2. *Fractio panis. Die älteste Darstellung des eucharistischen Opfers in der 'Cappella Greca'*. Freiburg im. Br.-St. Louis (Mo.): Herder, 1895.

3. *Die gottgeweihten Jungfrauen in den ersten Jahrhunderten der Kirche* (Nach den patristischen Quellen und Grabdenkmälern dargestellt). Freiburg im. Br.-St. Louis (Mo.): Herder, 1892.

4. *Die Katakombengemälde und ihre alten Copien. Eine ikonographische Studie*. Freiburg im. Br.-St. Louis (Mo.): Herder, 1891.

5. *Die römischen Mosaiken und Malereien der kirchlichen Bauten vom IV. bis XIII. Jahrhundert*. Freiburg im. Br.: Herder, 1916.

Concerning Wilpert cf.:

1. Kirsch, J. P. "Josef Wilpert und die heutige Katakomben-forschung," *Hochland* (München), 7. Jahrg. (1910).

2. Raitz von Frentz, E. Freiherr von. "Josef Wilpert," *Kölner Zeitung*, Nr. 81, 1944.

WINDELBAND, WILHELM, German philosopher, was born in Potsdam on May 11, 1848, and died in Heidelberg on October 22, 1915. He taught philosophy at the universities of Leipzig (1873), Zürich (1877), Strassburg (1882) and Heidelberg (1903 until his death). His philosophical-historical writings, all of an extraordinary literary quality, exerted a significant influence on his contemporaries. He systematically represented the point of view of a critical philosophy of value judgment that found its source in Kant's theories of ethics and cultural philosophy. His separation of the sciences into nomothetic and idiographic groups (axiology) can be said to have given the initial impetus to the later division of the natural and the social (humanistic) sciences.

Some of his major writings include:

1. *Einleitung in die Philosophie.* Tübingen: Mohr, 1914.

2. *Geschichte der alten Philosophie.* München: Beck, 1888.

3. *Geschichte der neueren Philosophie in ihrem Zusammenhange mit der allgemeinen Kultur und den besonderen Wissenschaften.* 2 vols. Leipzig: Breitkopf & Härtel, 1878–1880.

4. *Lehrbuch der Geschichte der Philosophie.* Tübingen: Mohr, 1892 (14th edition 1950; this work was the first attempt to produce an historical account of philosophy based upon specific problems instead of upon important figures per se).

5. *Platon.* Stuttgart: Fromann, 1900.

6. *Zu Platon's Phaidon.* Straßburg: Trübner, 1901.

Concerning Windelband cf.:

1. Daniels, Georg. "Das Geltungsproblem in Windelbands Philosophie," *Philosophische Abhandlungen* (Berlin), Heft 7 (1929).

2. Hoffmann, Arthur. "Das Systemprogramm in der Philosophie der Werte," *Beiträge zur Philosophie des deutschen Idealismus* (Erfurt), Beiheft, Folge 9 (1922).

3. Jakowenko, Boris. "Wilhelm Windelband," *Internationale Bibliothek für Philosophie* (Prag), Vol. V:1 (1941).

4. Kronfeld, Arthur. "Über Windelbands Kritik am Phänomenalismus," *Archiv für Psychologie* (Leipzig), Vol. XXVI (1913).

5. Lass, E. "Wilhelm Windelband," *Vierteljahrsschrift für Philosophie* (Leipzig), Vol. VIII (1884), 1-17.

6. Rickert, Heinrich. *Wilhelm Windelband*. Tübingen, 1915.

7. Ruge, Arnold. *Wilhelm Windelband*. Leipzig: Barth, 1917.

WINKLER, FRIEDRICH, 1888–

1. *Albrecht Dürer, Leben und Werk*. Berlin: Mann, 1957.

2. *Altdeutsche Zeichnungen*. Berlin: Mann, 1947.

3. *Die altniederländische Malerei. Die Malerei in Belgien und Holland von 1400 bis zum 1600*. Berlin: Propyläen, 1924.

4. *Castruccio Castracani, Herzog von Lucca*. Berlin: Ebering, 1897.

5. *Die flämische Buchmalerei des XV. und XVI. Jahrhunderts. Künstler und Werke von den Brüdern van Eyck bis zu Simon Bening*. Leipzig: Seemann, 1925.

6. *Hans von Kulmbach, Leben und Werk eines fränkischen Künstlers der Dürerzeit*. Ed. by Georg Fischer. Kulmbach: Freunde des Plassenburg (Stadtarchiv), 1959.

7. *Le Valère Maxime de Leipzig*. Leipzig: Seeman, 1922 (Avec une introduction sur les commencements de la peinture de genre aux Pays-Bas).

8. *Der Meister von Flémalle und Rogier van der Weyden*. Strassburg: Heitz, 1913 (Vol. CIII in the series "Zur Kunstgeschichte des Auslandes").

9. *Mittel,-niederrheinische und westfälische Handzeichnungen des XV. und XVI. Jahrhunderts*. Freiburg im. Br.: Urban, 1932.

10. *Die Zeichnungen Albrecht Dürers*. Berlin: Deutscher Verein für Kunstwissenschaft, 1936.

11. *Die Zeichnungen Hans Süss von Kulmbach und Hans Leonhard Schäufeleins*. Berlin: Deutscher Verein für Kunstwissenschaft, 1942.

WITTING, FELIX (1873–   ), German art historian. Unfortunately I was unable to locate any biographical information concerning the life, activities and major events in Witting's career, nor was I able to uncover any secondary material relating to his works and/or influences upon his intellectual development and goals.

Of his various published volumes listed in the *Deutsches Bücherverzeichnis*, the following seemed most pertinent to Dvořák's comments:

1. *Die Anfänge christlicher Architektur. Gedanken über Wesen und Entstehung der christlichen Basilika.* Strassburg: Heitz, 1902 (Heft 10 of the series "Zur Kunstgeschichte des Auslandes").

2. *Kirchenbauten der Auvergne.* Strassburg: Heitz, 1904 (Heft 28 of the series indicated above).

3. *Michelangelo da Caravaggio.* Strassburg: Heitz, 1916 (Heft 113 of the series indicated above).

4. *Michelangelo und Beethoven.* Strassburg: Heitz, 1916.

5. *Piero dei Franceschi. Eine Kunsthistorische Studie.* Strassburg: Heitz, 1898.

6. *Von Kunst und Christentum. Plastik und Selbstgefühl.* Strassburg: Heitz, 1903.

7. *Westfranzösische Kuppelkirchen.* Strassburg: Heitz, 1904 (Heft 19 of the series indicated above).

WORRINGER, WILHELM (1881–   ), German art historian, was born in Aachen, January 13, 1881, and at present resides in Munich, Heidelbergerplatz 3. In 1925 he became a professor of art history in Bonn, taught in Königsberg (1928), in Halle (1946) and since 1953 in Munich where he has taken up permanent residence.

His major historical research has been dedicated to the psychological interpretation of various styles of art; he has endeavored above all to formulate in unambiguous terms the essential characteristics of medieval Gothic sculpture and painting. His *Geistesgeschichtliche* interpretation of Gothic art proved to be most fruitful to contemporary criticism, but it has not been accepted unconditionally from all quarters—viciously attacked by some and unreservedly praised by others. In his most important work, *Abstraktion und Einfühlung. Ein Beitrag zur Stilpsychologie*, he attempted to demonstrate that these two concepts (abstraction and empathy) form the polar bases of all artistic creation, the latter in a sense being conceived as the necessary complement to the former which provides the initial point of departure (and ultimately the final point of destination) of any theory of art and its realization in concrete products. To a degree Worringer might be considered a popularizer of the theories of Alois Riegl (q.v.) concerning the justification of nonrealistic art (*gegenstandslose Kunst*)—be it of the past, especially northern Gothic art, or contemporary versions thereof.

His basic writings:

1. *Abstraktion und Einfühlung. Ein Beitrag zur Stilpsychologie.* München: Pieper, 1908; English translation: *Abstraction and Empathy. A Contribution to the Psychology of Style.* Translated by Michael Bullock. London: Routledge and Kegan Paul; New York: International Universities Press, 1953.

2. *Ägyptische Kunst. Probleme ihrer Werte.* München: Pieper, 1927; English translation: *Egyptian Art.* Edited by Bernard Rackham, *et al.* London: Putnam's Sons, 1928.

3. *Die altdeutschen Buchillustratoren.* München: Pieper, 1912.

4. *Die Anfänge der deutschen Tafelmalerei.* Leipzig: Insel, 1924.

5. *Formprobleme der Gotik.* München: Pieper, 1911; English translation: *Form Problems of the Gothic.* Authorized American translation, New York: Stechert, 1918; authorized British translation, London: Putnam's Sons, 1927.

6. *Griechentum und Gotik. Vom Weltreich des Hellenismus.* München: Pieper, 1928.

7. *Käthe Kollwitz.* Königsberg: Gräfen und Unger, 1931.

8. *Künstlerische Zeitfragen.* München: Brickmann, 1921.

9. *Lukas Cranach.* München: Pieper, 1908.

10. *Problematik der Gegenwartskunst.* München: Pieper, 1948.

11. *Über den Einfluss der angelsächsischen Buchmalerei auf die frühmittelalterliche Monumentalplastik des Kontinents.* Halle: Niemeyer, 1931.

Concerning Worringer, cf.:

1. *Neue Beiträge deutscher Forschung. Wilhelm Worringer zum 60sten Geburtstag.* Edited by Erich Fidder. Königsberg: Kanter Verlag, 1943.

2. Read, Herbert. "Introduction," *Form in Gothic.* Translated and edited by Herbert Read. London: Tiranti, 1957, pp. ix–xiii (First English edition, London: Putnam's Sons, 1927).

INDEX

abbreviation of reality: 36
Abelard: 106
abstract unity: 148
Altaner, B.: xiv, 186, 196, 199, 230
Altdorfer, A.: 104
Amalric of Bena: 154n., 175
Amiens, Cathedral of: xi, 25, 93
Anselm of Canterbury, St.: 28, 176–178
anthropocentrism: 15
Aquinas, St. Thomas: xxvii, xxviii, 32,
    48, 49, 76, 83, 110, 156n., 157n.,
    158n., 159n., 160n., 161n., 162n.,
    163n., 164n., 166n., 181, 196, 218
architecture (see also classical, Ba-
    roque, Gothic, Renaissance, Ro-
    manesque)
    compositional limitation: 140
    compositional structure: 144
    curves: 58
    ecclesiastical structures: 51
    Grecian: 23
    heavenward flight: 58, 59
    monumental harmony: 29
    resistance force: 72
    rhythmical arrangements: 53
    rhythmical forms: 51
    rhythmical sequences: 68
    symmetrical harmony: 98
    union in time and eternity: 53
    vaulted lines: 56
    vertical lines: 58
    vertical schemata: 53
    vertical stance: 58
Aristotle: xxviii, 21, 119
art (see also classical, Gothic, Renais-
    sance, Romanesque)
    ancient development of: xxii

Augustan: 108
Baroque: xxv, 7, 24, 56
Byzantine: xxiii, 7
decorative form of: 26
didactic meaning of: 32
Egyptian: 22
figurative: 26
formal aspects of: 129
modern: 28
oriental: 28, 92
permanent principles of: 122
representational: 33
Romantic: xxii
artistic
    dualism: 114
    form: xxvii
    imagery: 22
    microcosmos: 130
    perception: 144
    truth: 37
    will: 24
assimilation process: xxiii
Augustine, St.: 21, 32, 83, 135, 153n.,
    162n., 176, 204, 231, 232
Averroists: 110

background (see also painting)
    depth: 61, 62
    depth-orientation: 63
    detachment from: 63
    directional path: 55
    elements: 74
    importance of: 72
    neutral coulisse: 72
    plane: 67
    scenery: 71
    staging: 63